THE FUNCTION
OF RELIGION:
AN INTRODUCTION

Louis B. Jennings

University Press
of America™

Copyright © 1979 by

University Press of America™
division of
R.F. Publishing, Inc.
4710 Auth Place, S.E., Washington, D.C. 20023

TO IRENE

A persistent question confronts man, What is religion? This phenomenon has taken so many different forms that it is difficult to find common elements. A simple solution is to state that whatever one acknowledges as religion is to be accepted. Edmund Burke indicated this approach in colonial America when he said that in that country "every man's hat is his church."

It is against this background that the present approach has been taken. The general thesis is that religion emerges as a functional vehicle to interpret the manifold diversities of life. It will fulfill its purpose only as long as it is capable of serving this role. Hence, the history of mankind depicts the rise and fall of religions on the basis of their ability to respond to the human quest for a meaningful, fulfilling, and purposeful life.

Consequently, certain presuppositions are accepted as underlying principles. First, all persons are religious. It has been said that "man is incurably religious." Therefore, it is not a case of religion or no religion but what sort of religion. One possible qualification may be made to this assertion. Some people who commit suicide appear to do so because of a complete loss of religion. They reach a point where there is a total lack of meaning to existence, and they can find no justification for preserving the latter. Apparently, however, some individuals engage in this act of self-destruction as a part of their faith. It occurs, most generally, when there is a strong belief in a more attractive life after death than can be experienced in the present order.

Second, it is postulated that only persons are religious. It is a distinctly human phenomenon. One can say that it is a feature which gives uniqueness to the human species and sets man apart from other creatures. Animals, especially those which have been domesticated, sometime respond in ways which approach religion. They appear to embody a type of religion categorized as prehuman. For example, a dog can reflect a sense of purpose and commitment. Unlike man, how-

ever, it does not appear to be a trait which is indigenous
to the creature itself.

Third, everyone begins with an inherited faith. In the
beginning of life the content of his religion is determined
by the society where he is born. In a general sense, one can
say that all people in the United States are "Christian."
That is, there are certain ingredients in our society which
have been bequeathed to it by Christianity. They have become
so secularized that they have ceased to be identified as religion. For example, it can be argued that the form of our
government was determined by the organization previously existing in the church.

Fourth, this initial religion will fail to meet the needs
of the person. In the individual's confrontation with the
demands of life, his faith will be subjected to the crucible
of experience. The outcome will be religion in a new dimension. Adjustments will be made. If his traditional religion
is not capable of responding to the new conditions, it will
be sloughed off or relegated to a superficial status. Actually,
it would appear that for many people religion falls into a two-
dimensional expression. On the one hand, there is the con-
fessional faith which embodies the comprehension of life which
has been established in the course of history. The person may
relate himself to it and believe that it is his faith. In
actuality, however, he professes, in his daily pursuits, a religion which has been created in terms of the issues which
confront him daily. It will not deny many features of the
inherited religion; but they must be functional in daily life.

Therefore, finally, genuine religion is a uniquely personal
phenomenon. It must emerge from an individual quest for, and
discovery of, a value focus whereby a meaningful existence can
be acquired. Since, however, life experiences are constantly
changing and new dimensions of outlook come into view, the religion will become moribund just as assuredly as an inherited
faith. Growth and decay are just as much a part of religion
as they are found in physical existence.

While the basic function of religion is related to the personal life, by the sheer fact that human beings are essentially

social creatures means that there will emerge group relationships wherein it will be expressed. Individuals will become
identified with others and discover that they share much in
common in matters pertaining to faith. Further, the interaction will contribute to the enlarging dimension of the person's religion. Therefore, as will be shown later, religion
cannot avoid a social character.

In an introductory work of this nature, it is always difficult to determine the materials to be included and those
which are to be excluded. This problem is especially evident in relation to the five dimensions of life with which
religion is related. Each of them has many positions which
should be included in a comprehensive analysis of the subject.
I can only request a certain measure of charity on the part of
those persons who are most knowledgeable in these disciplines. A major goal will have been achieved if there can
be carried further a dialogue between spokesmen for religion
and representatives of the other fields. Thereby, a provocative interchange may be created and new insights achieved
by everyone.

Obviously, there are other dimensions of life than those
which are represented by philosophy, ethics, economics, politics, and science. Moreover, the very nature of religion,
as here presented, indicates that it would interact in these
other areas. The limitations of the present work in not
demonstrating a correlation is regrettable. This factor is
especially true in the realms of literature, art and music.

Production of a work of this nature is achieved only
through the assistance of many persons. It is impossible to
acknowledge the contributions of everyone. Several groups
and individuals, however, must be given recognition. First,
the Fund for the Advancement of Education of the Ford Foundation awarded a fellowship which made possible the initial
study upon which this work is grounded. Subsequently, it has
been used in typed form with my students at Marshall University where the study has proven itself in actual classroom situations. Through this process, substantial revisions have been
made necessary. A series of studies over several years with
members of the Judge Warth Sunday School Class at the First

Congregational Church was most productive and instructive.
The incisive and thoughtful responses of the men and women
of this group contributed immeasurably to a reconstruction
of the work. My wife, Irene, and daughters, Carolyn and
Sharon, have been helpful in their own supportive ways in
encouraging the project. I wish to thank the staff at the
University Press of America for providing helpful guidance.

Marshall University   Louis B. Jennings
Huntington, West Virginia

x

CONTENTS

CHAPTER I

INTRODUCTION

Man lives in a world which is experienced as complex. This premise is generally recognized for both the past and the present. Human beings have not been able to put the vast number of individual ingredients brought within the context of their lives into some type of organized perspective in order to achieve a meaningful and purposeful wholeness.

Everyone seeks to derive a principle whereby the particulars can be put into a comprehensive and universal pattern. Each person accomplishes this objective to a greater or lesser degree. But no one succeeds in arriving at a principle which is adequate for all of his encounters. Hence, there are elements of human living which have to be left on the periphery or in the realm of the nonunderstood. Such ingredients provide the bases for man's continuing quest for more complete knowledge and understanding. But even as he is succeeding in reducing some aspects of his life to an orderly exposition, other items begin to appear and to call for examination. Thus the experiences have gone on and will undoubtedly continue in the unfathomed tomorrows.

A. BASES FOR MODERN COMPLEXITIES

But modern man seems to have an unusual awareness of the problem as it confronts him in his own world. There seems to be such an overwhelming complexity that he is quite certain that his age is unique in respect to the demands made upon him to try to cope with his universe. There are many factors which contribute to this reaction.

1.FULLNESS OF LIFE. The world of man reveals itself in such a manner that the opportunities for selection seem to be almost unlimited. For every possibility which was available in the past one will find many today. Every dimension of human living and experience has this enlarged scope as a distressing characteristic. Each area has been exposed to extensive study and examination. As this operation has proceeded, new features have been unveiled. This achievement has been made possible by the vast increase in the amount of time available for expressing human inquisitiveness. For example, the numerous choices which an American has in his food are sometimes bewildering. To a considerable extent the same complexity is evident in most areas of life. Further, there seems to be no relaxation in the enlarging of this fullness. Even more significant is the fact that this fullness is becoming known. Our modern methods of communication make possible an acquaintance with these possibilities. For everyone this factor operates in the more material aspects of life which can be apprehended through the sensory faculties. But as literacy has become more widespread, the same exposure appears in the more intangible features of human experiences. Even ideas have a way of filtering throughout the nation and the world. Thereby, a new dimension of choosing is forced upon the individual. Through techniques of audio-visual devices, even abstract ideas can be presented so that they can be apprehended by individuals with only modest achievements in intellectual endeavors. The sheer magnitude of the possibilities seems to be staggering.

2. VARIETY IN LIFE. But the problem is enhanced by the very great variety of these experiences. There seems to be no end to the possible courses of action which are open to each one. Moreover, each approach can often be made attractive and appealing. One seems to be torn asunder as to which road to follow. This predicament may not be too significant in some areas. If one has mashed potatoes today, he can have home-fries tomorrow, or even later today. But it is more difficult to follow a course of non-violent protest today and a violent one tomorrow - and especially in the reverse order. Once force has been accepted as a method to cope with some situation, it is extremely difficult to choose another direction. The conflicts which have erupted throughout the world illustrate this predicament all too vividly. It is in these areas of social responses where modern man is in a particularly disturbing dilemma. He hears the din of voices advocating all types of panaceas for living life. Each of these advocates of a program can present a very telling case in behalf of his ideas. Hence, it becomes increasingly difficult for one to select a particular path for himself.

3. FREEDOM. The problem is compounded for modern man since he has a considerable measure of freedom. As a matter of fact, he can scarcely escape making a choice. First, there is the freedom of exposure. In one way or another the message comes through. Unfortunately, it is not always clear, though perhaps loud. The proposals are not always presented with that candidness which one might desire. Either consciously or unconsciously there is some limitation on the presentation. In making the choice of potatoes in the restaurant the patron does not receive

2

a sample, He must, rather, depend on the printed word as seen on the menu. Obviously, the advocate of an idea is not expected to give full weight to the weaknesses of his proposal. Actually, he may be so blinded by his own understanding of his idea that he may be incapable of seeing its limitations. Where a more activist role is being sought, the effort to limit the presentation to one side will be even more strenuously carried out.

Second, there is freedom of examination. One has the opportunity in the modern world to direct some attention to the several possibilities. Again, ther may be some handicaps in this operation. One approaches the viewing with his own being having been prepared by all the experiences from the past. In other words, he does not approach it without some predilections. His "prejudices" will be there to influence the examination. There is a considerable measure of blindness involved in every phase of human living. Efforts may be made by the individual hmmself or others who seek to help him in his examination to overcome the limitations. To some extent this endeavor will be successful. It is the way we grow. But the hindrances will never be more than partially met. Nevertheless, we do succeed in making various examinations.

Third, there is the freedom to choose. Man's ultimate decision is his own notwithstanding the limitations imposed by varied circumstances. The person may choose to give his wallet to the thief because the latter holds a gun. But the decision is that of the individual. He could have chosen otherwise even though it meant death. Obviously, there have been those who did choose to die rather than to take some other course of action. Hence, no matter how we attempt to explain the bases for our choice of action, we do have to accept the fact that we made the free decision.

Fourth, there is the freedom of action. Often we make a choice but go no further. There is no implementation. It is at this point that modern man may have his most excruciating problem. He is drawn in a certain direction but is stymied in carrying forward his resolves. He lives in two dimensions - what he has chosen to do and what he actually accomplishes. It really means that he has made two choices. One is on the level of the examination of a potential achievement; the other is at the point where other ingredients intrude. One may resolve to give one million dollars to the starving Armenians; but he finds that his bank account does not provide the means for this course of action. He chooses to give up his good intentions rather

3

than to seek to find other approaches whereby his first resolution was made. Nonetheless, he cannot escape all the ingredients which entered into the first resolve. Consequently, he suffers some measure of conflict. If this latter is not resolved, it may lead to some psychic difficulties.

B. DANGERS IN COMPLEXITY

1, SPREADING ONESELF TOO THINLY. As modern man finds himself confronted with the many and varied alternativon, he is subject to a number of potential dangers. One of these is that he will attempt to follow as many of the alternatives as possible. He lives a smorgasbord type of existence; he simply moves from one point of life to another. But the possibilities are so extensive that one of the primary demands confronting him is speed. There is no time to lose. Hence, a great effort is directed into the development of techniques through which movement can be achieved most effectively. Modern gadgetry often has its primary value derived from the fact that it provides acceleration. Even a few short years ago our grandfathers would not have been too disturbed if they missed their train even though another would not be through their town until the next day. In our modern world we get upset if we miss our turn in a revolving door. The primary objective is to accomplish whatever is undertaken in the least possible time whatever the cost may be. One can often see a car speeding down the highway only to turn into a house; then the driver, having arrived at his destination, would have great difficulty in providing an explanation for his hurry. There is a restlessness about life. We must be on the move and do it as rapidly as possible.

2. PARTAKING ONLY OF SURFACE VALUES. Under these conditions of movement, it is scarcely possible to do more than skim the surface of life itself. We receive only a fleeting glance of the passing parade. There is no time to experience fully any facet of life. Rather, we gain only a rather blurred view of the individual segments and put them together in a totally inchoate whole. Further, we miss a very great deal in the process. One might do well some day to take a leisurely travelled trip between his home and his place of employment and to make a conscious effort to observe the scenes on the way. It would probably be an astounding experience. One often hears the remark, "Well, I just never knew that was there," although he had passed that way day after day for many months or years. We really develop an incapacity to observe. This deficiency be-

4

comes even more marked with respect to human beings and values.
We are inclined to isolate ourselves from human relationships.
People become not individual persons in our lives but masses of
human beings. We think in terms of group identities instead
of personal entities. Our attitudes are formed on the basis
of the group characteristics instead of those reflected by the
particular individual.

3. LITTLE OR NO PROGRESS IN PERSONAL DEVEOPMENT. Since we
simply move from one point to another, there is little opportunity for more than a casual understanding of, and appreciation for, the various ingredients of our living. We tend to
view things but do not gain a perspective. Further, there is
gradually eliminated any real interest in formulating any comprehensive view of things. There is insufficient time; too
many items demand our attention. Modern man becomes so involved
in his extensive round of activities that it would probably
frighten him to question the reason for these interests or to
probe into the meaning of life.

4. NEGATIVISM AND PESSIMISM. Given the course of life as
it has been portrayed, there is the probability that the person will lose zest for life itself. He begins to sense a feeling of frustration as he carries forward his daily round of
engagements. Eventually, these affairs may become devoid of
any meaning. Life becomes futile and empty and begins to
take on a negative hue. He can see only the ills. In the
words of the well-known cliche, man observes only the hole
in the doughnut. Criticism is defined in terms of discovering what is wrong instead of its semantic meaning, "being
able to discuss." The ultimate result is an entirely pessimistic view toward existence. Everything turns sour. The
words of Koheleth sum up his basic philosophy: ". . . vanity of vanities! All is vanity."[1] The ultimate result is
suicide. We read about the substantial number of individuals
who succeed in snuffing out life or attempting to do so and
fail. Undoubtedly, there are many more who do not become
recorded in the statistics. For example, it has been suggested that many automobile accidents result from the inten-
tion to cut the cord which ties one to this world.

C. SOME SOLUTIONS

1. ESCAPISM. Some persons recognize the problems and blame
it on modern civilization. Hence, there is an effort to escape this mode of existence. The study of man in primitive

5

societies, especially those from the ancient past, has contributed to this point of view. These people have been seen as not subject to many ills and tribulations which are present in modern experiences. They surely lived an idyllic existence. Their needs were few in number, and they moved beautifully through the world, joyously partaking of all its goodness. There is an element of truth in this picture. It is true that primitive man lived a restricted life. He could, therefore, concentrate on a limited number of goals. To this extent his life was well organized, and he moved forward with a measure of certainty toward its fulfillment. Unfortunately, this depiction presents only one side of the situation. His means for coping with the necessities of life were so limited that he had considerable difficulty in surviving. Hence, he was caught up in a vast area of the unknown. Even in the very essential world of procuring food, there were so many uncertainties that they made his life full of perplexities and anxieties. It is not surprising that ancient deities were frequently pictured as fertility gods and goddesses.

In essentially the same fashion, the person who, today, seeks to "get away from it all," discovers that he must find ways to cope with the demands of life. Only the most persistent continue in this type of existence for an extended period of time. The more general approach is to engage in this mode of living on a more limited basis. We go on a "vacation." Sometimes we do, in fact, vacate our normal patterns of life. We might even "rough it." But these periods are short and provide nothing more than an interlude in an otherwise civilized type of life.[2] The vast majority of people simply escape one form of civilization to partake in another. Actually, the opportunities for a genuinely isolated type of existence are rapidly becoming nonexistent.

2. AUTOCRATIC SOCIETY. A more common type of solution is to be found in establishing some form of dictatorship. By this method, the patterns for living are formed by some one individual or by a small group. The mass of persons simply follow the direction which is given by those who are entrusted with control. Throughout the history of most civlizations this type of social structure has been most evident. In many respects it is still followed in modern life, even in so-called democratic societies. At intervals we may go to the polls to elect our representatives. But in the ensuing intervals we simply follow the patterns which they establish for us. In the realm of economics, we put our services at the disposal of an indi-

vidual or a corporation and assume our role as it will be assigned to us. There is no particular meaning or value in these forms of living. But, at least, they provide a social frame of reference whereby we, and our fellow men, can survive without concerning ourselves overly much with the social order or our own individuality within it. The employer provides for our economic needs more or less satisfactorily. As long as no one promies us something better, we are reluctant to seek to effect any changes.

For the major part of mankind the dictatorship is more stringent. Since their experiences, however, have not been essentially otherwise, there is a meek acceptance of the process. Only with the growing recognition that some other course of action may offer fulfillment is there an advocacy for change. For example, in Europe there arose the monarch to offer some relief from the complexities of the feudal age which had led to interminable warfare. But, as time passed, the power of the king was increasingly circumscribed with another type of power structure. It is questionable, however, whether the ordinary person received any appreciable enlargement of human values through the new mechanism. The last European monarch of any consequence is Prince Ranier of Monaco, and news in recent years suggest that his power is being questioned. Nevertheless, all too often some new form of dictatorship emerges to take control. This process has occurred most obviously in the establishment of Fascist and Communist dictatorships and usurpation of control by the military. Moreover, even in countries with strong democratic traditions, the pressures of modern life seem to offer no alternative except some form of far-reaching governing power which directs the lives of the citizens in a country.

The United States has not escaped. Whether our democratic institutions can stand against the stresses and strains which are being exerted by present-day civilization is questionable. Our form of dictatorial power may be the computer. For example, can an individual person be permitted the luxury of deciding how to fulfill his economic role on the basis of personal choice? Does he not have to subject himself to batteries of tests which will determine his appropriate place in the economic system? With our knowledge of genetics, is it really sensible for human beings to be given a free hand in the determination of their offspring? Does the individual have the "right" to control the operation of his own automobile on the

7

highway instead of being controlled by devices which have been
built into the roads?

3. CONFORMISM. One of the most common patterns whereby
modern persons seek to simplify their existence is through the
process of conforming to styles of behavior as they are socially set. To deviate from the established norms would incur the
disapproval of others who are conforming. Western advertising
illustrates this approach very strikingly. The manufacturers
of the various products establish the styles and then utilize
extensive appeals in order to bring the buying public to accept them. A television commercial produced for an automobile
manufacturer will direct primary attention to the stylistic
features of the car. Even the other characteristics have to
do with the components which will make it possible for one to
be in line with the rest of society. The motor has a certain
number of horsepower; there are power brakes, power steering,
power windows. "Power" is the word which says it all. As we
have come to depend more and more on mass production, this emphasis on conformity has increased. Both essentials and luxuries are provided in this manner. Consequently, there is
scarcely any basis for the expression of the individual personality. It is almost inevitable that we think as other
people; we hold to the same set of values; we read the same
books - the ones which are on the best-seller lists; we watch
the same television programs - those which have achieved the
highest Nielsen rating; and, in many other experiences we seek
to keep up with the modes of outlook and behavior which appear
to have been prescribed for us.

One very interesting phenomenon in recent years has been the
emergence of the "Hippie." Here was the person who had become
disturbed by the continuing demands that people follow an established course. Hence, he wished to be different and to follow a more independent course of action. And he did. He
simply related himself with others of like mind who proceeded
to set up some codes of thought and behavior. The emphasis was
to make it unique and distinguished from what was found in the
rest of society. In its actual operation, there was a singular
uniformity. It has been observed that this movement is disap-
pearing. It is lacking in any substantial wrestling with the
problems of human living. The attack has been made on the
superficialities. Then another set of external features has
been substituted with the accompanying requirement that they
must be followed.

8

4. SIMPLICITY OF SELF-IMPOSED NARROWNESS. Another approach
to the problem is through a very carefully contrived narrowing
of one's relationship with life. The person is in society and
is doing whatever may be necessary. But he is primarily operative in one very specially circumscribed area. Our modern age
encourages this approach. We live in the time of the specialist. It is the person who is an expert who is given status.
Consequently, each one is attracted to this mode of performance.
This characteristic is found especially in those individuals
who are ambitious to advance in their professions - and for
the financial rewards which accrue therefrom. No longer can
one be a general practitioner and treat the whole person.
Rather he must become specialized in a particular discipline.
Admittedly, this emphasis is almost irresistible. The knowledge required today is so extensive that one almost of necessity must confine himself to a limited area. The field oftentimes becomes circumscribed and complex to the degree that it
is difficult for those in related fields of endeavor to understand one another.

Since the dominant spirit today is science, it is discouraging
for a person to direct his attention to anything which does not
reflect this emphasis. One of the rather unfortunate features
of modern society is the fact that men and women in the several scientific specialties have comparatively little knowledge
of other areas of human living. Nevertheless, they may become
spokesmen for movements which will have vast influence in the
lives of people. Further, their position in society results
in their opinions in areas other than their expertise being
evaluated very highly.

D. UNIFYING FACTOR

1. NEED FOR IT. If our analysis of the predicament confronting modern man is correctly given, it can be said that his
greatest need is for some means to be effected whereby his
life can be made whole. But, actually, this requirement for
human fulfillment has been evident from the most ancient times.
Religion originated in order to meet this need. This uniquely
human phenomenon has been found as far back as history can be
traced. There has always been a seeking for some basis whereby there could be a correlating and giving direction, meaning,
and purpose to human existence. Even in the most primitive periods, when we think that life was simple, it can be said that
man was most definitely religious in his confrontation with
life. The simplicity, in fact, was there only as seen from the

9

perspective of modern experiences. Actually, it may not be incorrect to assert that life for our primitive forebears was even more complext than that of their kinsmen who have followed in a later era. The vast realm of ignorance made him very dependent on the gods or spirits which could solve the intricate problems which were beyond his comprehension.

Modern man has become knowledgeable in these areas - at least some of them - and can move with greater confidence. That is, he knows about them. But the difficulty is that he becomes involved in the minutiae and is overwhelmed by the difficulty in finding some way to correlate them. It is the knowledge of the great diversity of life which provides the obstacle for him. Since he wishes to live life in a manner which will reflect his own utilization of the many and diverse areas, he must have a basis for making decisions. We are constantly confronted with the Old Testament injunction, Choose ye, this day. To what ends will one give himself as he lives his days?

This need is felt not only by the individual's propensity toward this quest but, also, by the several groups in their need for social formulations which can guide their existence. Here, too, there is the ever present danger of being torn asunder as conflicting and uncoordinated efforts are carried forward. Especially do the organizations which correlate the endeavors of the members who compose the groups need this type of unifying goal and sense of purpose. Otherwise, small groups break up into factions, and the aggregations come to develop a constant state of conflict among themselves. The whole order of human beings becomes a mass of people with each one ultimately seeking to follow whatever proves to be of momentary attraction and value to him.

It is in this state of affairs with all its diversities, contradictions and conflicts that modern man seeks some basis for unification.He yearns for organizing motifs which will serve to relate the individual or group to the manifold areas of experience. But, even more, it will weave the particulars into some meaningful pattern and give a total perspective to life itself; it will serve to provide some basis for expanding his life more profitably so that the new ingredients can be accomodated into the context of the determinative principle.

2. RELIGION. It is at this point that man's religion enters onto the scene. Its purpose has always been to provide him with the basic frame of reference within which and by which

10

life could be determined. He has always had it in one form or another. Essentially life cannot be lived without it. Hence, it is not a case of religion or no religion. Rather, it is the type of religion which is the key question. All too often man has given some overt acquiescence to a stated faith, but his life was really built in terms of something far different. Nonetheless, the religion was there. His day-by-day life and its activities were being guided by some form of orientation. Whatever meaning and purpose were found were due to the presence of a more or less clearly defined faith. To be sure, too often man has not been particularly cognizant of the nature of the organizing principle of his life. In part, this has been due to the commitment in an outward form to some established religious pattern. But, in truth, this latter had only modest influence on his life. On the other hand, it did serve to make the person uncertain concerning the place of his religion. His own identification would be in terms of the accepted faith. At the same time, he was all too aware of his failure to follow the projected pattern in his life. The usual basis has been to explain the deviations from the traditional pattern as sin since it seemed to involve a missing the mark set by an accepted order. There was truth in this explanation. Unfortunately, it did not serve to account for the procedures which were followed.[3] What had really happened was that man's life had outstripped his religion. The latter could no longer perform its integrating task; it was so tightly constructed that new insights and perspective were unacceptable. Only the forced demands of life, as they continued to be made, eventually brought the religion to its proper position. Historically, the inadequacy has not been disastrous for religion. It has been so closely knit with other patterns of life, as they had become organized, that it could persist in its established norms without being confronted with any other force which could question its status. Since the learned and leading men of the society were identified in positions of religious leadership, they dominated the course of human existence. Eventually, some of them would begin to point in new directions as they met the exigencies of human living. Therefore, the religious order would be able to move ahead of other forms of life which might give the new direction for a reconstructed religion. With some exceptions even the institutional forms of religion have had their position in the life of man questioned.[4]

In the modern era, traditional religions have been, and are, very much on trial. Today the same complexities of life are

11

met by man. New worlds are being opened to him. His religions
seem to be altogether inadequate to give meaning and direction
in his new environment. Even more significantly, there are
new forces at work which would do this task from the vantage
point of a particular facet of the new outlook and perspective.
In the course of our examination, a number of these new forces
will be met. It will be seen that they are not just presenting raw materials for man to use in his daily living. Rather,
they are seeking, directly or indirectly, to elicit a response
which, for all practical purposes, amounts to a call for loyalty and commitment to their point of view. Everything is to
be done in terms of the particular discipline. Consequently,
established religions thoughout the world are being confronted
with the most formidable challenges they have ever had to meet.
In every instance it can be said that there is a distinct cultural lag as a consequence of this challenge. Established
religions tend under these circumstances to be followers of
the other components of human living instead of moving forward
creatively in terms of the new world outlook which is emerging.
Whether they will be able to take the initiative again and
carry forward is a major question of our times. Some observers
of the present scene are rather pessimistic. The movement
which has expressed its position with the words, "God is Dead,"
reflects this evaluation. The effort of this study will be
to suggest that it is not a case of God being dead,but a demand, as always, that this Being must be adequate for the total scope of human experience. The need for the integrating
work of religion is very much with us. It must, however, be
a faith which is cognizant of the twentieth, or even the
twenty-first, century. Otherwise, man will turn to another
movement like capitalism, democracy, fascism, communism or
cybernetics. It is improbable, however, that any one of these
"faiths" can serve man adequately to provide him with that requisite guidance for life. Each of them suffers from a common
deficiency in being turned within itself to achieve its own
individual objective. An adequate religion must direct human
beings outward toward a fulfillment in the entire universe.
It must be a cosmic faith which embraces the entire scope of
reality.

Religion, moreover, must be abreast of the times in which
its exists. It must move courageously forward in terms of
the many and varied influences which enter into human affairs.
It cannot stand on the sidelines and refuse to become involved
in the daily happenings. To the contrary, it must be able to
interrelate with every facet of personal concerns and interests.

12

It must be that which permeates and becomes the order-giving factor of human existence.

One of the real problems in this form of religious expression is the organized cultus wherein it will operate. There can be no overt expression of religion which will be adequate for all persons. We live in a much too high diversified universe for that sort of thing to be successful. Consequently, the particular religion which will be dominant in the life of a person must be peculiarly his own in terms of his individual relationships with the many features in his life. To insist that a person must conform to an established pattern will mean one of several things. Either he will be honest and reject it; or he may be willing to give outward conformity and push it to one side in the actual confrontation with life; or he may seriously accept it and push ahead into life and meet insuperable difficulties without understanding why his religion does not satisfy. The solution would seem to be that organized religion should serve as a reservoir or storehouse wherein there exists many and varied options which will serve as germinal seed for the production of individual and personal religious faiths. Perhaps, even more, it should serve as the motivating factor in assessing the need for a faith. In this latter role, it would have the whole religious heritage of human history to draw upon to serve as inspiration for a viable faith in the current age even as the faiths of past eras have done. Thereby, the social structure might better be construed as a fellowship of those who yearn after righteousness and are bound together by a recognition of the incompleteness which characterizes the achievements of the moment. Therein each one would be in a position to encourage the other in the common quest but with no necessity to arrive at the formulation of a set pattern of faith itself.

CHAPTER II

PERSONAL CULTURE

1. THE TERM. Culture is a word which is used with a variety of connotations. On the one hand, we use it in different ways to describe the nature of individuals. In this usuage, the general emphasis is to make a comparative statement. That is, some standard is held in mind and used as a basis for determining whether the person is to be considered a cultured or an uncultured person. The measuring device may be a set of specific items, or it may be a vague understanding. To a great extent the determinative factor is whether the other person conforms to one's own personal tastes. Consequently, it is a highly variable symbol.

On the other hand, the term may be used to describe groups. At its best, this usage can be rather precisely employed. Specific features rather than emotional concepts will be utilized. That is, the group is recognized for its own distinctive characteristics as the determinative items in making it an independent and unique society. From this point of view there is an almost unlimited number of types of cultures. But some measure of classification is possible since groups do share common elements in their contruction. Obviously, the categories which are used have to be rather broad in scope. We can speak of some societies as having a primitive culture. This statement means that they lack certain features which are present in more complext societies. But an examination of so-called primitive cultures will reveal the most strikingly varying traits.[1]

The feature which is most interesting about this concept is that there is a close parallel between the culture of a society and that of the individuals who compose it. The latter reflect many of the distinctive traits which are associated with the group. As a matter of fact, he will probably make an effort to conform to features of his society. At the very least, he will observe the more insistent elements of his society and those which have a long history. The society, too, will bring pressure to compel a substantial degree of social conformity. But, to an even greater extent, his adherence will be due to the fact that the ordinary individual does not conceive of an alternate pattern unless certain conditions direct his attention to it. A variety of factors may bring about the alteration - contact with other cultures, new environmen-

15

tal conditions, etc. In actuality, the uncertainty may be
nothing more than a vague and not too clearly expressed feeling
that there are incongruities. Especially will this be the likely situation if culture is seen primarily in terms of the traditional bases of society. That is, basically, the individual
will mirror the social culture of that society to which he be-
longs.

But even as a person will have the physical features which
are very similar to those of his parents and yet there will be
differences, in a similar manner the cultural pattern is manifested. A careful comparison of individuals in a group will
convey certain individual idiosyncracies. These characteristics may not be of major importance as far as the social culture is concerned. But, in some instances, they will be effective in bringing a change in the social complexion. In
the past these transformations have been achieved very slowly.
Primitive societies are described as static. But the same
term may be applied to some civilizations. As social groups
become more complex and interactions take place more rapidly,
there may appear a greater and more pronounced change in the
social characterization. But the point of major significance
is the fact that there is considerable interdependence between
the two expressions of culture. A person operates within the
cultural pattern established by his group or groups. Then he
manifests facets of this social character in his own life but
with that degree of individuality which identifies him as a
distinctive person. Some of his uniqueness may be transmitted
to the social order. Consequently, the culture of the society
will be different in the subsequent period. From this analysis
a very broad definition of culture is possible. <u>Culture consists of those distinguishing characteristics of a society
which are reflected in the lives of its individual members
with that degree of modification which will determine the future nature of the society.</u> Therefore, the term must be considered as a dynamic quality because of these interactions.

   2. THE NATURE OF PERSONAL CULTURE. In order to delineate
the special features of cultures with which we are concerned,
it may be useful to look at several different identifications
of the term when it is applied to the individual.
   a. <u>Etiquette.</u> One very popular usage of the term is to
apply it to a person's outward expressions, especially as seen
in his actions. Social interaction brings with it common means
whereby one engages in the everyday activities of life. These
standards contribute to greater ease and comfort in interper-

sonal relationships; one knows what the other person will do and how he will carry out the action. Furthermore, he knows that his own responses will be essentially like those of his fellows. Altogether there is the basis for congruent relationships. On this basis a cultured person is identified as the one who conforms to behaviorial patterns which are acceptable in polite society. This concept of culture has great value. It is conducive to harmony in the process of social intercourse. It is, therefore, by no means inappropriate to inculcate these forms in the lives of members who are joined together in society. It loses its value, when, as too often happens, there is a lack of any degree of flexibility in establishing and maintaining these forms. Too often they achieve the opposite of the intended results. They become rules to condemn the person who fails in his performance and, thereby, elicits discomfort in the associations.

Moreover, there may be a failure to recognize that rules of etiquette vary in different societies. As a consequence, a tone of superiority may emerge and counteract the intended result. Even physical or psychological cruelty may be inflicted. Equally unfortunate in this type of rigidity is the fact that little provision is made for modifications of the standards.[2] It is especially unfortunate in our age of creativity when technology is constantly introducing new tools for human living. The diamond ring must be genuine although it would take an expert to distinguish it from a carefully prepared substitute.

Upholding customary patterns of human behavior is desirable as long as they contribute to the fulfillment of the intended smoothness in association. We probably should make a more systematic effort to prepare individuals for the various life situations which they will meet. Consequently, the employment of the term culture in this context is not to be deplored. It will, in fact, be implied in the comprehensive meaning given below.

b. The arts and literature. Sometimes the term can be applied to the person who has developed a knowledge of, and appreciation for, what we call the "finer things of life." Ordinarily, we think of persons who have an acquaintance with the creative genius of society as a cultured person. They have attained that degree of sophistication which makes it possible to be conversant with those who have attained a similar status in society. It may even apply to one's appreciation

17

for things in an ordinary area of life but having a distinctive character. For example, one may think of a genuine gourmet as a cultured person. Of course, it is highly unlikely that this person would be devoid of "good tastes" in other areas. It is doubtful that he would be so rated if this were not true. At any rate, the usual meaning of the term when used in this context refers to that person who is at home with whatever society considers to be the best expression of art, music, and literature. It should be noted that these assessment have come to be made by the society at large. Therefore, the individual may not necessarily agree with all the evaluations. He would be suspect as a cultured person if he did. But he does draw forth for his own choices those items which fall into the general category of group acceptance. But he can be creative by utilizing his insights in evaluating new productions and thereby altering the nature of the social culture at a later date.

Again, there are real dangers in this approach to culture. It can be used to condem new forms of artistic creation.[3] The greatest danger in our day is the proclivity to fail to appreciate the arts of other cultures. This narrowness can be especially damaging in interpersonal relationships among varied groups. It means, therefore, that our education in the fine arts and literature must be substantially broadened if we are to be cultured in the new world which has come upon us.

c. Philosophy and religion. The usage of the term which will be the basis for this study will not exclude the preceding connotations. It will attempt to be more inclusive. It will involve the idea of the culture being that which embraces the total person and especially as it will reflect the social perspective - the culture of the society from which the ingredients for the individual are obtained and to which his expressions will contribute. Further, the emphasis will be placed on the phenomenon as being a quality within the person rather than its mere external expression. Moreover, it is here, in the inner being, that philosophy and religion have become most forcefully operative. These two discipline, it will be argued, constitute the real basis for culture. In short, the person who is identified as a cultured person is he who reflects the spirit of his society as expressed in its most mature philosophy and noblest faith. The relationship and contribution of the two items will be discussed later. It will be contended, too, that the nature of philosophy and religion - especially the latter - must be determined in the

18

confluence of the wide range of elements and forces which operate within the society. It will gather the constituent parts in a group and form a wholeness for them. Therefore, religion will not be simply that expression of faith which is found in the institutionalized organization Rather, it will be that which is discovered in the interaction with all the myriad expressions of life which are found in the marketplace of the society. The ultimate result will be to produce an inner spirit of unification in the lives of the individuals concerned.

3. VALUES OF PERSONAL CULTURE. This conception of culture, and of religion as the nexus for it, can contribute substantial values to the individuals concerned. It is designed to bring to the person that unification, direction, and purpose which can be achieved in no other way. In religious terminology it can bring salvation to man.

a. First, it can achieve for the individual a sense of unity within. As it has been indicated previously, the predicament of man at all times in history and especially in the modern age is the tendency to have a sense of being overwhelmed by the complexities of life. He is torn in a variety of directions. These complexities cannot be escaped. One may ignore them; he may attempt to run away; but they will still be there ready to disturb when the individual is willing to be aware of life. The solution must be to find some focal point around which the diverse areas of life can be organized. In one way or another this role has been the responsibility of religion. Unfortunately, the latter has fulfilled its duty too often by presenting a too limited commitment. It has rejected whatever was uncongenial to a basic position which had been prescribed, or it has essentially denied the presence and value of disturbing features. Notwithstanding this inadequacy, the purpose of religion was served. Man did find some grounds for integrating his life and achieving a measure of fulfillment. Consequently, the present presentation with its cultural emphasis stands in the tradition of religion. But it does so with the proposal that a more comprehensive role be assumed. All relationships of man with life must be taken into consideration. The ultimate result will be that same sense of inner poise and stability[4] will be obtained even as the man of faith has achieved it in the past.

b. From this stance of poise and stability will flow the order for directing the course of man's living. His activities

19

will be guided by that sense of direction which he will possess. He will have a base from which he will proceed, and it
will serve as a guide in his relationship with the actual performances of his life from day to day. Consequently, he will
not fear to venture out into new areas of experimentation. Insofar as the new areas open up avenues for a greater enrichment
of his major perspective, they will make their appeal. There
is, too, the guidance for reformulating the structured foundation for his life. The reconstruction will be carried out
conscientiously and carefully to the extent that the exposure
of his religion to the life's processes has shown wherein it
is inadequate.

c. When one has achieved this cultural integrity, he will
be in a position to <u>relate</u> <u>more</u> <u>adequately</u> <u>to</u> <u>the</u> <u>social</u> <u>order.</u>
The original source for his religion was society. It had bequeathed to him a rich religious tradition. This factor had
established an initial base for belonging. Insofar as he departs from the religious heritage, the purpose will be to discover a more comprehensive basis for life. Under these circumstances he can scarcely feel a sense of estrangement. Rather, his reformulation must inevitably be in the nature of a
synthesis. The old and the new will come to be correlated so
that he will always feel a sense of relationship to his fellowmen in the group. Even if the latter reject him, he will
yet feel an underlying spiritual unity. One of the most interesting examples of this phenomenon is to be found in the
case of St. Paul. His Christian faith was so great a departure from his Jewish heritage that he would be decisively rejected by his fellow Jews; nevertheless, Paul was always conscious of the fact that his Judaism was not unlike that of
those who opposed him. In his Letter to the Romans he tries
to give a rational explanation for this turn of events by
saying that what has happened has been God's way of bringing salvation to the Gentiles. Eventually the Jews will
become responsive to the new faith.

This sense of social identity is a very necessary ingredient
for human fulfillment. Man is the most sociable of animals
and can achieve his real nature not as a solitary individual
but in society. The discovery of himself as a person must be
through religion even as the latter is characterized as a social
phenomenon.

d. Therefore, it can be said that religion as the determiner of culture enables a person to have that understanding

20

of himself and of his environment which ultimately gives clues to the age old query, What is the nature of things? He finds the solution in terms of what he has incorporated into his religious faith. He can know essentially where he stands in terms of the ultimate realities of existence. There is an assurance and confidence since the materials out of which the answer has come will have been derived from the relationships experienced with the several areas of human living. Hence, there is a sense of unity which is found in the congenial relationship which exists between his religious faith and the other areas of his life. Further, there is an awareness that, as new understandings are arrived at in the several areas of human experience, his religious faith can and will be adjusted accordingly. Consequently, he will never be crowded into a corner from which he will have difficulty in extricating himself.[5]

    e. Most importantly, however, the person has the means whereby he can direct his life into the several areas of daily living. His religious faith is operable in all the concerns and interests which he experiences. It is, indeed, a viable faith. The achievement has great value for himself since it provides for the determination of his own life in a more significant and purposeful manner. Moreover, he is able to contribute more substantially to his fellow men. His own example, whereby he conveys a sense of direction, can have immense value in conveying to others that understanding of purpose whereby some achievement of meaning is required. He stands forth as a pillar of strength. He becomes, indeed, the "salt of the earth . . . the light of the world."[6]

    4. COMPOSITION OF PERSONAL CULTURE. How is personal culture formed? What is the procedure by which it is achieved?

    a. Knowledge. One begins the process by becoming acquainted with the nature of things. The materials will be supplied by the several disciplines which provide a comprehension of the universe. At this point, however, a serious problem arises. It is the immensity of the facts which are now available. The amount of knowledge has increased tremendously in the modern period and the future projects an even greater quantity. Consequently, the mere acquisition of the materials is no longer feasible as a workable basis for gaining knowledge. A high degree of careful selectivity must be attempted. No longer can one be a "walking encyclopedia." Furthermore,it is not necessary since there are adequate resources which are usually available and capable of supplying whatever materials may be needed at any given time. One of the major requirements in our educational system is the teaching of students how to seek out information when and as it is needed for a specific purpose. Furthermore, considerable more effort should be devoted by the specialists in the several disciplies to provide compendiums of knowledge in their areas. Then the ordinary person, as he is working out his own way of life, can use these resources to the extent necessary in order to achieve an understanding of the world around him. Consequently, the process of gaining knowledge will be a highly selective one wherein a person will utilize those elements which he can weave into a comprehensive understanding of the universe. It should be hastily added that this approach does not mean a refusal to give consideration to, or to deny arbitrarily the truthfulness of, any particular ingredient. On the contrary, one will open to, and interested in, all human experiences as they come to be made available. Further, he will be a highly inquistive individual constantly seeking for additional knowledge. In the final analyis, however, that which enters into his own system of thought will be whatever can be interrelated into a comprehensive system of understanding. He will be always working toward the integrating of knowledge into a basic pattern of ideas which is consistent with itself. When it has been adequately established, he will be able to make his religious commitment accordingly. In an overly simplified description, the methodology will be to proceed from the concrete observations as these are provided by the several disciplines and areas of life to the philosophical system which will unify them into a total perspective to the religious dedication which will be appropriate.

There are several complicating factors in this picture. The materials which are provided by the many specialized areas of study make their contributions from the standpoint of some religio-philosophical point of view. This situation is unavoidable. As the logician asserts it, Not all propositions can be proven. Premises underlie àll knowledge. Consequently, facts reflect considerations which are not facts but presuppositions. Nevertheless, so long as the channels of communication are left open, not only the facts but the premises can be examined and their strengths and weaknesses assessed. Furthermore, knowledge is no longer consider a static affair but a dynamic one. Man continues to probe and make discoveries in an ever enlarging realm of existence. Therefore, the person who wants to become knowledgeable must maintain an open mind and be alert to new apprehensions as they come from all areas of human experiences. The fact of the present may become, for all practical purposes, the superstition of tomorrow.

The major stipulation is for man to have a considerable degree of unification in the varied elements of knowledge. He must live in a universe and deal with it in terms of an overall comprehensive understanding. Consequently, at any given time he will live in terms of an interwoven and coordinated system of data. As new gains are achieved, he will be able to rework his overall comprehension gradually, methodically, and continuously. This methodology may very well result in a considerable change taking place over the total period of his life. But the modifications will have taken place so gradually that there will be no perceptible disruption of the unitary nature of the knowledge by which he guides his life. Unfortunately, there will be those who will, on occasions, have to make some more drastic reconstruction. Some will have begun this program with a substantially out-moded set of materials so that when they have been exposed to more current knowledge, a revolutionary reworking will be required. It will mean a discarding of considerable amounts of earlier accepted facts. There is even the possibility of a rude awakening which can be quite traumatic. One who has accepted some previous understanding as final will almost certainly suffer growing pains. This type of person will be tempted to reject categorically all new knowledge when it stands in opposition to truths which have been accepted. The source of this difficulty may be organized religion. When the latter has been formed according to some restricted view of the universe as it was derived from an earlier period and is no longer feasible in the light of later disclosures, it can be a severe hindrance to its constituents. In this type of situation the person may be forced to reject this inherited faith and to seek a more appropriate one. Sometimes religions do not instill within the person the need for a constant reexamination of his perception of the universe. The problem is an understandable one. The very nature of institutionalized religion is to seek to bind people together into some essentially harmonious expression of faith. The Latin root for the English word religion conveys this idea. When a measure of unity has been achieved, there is a reluctance to break the solidarity by introducing other ideas. It will be a major improvement when organized religions refuse to become bound to any absolutes. In the place of the latter would be a substantial flexibility and even encouragement for the adherents to

23

express disagreements while maintaining a common fellowship designed to seek for a dynamic expression of faith.

b. Taste. The Psalmist advises us to "taste and see that the LORD is good."[7] It is this operation which must follow upon knowledge. If the latter is formulated into a unitary comprehension of things and goes no further, it is scarcely worthwhile. The determination of its worthfulness emerges when it is exposed to the world and its demands. Knowledge must lead to some kind of realistic apprehension of that which is known. One must partake of that which knowledge discloses. This action can be accomplished in several ways.

(1) The person can act in accord with that which is known. He will simply live his own life as it will be directed by the attained knowledge. He learns the law of gravitation and proceeds accordingly.

(2) Through continually increasing his experiences, he can more deeply inculcate the knowledge which he possesses. It becomes more fully operative in his life. This procedure can be carried out by seeking to make the knowledge work more adequately in his varied experiences. For example, the person may learn that harmony contributes significantly to life; then he seeks to find the many and varied ways in which this quality can be expressed.

(3) He can enlarge his appreciation of that which is known. The process of making his knowledge operative will point toward an enlarged appreciation of the phenomenon. One may have experienced flowers throughout his life, but the experiences should gain immensely through a study in botany. The intricacies of the biological analysis could serve to effect a greater sense of wonder and awe in the presence of life itself. From this position it would be possible to extend the apprehension to all expressions of biological phenomena. In the final analysis, life itself would bring a remarkable meaning to the observer.

(4) This process can be extended substantially when one assists others in partaking of things which are known. There is perhaps no greater test of the adequacy and significance of knowledge than teaching another person. There is the need for greater clarification so that the other individual, too, can grasp the reality embodied in the phenomenon. The interchange of ideas in the several areas will bring a deeper penetration

into the knowledge. It is this social sharing of knowledge which achieves the ultimate test of its worthfulness.

c. Discipline. If culture is to be achieved, there must be some form of control exerted upon the person. The inclination is constantly at hand to move haphazardly in accord with the momentary impulse. Far too often there seem to be immediate values which we desire to achieve. The resulting disorder, however, is the very antithesis of culture. Culture requires maturity, that sense of fulfilling life in accord with the demands which are expressed in its composition. A lack of discipline must inevitably result in chaos. The individual has no basic sense of direction or self-control, and the social forces are not adequate to give the requisite guidance. In society this problem may be solved by establishing a form of external discipline. It may be established in the family where the parents exert a rigid authority. In the ecnomic realm, the controls created by the employer over the employees may be exceeding stringent. In its most complete form, the political state will establish an autocracy in which the full power of the organized group will be imposed on the lives of the individuals. Traditional religion has often served this role.[8] God has been portrayed as the Supreme Dictator. Any deviation in these several areas will bring with it the full expression of the power which has been asserted.

But the discipline which is most needed must come from within. It may be argued that this type of control is the only form which is ultimately effective. Even in an autocratic society the external controls must somehow be transformed into internal forces. Usually this operation is accomplished by some form of fear which prevents the individual from deviating from the established patterns. In a more creative way, however, the formulation of culture depends on the willingness of the individual to build his life positively in terms of that which is known and has been tested in the confrontation with life itself. Thereby his life becomes self-directed. It is the pattern which is attempted in societies which are genuinely democratic. The individual will be left to his own devices until the point is reached where his affairs interfere with those interests of other citizens and prevent them from achieving their own fulfillment. When that point is reached, some form of compromise or of consensus must be achieved. It is hoped that this decision will not unduly restrict one. Nevertheless, society must provide the setting wherein personal achievements can be arrived at by all members of the group. In actuality, the genuinely cultured person will not be unduly affected by these restrictions since he will be utilizing this form of experience in achieving his own adjustments to life itself.

CHAPTER III

SOCIETAL CULTURE

It has been emphasized that culture involves a very close interrelationship between the individual and society. A considerable part of a person's culture is determined by the fact that he is identified with a particular society. On the other hand, his own cultural pattern is meaningful only insofar as it operates in a group environment. Otherwise it becomes a rather sterile basis for private living and individual satisfaction. Nevertheless, in the course of the individual's living in the group context, his culture will become modified by influences of various types which are operative there. Furthermore, he is consciously or unconsciously making some contributions to the type of culture which will characterize the society in the future. No one really escapes either of these poles of actions and reactions. Even in the rather small, rigidly limited groups there is the operation, to a degree, of this process. With respect to an ever increasing number of people today, the action takes on much wider and more significant consequences. Modern man has been caught up in the turbulence of very complex and multiple cultural patterns; and no escape is possible. Even areas where primitive groups have resided in self-contained environments for centuries are being exposed to the complexities of modern life. Anthropologists have increasing difficulty in finding a group which can be said to approach very closely to a "pure" primitivity.

As a result of the breakdown in individualism and isolation, it is not surprising that the emphasis today is on societal culture. We are becoming increasingly conscious of group values and characteristics. The old age of "rugged individualism" has become passe, even if it existed in the past. The latter may be denied. The anthropologist and the historian do their work from the vantage point of social movements rather that that of particular individuals. The latter really achieve their status as leaders because they reflect in their own ideas and actions those items which embody the concerns and interests of the social order and appreciate the direction in which it is moving. They may give some guidance to the actual process, but their real value is to symbolize and to solidify the underlying feelings and attitudes of the society. In other words, they must be basically synthesizers. It is the environment which produces the great persons in history as much as it is the creative genius which they contribute to the order of things.

One may question whether a particular person who is honored as a great leader of history would have been heard from had he appeared a half-century before or after his day. Had he been heard from, it would almost certainly have been in a different setting and with other forms of contributions. It should be noted that this assessment does not deny the creativity of the heroes and the heroines. Rather, it enhances their value in that the greatness of these individuals is to be seen in their ability to guide the course of events but, also, in their understanding of the direction that events need to be guided and are, in fact already moving. Consequently, individual greatness should be recognized but from a different point of view. Leadership is required; and blessed is the society which has a person who is capable of assuming the obligations at the moment.[1] Nevertheless, he must be the person who has the insights and feelings which are reflected in the course of the social movement with which he is affiliated. Actually, his work will be successful in no small measure as a result of his ability to attract associates who will bring about a coalescence of the forces which the social order represents.

A. COMPONENTS OF SOCIAL CULTURE

1. INHERITED CHARACTERISTICS OF THE GROUP. In analyzing the composition of group culture, the initial element must obviously be the inherited characteristics of the group. At any particular moment, a society will be largely characterized by the ingredients which have been bequeathed by its ancestors. There is a great indebtedness to the past. Its forebears have struggled in their own day to formulate those ideas and values which have become ingrained in the very essence of the group. But this inheritance developed as the people of the past wrestled with the problems of life in terms of the conditions which prevailed in their day and, in particular, according to the limitations set by the knowledge and understanding which were available. The succeeding generation will find it necessary to eliminate some features which have been transmitted. This process should be carried out carefully and with a high degree of appreciation for the efforts which were made to enrich human living. One of the great values of historical studies is that an assessment of the past can be made in the context of the era when the developing world was doing its creating. Historians will seek out not only the course of the events, but they will attempt to give an understanding of the productive agencies and the varied influences which stimulated the achievements and failures.

28

It is most important that a later generation recognize that it must begin with its past. There is no possibility of denying its presence and its impact upon the current events. Further, it is ready to provide guidance for the new generation. Any changes which are wrought in the society must be done in the context of the prior developments. In other words, one cannot wipe the slate clean and begin anew. There is, also, the unlikelihood that this process would be profitable even if were feasible. In order for the inheritance to be used most successfully, there is required as accurate description of the social bequest as can be accomplished. Only through this very delicate process can a group know where it has arrived at the moment so that it can build effectively on that foundation.

The transmission of the contributions from the past is accomplished through institutions. They provide a relatively easy basis for understanding the status of a society's culture at a particular time. Moreover, the most orderly way for effecting cultural reordering will be by working within the established institutions. It is a slower process but, generally a more lasting one. A radical approach will ultimately require a restoration of many traditional patterns of group behavior. There are occasions when institutions become so inflexible that they must be uprooted. Too often a reexamination of this procedure discloses a disconcerting view. The question will then be asked, Was that move actually necessary? Who really won the war?

2. INFLUENCES ABSORBED FROM OTHER SOCIAL ORDERS. At a very early date man began to have contact with groups other than his own. It is even questionable whether any society has been able to maintain a complete isolation. The nomadic nature of primitive man contributed substantially to the interrelationship of groups. All societies are affected by this process. In recent times, with greatly improved modes of communication, it has been greatly accelerated.

In the same manner that there are differences among individuals relative to their personal traits, so there are variations among social aggregations. When two individuals or two societies have associations with each other, there will be the inevitable exchange of ideas and attitudes. Efforts may be made to maintain the purity of the group mores, but they will be futile. Additionally, these contacts will introduce new problems. They will require the introduction of changes in the social characteristics in order to meet them.

29

Very often social contacts have created conflicts between groups. The ensuing war will bring victory to one side, and the conqueror will attempt to impose his will on the other, including conformity to his social values. It is remarkable, however, how often the process has ultimately turned out essentially opposite. The pattern of life characteristic of the defeated group has been adopted by the so-called superior society. A part of the explanation is that military operations reflect a primitive form of culture. It is an animalistic form of behavior. Superiority in this activity reflects a lower cultural plane in comparison with that of the people who are defeated. The life-style of the defeated group will prove to be more attractive and will be absorbed by its master. The conqueror becomes the conquered. Undoubtedly, there are exceptions to this generalization. Nevertheless, history is replete with examples which support it. When the Hebrews invaded Palestine, they found a culture which was far superior in many ways (religion and morality were probably exceptions). Eventually they conquered the Canaanites. But, subsequently, Hebrew life changed substantially. Similarly, the story repeats itself in the invasion of Greece by the Hellenes; later, the Romans proved to be militarily victorious over the Greeks and, thereby, provided for the infusion of Greek civilization; in a subsequent period, the Germanic tribes invaded the Roman Empire and sacked Rome itself, but their life would never be the same again. In each instance, the defeated group proved to be superior in cultural factors.

The point of major consideration is that the interrelationship among groups will bring new cultural ingredients into the social situation. The nature of the culture will be altered by this form of association. Some features will lose their significance, novel elements will be appropriated, and a general reworking of the social picture will occur. Each group must recognize an indebtedness to other societies.

3. NEW CONTRIBUTIONS FROM EACH AGE. No society is a completely static one. Each generation must live its own life in the light of certain situations which exist at the time. To an overwhelming degree, it will certainly appear that the major determinants of culture will be the inherited characteristics of the group. Past experience will be the major guideline. Some adjustments may be required by the advent of intergroup relationships. Nevertheless, even the daily confrontation of the individual persons and the group with demands emanating from life itself will necessitate some

adjustments. In a stable age, these changes may be almost imperceptible and require a number of generations before any notable changes will become observable. Nonetheless, they will have continued.

The leaders of the group must be sensitive to the situation if they are to fulfill their roles in a successful manner. The challenge is presented more insistently when there is present someone who serves as the "devil's advocate." If the accepted modes of procedures do not achieve their goals, the rebel is ready to take advantage of the embarrassment. Unless the heads of the organized order can take hold of the situation and grasp it firmly by making the old order work or, failing that, introducing the necessary modifications which will bring success, their days will be numbered. The cultural pattern will then begin to undergo transformations so as to reflect the new situation. It may be that, in a particular case, the old order will be able to assert its prerogatives. The opposition may be removed. It is unlikely, however, that the contribution of the rebel can be completely discarded. Somewhere along the line of historical development a synthesis between the inherited emphases and the contributions of the new generation will take place.

4. THE CULTURAL UNIFIER. It is in the context of the ingredients as described above that there emerges that need for a creative force which can serve to bind all these elements into a unified whole. The real genius of the society will be discovered at this point. The several diverse facets must be woven into a reasonably concentric mode of social identity if the real meaning of the society is to be achieved. If the potentially discordant elements are not harmonized, the society will be in danger of losing cultural identity. It is the religion of the society which will determine its well-being and its cultural integrity. Unfortunately, this part of the social order oftentimes has great difficulty in fulfilling its appropriate task. The fact that it may be so closely identified with some particular part of the group affairs that it will prove to be ineffectual in achieving its designated role will often mean that its responsibilities to the order will simply go unfulfilled. Consequently, the real cultural attainment may be lost. The society may be dissolved into an inchoate amalgamation. The crux of the problem usually is that the religion, through its own institutions, becomes a special pleader for some one or another segment of the whole.[2] Or it may become so concerned with its own organizations and their status that its main interest will be to preserve the established patterns

31

of the group so as to retain its own structure. If this procedure is rigidly adhered to, the time will come when there
will be a complete loss of its effectiveness. The biblical
warning reflects this danger when it says that Christianity
must be "in the world but not of the world."[3] Too often discrete patterns of religion and religious institutions have
been able to retain their position in a society long after
their period of usefulness has passed and the people were
actually following new forms of religious expression in the
living of their lives.

Second, a religion may be formulated on the basis of being
completely new and different. It is questionable whether it
has ever actually occurred. The common approach has been to
introduce new features and to place so much emphasis and attention on them that the impression has been conveyed that the
religion was a completely new entity. It may even convince itself of this assessment. It may direct vigorous opposition to
the systems which had been previously established. A closer
examination would reveal that the amount of novelty was rather
small. Its eccentricity may be sufficiently attractive to make
an appeal to others, especially if these items bring into clear
justaposition some of the most archaic features of the traditional orders. If the group, however, were so radically new
that it rejected totally the forms and processes of the inherited faith, its attractiveness would be decidedly lessened.
The gulf between the old and the new would be so great that
few would be capable of responding to the latter notwithstanding
a growing disaffection with the old.

Third, there is the middle course which is the genuine approach if a religion is to fulfill its function in a society.
Its starting point is to accept in an appreciative manner the
faith which has been operative in the group. As far as possible
it will adhere to the ingredients which are present within it.
These elements will have been tested in their service to several
generations of participants. Oftentimes a particular item can
be retained in spite of its apparent inappropriateness in the '
later period. It may require some simple adjustment so that it
will embody the new insights which have been achieved. One of
the most remarkable features of the Old Testament is the manner
in which some of the most ancient features of religion, even
very primitive ones, are carried on its pages. The task was
accomplished by encasing the traditions in the forms which reflected subsequent developments.

32

The success of a religion will be its ability to manifest that flexibility which will permit the admission of new ideas and values. But they cannot stand alone; there will be the need to synthesize them with the heritage so that they will reflect the needs of life as actually lived in the group. Ideally, the religious organization will place its primary emphasis on certain broad, general principles with no demand for a specific implementation. The latter will be determined within the context of the lives of the individual members as they relate themselves to the society. When a religion becomes deeply involved in the minutiae of daily existence, and especially when it attempts to direct life at this point, it runs the risk of losing its perpective and becoming another power structure. The ultimate result may be an institution so rigid and inflexible that it will become moribund and worthless. Faith must be a living reaility which constantly moves onward to larger outlooks and more comprehensive values. It cannot ignore the concrete issues of living, or it will become irrelevant. At the same time, it must not become so involved that its energy and enthusiasm will wane as the details of life become overbearing. It must retain its ability both to inspire and to challenge.

B. DEGREES OF CULTURAL ATTAINMENT

On the basis of the fourth item in the determination of social culture, degrees of cultural attainment can be identified.

1. UNASSIMILATED CULTURE. In terms of our previous analysis, this society would be a group which is lacking in an effective philosophy and religion. Therefore, it would have no basis for determining the direction which the people should go. In the absolute sense, it is probable that no society which has ever existed fits this classification. The process of the initial association would have required some cultural base. Moreover, the accumulated traditions, however limited, would provide some guidelines and inspiration. Nevertheless, some groups do appear to approach perilously close to this state of existence. The situation emerges when the religion is so inadequate that it proves to be rather ineffectual as a dynamic power for the people. There is danger of chaos with the breakdown of any substantial ordering of the people through an inner devotion to a definitive pattern of life. The Old Testament records a summary statement of a period in Hebrew history which expresses very succinctly this situation. ". . . every man did what was right in his own eyes."[4] The author of this statement does pre-

sent evidence which demonstrates that these words were not a
completely accurate description of the condition. The Hebrews
possessed a religion which they had brought in from the desert.
It did give a basis for solidification and group identity. On
occasions it served as a rallying cry for the people. The slo-
gan during the time of Gideon was conveyed in these words: "A
sword for the LORD and for Gideon."[5] Nevertheless, the other
statement described approximately the actual situation. The
people were unquestionably in a distinct quandry. The religion
of the desert was simply not suited for the environment which
they found in the land of Canaan. The everyday life of the
people was undergoing a change, but the religion was not adjusting itself to the new conditions. Specifically, the people
needed a god for the agricultural life. Since the God of Sinai
was a desert deity, he proved to be incompetent. At the same
time the traditional religion forbad the adoption of any other
faith. It would be centuries before the inherited religion
would become suitable for the new form of life. In the meantime there was apostasy - an inescapable necessity. The religion of the Canaanites had to be adopted in order to provide
for the daily pursuits of life. It is most remarkable that
the inherited religion did not disappear altogether. This
factor indicates the strength of the Sinai Covenant and the
impact which it had on the people. It could be maintained
in the face of tremendous difficulties until men of unusual
religious insight could update it. In the interval it could
be said that the ordinary Hebrew gave little more than verbal
acquiescence to the religion of his forefathers.

The same phenomenon can be observed today. The newly emerging nations of the world reflect the same predisposition. They
have their cultures which are old and well-established. Currently, however, the people dimly foresee the possibility of
identifying with more advanced civilizations. Consequently,
there is the inescapable dilemma since their heritage makes
this development extremely difficult. Their religious patterns
are simply not too well-geared for the demands of the new age
which is breaking in upon them. On the other hand, there is
no other religion which is suitable for the crisis. As a result, there is the basis for turmoil as the people move be-
wilderingly into the new order. This phenomenon is especially
observable among the youth who are attracted to the new prospects. But they see their leaders responding in a more traditional, quietistic fashion. A form of religion must emerge
which will not ignore the ideals and values which have been
perpetuated from the past. Concurrently, they must be inter-

woven with outlooks and perspectives which can give guidance
and purpose in terms of the advancing civilization. This process will be a long and torturous one requiring much patience
on the part of everyone who is involved. The most hopeful
sign is a demonstration by some Christian groups who are taking
a new approach in their relationships with these people. The
primary goal is not to convert them to the western faith. It
is to identify with them and work toward achieving religious
aspirations which will meet their needs. This form of missionary work is a very slow, agonizing, and discouraging
operation. In the long range of history it probably offers
greater possibilities for the development of a meaningful
life among these groups. A major problem is to secure support
for this type of religious leadership. If a religion does not
wish to secure converts to its faith, the need to spend money
for these activities may be questioned. Would it not be preferable to utilize the resources of the organization at home
where there are many missionary needs. It will be tragic if
this latter attitude prevails. The history of the exploitation in these countries, economically and politically, certainly should be compensated with some undergirding to support the people as they endeavor to become cultured in terms
of the new age which has burst upon them. The Christian missionary has not been an unimportant factor in both the exploitation and the thrusting upon them the new ways of life. He
can do no less than to make a sacrificial contribution in
this hour of need.

2. WELL-FORMED CULTURE. This form of culture is found in
that society which has integrated the many elements which constitute its nature. First, it knows and respects its past. As
it was stated previously, the heritage of a group provides
the foundation for any genuine expression of culture. The society must be thoroughly knowledgeable concerning the developments in its past history. More importantly, there is the
necessity to understand and appreciate the transformations
which have occurred. The most significant aspect of this
history will be the dedication and commitment which characterized the men of old as they entered into their labors.
The outcome should be a deep respect and appreciation for
all the efforts which have been made and the spiritual
genius which was manifested. At the same time, a true understanding will by no means close the door to a willingness to
set aside elements from the past which are incongruous for the
present and the future. Each generation has lived its life so
as to measure up to its responsibilities in its own day. The

present generation can do no less.

In the second place, there must be an awareness of the present order. To make an assessment at this point is a perilous undertaking. It is difficult to make since it is an evolving scene. Further, the observer lives so closely to it and is so much a part of it that there are limitations in seeing all the many and varied ingredients. This performance cannot be minimized as to its value since the cultural pattern must be formed so that it will be appropriate for those who are living in the present.

Finally, the society must not only plan for today but, also, for tomorrow. The future beckons, and the present will be meaningless unless it is geared to a continuing course of development. Naturally, it is impossible to anticipate the new demands which will be forthcoming. Therefore, what is created in terms of the present culture must be evaluated from the point of view that it will continue to serve. At the same time, this process should not be carried out with that finality which will impede the future in its own quest for cultural autonomy. The danger, based on past experiences, is that present concerns are met with the anticipation that they will serve henceforth to meet the requirements of the society. Thereby a group becomes too fully locked into a course of action which inhibits the adjustments which are required at a later day.

As these three ingredients are wrought out and expressed in some form of a social pattern, the spirit of religion will be able to enter and to give that sense of total meaning to the endeavors. In theistic terms, this process will mean that the society will build its life in terms of a cosmic significance which is called God. The latter becomes that Being who serves to elicit that sense of devotion as people fulfill their lives from the vantage point of the eternal process which is represented, in part, by the basic interests and concerns of the society. There should ensue a recognition that, however partial and imperfect human endeavors are, they do achieve a significance in the light of the eternal order of the universe itself. As human beings continue in this direction, they will be amenable to modifications in their program without losing confidence in the genuine creativity which is at work in the affairs. They know that man sees only in part and that his desire to see more fully encourages a continuing search notwithstanding the necessity to alter individual components. Hence, the cultural pattern will be worked out even

36

as the universe appears to be - in terms of an active, creative
process seeking to effect an ever greater attainment in reaching larger goals and aspirations. Therein the integrating
work of religion will be an active part of the social order
and will contribute to the formation and expression of culture.

3. DECLINING AND DECAYING CULTURE. The very nature of a
well-formulated culture makes it subject to the ever present
process of decay. Therefore, if a society is to maintain its
cultural integrity, the process of renewal must continue. In
particular, the religion of the society must keep from solidifying into some rigid and inflexible institutionalism stamped
with the traditional designation of being sacred and unchangeable. Unfortunately, the history of religion is quite discouraging at this point. The records suggest that, with few if any
exceptions, religion has been intent upon becoming wielded into
some final and absolute pattern expressed in a permanent institution with all the accompanying ingredients for this type of
establishment. The end result is a body which demands to be
preserved and supported without question. It becomes an end
in itself rather than a means to an ever enlarging apprehension of cultural values and their integration into the order
of society. When this process occurs, there is danger ahead.
The people will be required to give themselves to it rather
than seeking through it a higher status and a more purposeful
existence. Inevitably, a decline and decay of the social
culture will result unless and until the institution can be
sufficiently weakened to provide for the emergence of the
more creative work of a genuine faith. This description is
based on the challenge expressed by religious geniuses of
the past that religion must be expressed in terms of a giving and serving quality. Jesus expressed this idea when he
said, "For the Son of man also came not to be seryed but to
serve and to give his life as a ransom for many."[6]

Fortunately, history itself serves as a corrective at this
point. Sooner or later the entrenched religious society will
have to go so that the creative genius can have a free environment in which to work. Oftentimes the experience is a tortuous one since the power structure will have accumulated many
techniques which are designed to preserve itself. Nevertheless,
under these conditions there is usually no alternative but to
confront the establishment. If a more accurate understanding
of religion's true role in the formulation of culture were kept
in mind, it would make an occurrence of this nature unnecessary.
The religious order would be its own best critic. No part of

its nature would be so sacrosanct that it would refuse to be subjected to a careful examination and to change as the needs of the period would require.

C. TYPES OF SOCIETAL CULTURES

In the course of human history there have emerged numerous forms of cultural patterns. Each of these has exhibited an underlying structure wherein the several areas of human experiences could operate in some measure of cohesiveness. An external analysis suggests that this organized pattern was most explicitly expressed in its political organization. This assessment arises from the fact that the day-by-day concerns of a people in a society are managed by this part of the social structure. It is recognized that this function is a most important one so that a group would have difficulty, as will be shown in greater detail later in this study, existing without this type of organization. But the political role can be effectively operated only when it is congruent with the established pattern of the group. It is the society which determines the nature of the political order which is required rather than the latter imposing a structure on the society. The politics must reflect the underlying order which is created by the religious spirit guiding the people. This position is reflected in the statement that theology is nothing more than transcendentalized politics. The established political organization is only a mirroring of the more basic life of the group which is provided by its religion.

1. TRIBAL. One of the earliest groups to emerge in human history is the tribe. It coordinates the efforts and interests of a small group of families so that a more successful meeting of common dangers and a cooperative effort to achieve the positive values of their existence can be realized. This type of group can never be very large in size. Usually it will not be suitable to have a number greater than 100; the maximum seldom exceeds 300. When the size exceeds this figure, there may be difficulty in maintaining the attitudes which made the group operative in the first instance.

One of the basic requirements is a deeply imbedded spirit of group solidarity. The values and goals must be in terms of the society. The individual is expendable. When he interferes with the well-being of the whole, he must be removed. Should discontent among the tribabl members become too prevalent so that there is an interference with the stability of group, the solution can be achieved only by a division. The inescapable demand for this type of group is whole-hearted loyalty. There must be an unswerving appreciation for, and dedication to, the tribal traditions and to the established government of the group. The basis for both of these requirements is the tribal religion. The stories of the past reflect the concerns which have been manifested by the tribal gods and the successes and failures which have been achieved as a result of the ancestors' responses to these powers. When they were disobedient, they were punished. On those occasions characterized by harmonious relationships with the gods, the latter rewarded them with all the great expectations which they sought. Moreover, the political leadership has always owed its position to these same beings. Deities made the initial selection and continued to sustain them so long as they were approved. This factor elicited loyalty on the part of the citizens since indirectly it was an expression of worship given to the gods.

At this state the lives of the pople will be characterized by the utmost simplicty. There is little opportunity to achieve more than the barest necessities. Life is a very limited affair. Since these necessities are difficult to obtain, there is little complaint so long as there is no actual deprivation as seen from the standpoint of their standard of living. A considerable factor which contributes to this outlook on life is the fact that life is nomadic. Aside from the domesticated animals, they have to live off the land as food gatherers. A continuing search for the means of survival is required. Traveling from one oasis to another in quest of those things which make it possible to eke out an existence, they maintain a group consciousness. The social solidarity is supported by their religion since all members of the society journey forth together under the guidance of a common faith.

2. CITY-STATE. When conditions permit a more permanent type of settlement, the tribe will give way to a new form of social relationship. The city-state initially is scarcely more than the tribe taking its place in some particular geographical region which appears to offer adequate sustenance for its simple life. A settlement will be made in a carefully selected spot. Often it will mean dispossessing a group which had previously established itself. Consequently, protecting themselves against enemies becomes a major objective. A walled enclosure

serves this purpose. They can rest secure in their dwellings.
But the surrounding territory will be in their domain. It will
be in this area that they will provide for their economic requirements. The characteristics of the land enable them to
become producers of food. Thereby they gain control over the
processes of nature in a limited degree.

This order, too, will be thoroughly grounded in a religion
which is appropriate to agriculture. Their life is no less in-
secure and lacking in a need for divine assistance than in the
earlier period. The god of the state must be properly attended.
His dwelling will be situated in the center of the town or on
an adjacent hillside. The worship will be organized in accord
with the several periods of the farming calendar. Nothing will
be attempted in the most necessary parts of their life without
appropriate propitiation of the divine powers. Even lesser
concerns of the people cannot be ignored entirely by the religious order. It may appear that the religion is determined
by the economic needs of the society. On the contrary, it is
the people in their total requirements for living which serves
as the basis for faith and provides for its content. To the
extent that the people succeed in their endeavors, the religion will continue to exert a tremendous influence in their
lives. As long as the god is responsive to human needs, the
people will continue under this aegis. They are concerned
about the god; the latter cannot ignore the worshippers. It is,
indeed, a thoroughly integrated social order and the common
thread which binds it into a unified whole is the religion.

3. NATION. Through various processes, the city-states
become united. As this development occurs, there gradually
emerges that form of culture which is called the nation. To
the degree that the social entities which are incorporated in
the larger unit are reasonably well characterized by homoge-
neous cultural patterns, there is the basis for a considerable
advance over the earlier forms of associations. There is the
inescapable necessity that there will be those factors which
contribute to the assimilating process whereby a successful
amalgamation of the groups can be accomplished. For example,
if the language is approximately the same for all the inhabitants, the lines of communication will be open so that problems which arise can be solved. Further, there is the requirement for a reasonably well articulated philosophy which
will supply the common principles operative among the people.
The national faith will consummate the bonding process for the
enlarged group. To the extent that there is a deficiency in

these cultural ingredients, there will be difficulty in establishing a state. Discordant elements can be coerced into the social structure provided they are distinctly in the minority. It is even possible that many of the idiosyncracies which are reflected by individuals and groups in the nation will never become incorporated into the national order.

In the establishment of a nation, some strong central power is an inescapable requirement. It will have an especially unique status in the initial period. The difficulties which confront the socializing process at that time are many. They must be resolved rapidly and without faltering. Any substantial weakness at the starting point will generally have the effect of causing the people to fall back on the local powers which had served them earlier. As the integration is accomplished and experience is gained in the fusing of people together, increasing power may be passed into the hands of the people. Thereby a democracy may be established. Representatives of the people can emerge to direct the affairs of state.

4. EMPIRE. As the amalgamation of groups gains momentum, it is difficult to prevent its further expansion. The basic question concerns the method whereby it is accomplished. The simplest procedure is to achieve the next stage through military operations. It is not surprising that a very large part of human history is filled with war.[8] Nations take up arms against other nations in order to fuse disparate groups into a larger society. Through conquests temporary associations can be achieved. This mode of operation demands a strong military establishment with the power vested in a small, closely knit segment of the soldiers. At the head there must be the one person who will be capable of eliciting loyalty and devotion by the others.

But war begets war. Hence, it is virtually impossible for one group to conquer another without the latter being constantly alert for an opportunity to free itself. The empire is essentially an artificial and temporary accomplishment which will survive only as long as the ruling power is capable of maintaining a firm grip on the machinery of government. The empire not only establishes its will by force; it maintains its position in the same manner. As a consequence, there has normally been no inclination to effect a genuine integration of the people involved. There has always remained a distinct division betwen the ruler and the ruled. The latter has its own culture and retains it notwithstanding cruel efforts

41

designed to suppress it. Very little is undertaken to foster
a coordination along voluntary lines.

To the degree that there have been empires which have managed to effect a solification of the entire populace, it has
occurred as a result of the development of a common faith which
has received a reasonably wide acceptance. One of the most successful types of religion has been that which developed around
the emporor as a divine being. When this concept has been accepted, the power of the ruler has been substantially enhanced.
He acted not only in the name of the state but in his own right
as a superior being. When this form of religion has been
coupled with a strength of will and a successful grappling with
the needs of the people, it has proven to have the capacity to
establish a society which could continue for a long period of
time. Notwithstanding the reigns of incompetent rulers the political order has remained intact. There have been instances,
most notable in the case of the Roman Empire, when the time
span has been tremendous. Eventually, however, even this interrelationship between religion and politics has not staved
off dissolution. Coupled with the decline of the empire itself, there has been a new power on the horizon ready to take
advantage of the internal weakness.

5. FEDERATION. This form of culture shares a feature with
the empire. It, too, is composed of people who have diverse
heritages - customs, economic experiences, political patterns,
languages, and religions. The distinguishing factor, however,
is that it is formed through a voluntary association rather
than by force. Initially it may mean nothing more than living
in the same geographical area. Each group pursues its own
distinctive mode of living, including its religion, essentially isolated and independent. Increasingly, however, it will
become apparent that some measure of cooperation is necessary.
The groups begin to explore bases for relationships. It will
probably be a slow and gradually emerging process. As these
arrangements are fostered, it will mean that a two-fold operation is implemented. On the one hand, there will be a sur-
rendering of certain rights and privileges which had heretofore been possessed by each group. But there will also be
a retention of some arrangements which are unnecessary for
the larger unity. Insofar as the affairs can be worked out
carefully and gracefully, there will be a synthesizing of
cultural patterns so that the end result will be a type of
unified association. Eventually, the patterns of life possessed by the several groups will be so completely merged

that very few of the traditional characteristics will remain in their original form.

This type of development requires a large measure of patience and goodwill on the part of all associated groups and persons. Further, it will require the passing of several generations. It has been remarked that the most advantageous feature which contributes to human development is the fact that there are funerals. Through this process, obstructionist forces can slowly be eliminated. Since this form of cultural development depends on the efforts of many people, it cannot be imposed. It must come from within. It demands, too, that opportunity must be provided for personal development. The individuals will require substantial freedom. This priviledge, however, cannot be extended to the point that the liberty of one person or group will interfere with the same quality being accorded to other individuals and groups who are participating in a similar program of development.[9] The line between liberty and license is a very thin one, but, it must be found.

The positive ingredient which is needed for the federated culture is a sympathetic appreciation for other individuals and groups and their distinctive styles of life. When this attribute is actively present, there will be the opportunity to seek ways to intermingle creatively with other people who have their own characteristics so that a broadening of perspective can occur.

Ultimately, it will be the area of religion which will serve as the prime factor in the determination of federated culture. As far as possible provisions must be made so that different expressions of faith can exist without outside interference. In the course of this co-existence, the time will arrive when the varied groups will begin to reach out so as to establish more positive forms of relationships with others. Some areas of life will call for cooperation among the several groups. This personal contact will contribute to the sharing of religious perspectives. Eventually, there will evolve substantial consensus in creating a national faith. The several religions will contribute from their respective heritages toward this end. The national culture will become a reality. There may even be some progress in the unification of the organizations although this stage is the most difficulty to accomplish. It is possible only after the spiritual cohesiveness has been fully attested.[10]

6. COLLECTIVIST. This form of culture, too, shares many features in common with the empire. Military power is recognized as the keystone for establishing it. But there is a basic difference. Essentially, an empire is built up from the vantage point of one hegemony conquering another for purposes of advancing its power and control. The collectivist approach, on the other hand, is to build a society on the foundation of an ideology. The latter is projected as promising a Utopia wherein the constituents themselves will benefited. Further, to a greater degree than the empire, it is concerned to become the all-encompassing director of human experiences. It begins on a totalitarian basis in order to eradicate the values of the past and to direct the people onto the new road of salvation. Ideally it is supposed to result, ultimately, in a form of organized life in which the various members of the community will have that inner sense of commitment so that external authority will scarcely be required.

We have seen two major forms of this type of cultural pattern emerge in the twentieth century. They have appeared because traditional forms of social order have seemed to be incapable of meeting the needs which have become evident in this period. For example, the rapid developments in technology have had two results. On the one hand, there has emerged a severe internal struggle in the several industrial nations between the segments of the economy who were directing its operations and those who were controlled by the structures. The latter became increasingly restless and subject to identifying themselves with any group which offered some alternative order. At the same time the inability of nations to resolve their differences in the economic sphere became an equally disquieting factor. Both Fascism and Communism, each in its own distinctive program, presented solutions to these problems. Like the empires of old, strong central authorities were established to direct the fulfillment of the undertaking. Further, concerted efforts were made to eliminate vestiges of the past when they appeared to be incompatible with the new operations. Both features were designed to achieve a unity toward the plans and programs which were enunciated. It was asserted that a divided loyalty could not serve well in fulfilling the stated objectives.

One of the pressing needs for the collectivist system is to find a technique to elicit popular enthusiasm. The basic ideology is too abstract for this purpose. However, by the employment of religious techniques, the transformation of the

44

philosophy into concrete realities can be extremely helpful. Writings which are considered to be essentially sacred, ceremonies which can evoke emotional responses, statements of belief which are tantamount to creeds - these are the ingredients which are very persuasive. But, most important of all, they must have persons who have quasi-divine credentials. This form of identification proves to be most effective. The ordinary person can scarcely generate enthusiasm for a stated program even if it embodies great expectations for himself. If, however, a person represents that abstraction, he may become the solidifying and congealing factor for the group. Even the death of the individual does not destroy his status.[11]

7. SUPER-FEDERATED. The e appears to be a glimmering of one further possibility for cultural development. Technology has brought us to the point where some sort of international culture must be sought. The concerns and interests of many different people of the world interact at many strategic points. Intermingling of various cultural patterns is occurring at an accelerated pace. The future outcome must be to achieve a basis for human fulfillment in this larger context.

Theoretically either the Empire or the Collectivist system would be appropriate. The latter seems to be especially well equipped to meet the need. It makes a categorical assertion that it is. It attempts to build a world order wherein different people will commit themselves to a common goal. Up to the present time it has failed to demonstrate its capacity to accomplish this objective. The basic inadequacy is its insistence upon a too rigid formula. It has not been sufficiently appreciative of the diverse nature of people, their heritages, and their goals and interests. In other words, it is attempting to impose a culture instead of permitting it to evolve in a more natural pattern. Communism has been confronted with open expression of the problem. Conflicts have erupted among countries espousing this philosophy. Some of the eastern European states have made some daring efforts to express their dissatisfaction by asserting their own programs in the face of severe resistance from the Russians. The situation parallels too many forms of traditional religions. They profess the absoluteness of their faith; then they resist all efforts to bring it into a contesting relationship with other religions. If one is assured that his point of view is correct, he should be willing to expose it to alternative points of view.

Therefore, it may be that the best form for the new era will

45

be an extension of the federated idea so that it will embrace all or most of the varied cultures in the world. The diverse individual and social entities would work toward a form of interrelationship whereby each would make contributions in terms of the whole. Following its model, it would be necessary to provide for a large measure of personal and social freedom. More importantly, efforts would be made to discover new and improved methods for dealing with the manifold problems of this age. A positive search would be undertaken to find areas of cooperation and to discover agencies which could be established to make it operative in all the areas of association. Many efforts are being made in a halting fashion whereby movement toward this goal is being realized at this time. It can be asserted that this type of system is now evolving. The disturbing factor is that the technological advances are appearing so rapidly that it is difficult to await the arrival of this cultural pattern to provide for human living.

One of the principal hindrances is the fact that the several major religions of the world lack any substantial amount of communication among themselves. The new culture can scarcely be created without a federated system of religion. The situation is further aggravated by the fact that each of the major religions of the world is so badly fragmented that it is extremely difficult for mankind to be given the spiritual leadership which is required. The hopeful sign is that some of the faiths are making gallant efforts to heal the breeches by affirmatively seeking areas of association. Techniques which succeed on this smaller scale can be applied to the larger problem. There is some confidence that the very nature of religion, as expressed in the traditional faiths, will reveal a common unifying spirit which will foster and encourage an increase in this dimension of human fulfillment.

CHAPTER IV

SOURCES OF CULTURE

It has been stated that culture is a multi-faceted entity. It is composed of many different ingredients; these elements are products of varied forces at work in the life of the individual and his society. It is recognized, in other words, that culture is a complex phenomenon and manifests itself in diverse types. The question which is now raised concerns the sources of culture. What are the raw materials which contribute to its creation and composition? What determines that an individual or a group will have a particular pattern of living? Many answers have been presented to these questions. Efforts have been made to find some one creative factor which can be asserted as having the greatest impact on the course of life and giving to it a unique character. An examination of these answers will be made under three major classifications: Physical, Personal, and Spiritual.

A. PHYSICAL

1. GEOGRAPHY. An attractive argument can be made for various forms of physical sources as the determining bases for personal and social culture. It is easily recognized that these elements are significant features in every pattern of living. They are very apparent and serve major roles in the course of developing human experiences. The geographical characteristics in the environment are sources for man's creativity. The nature of the land, its natural resources, the climate, rivers, the location in respect to other areas are predominant in the analysis of any particular culture. They serve to guide the people in a region toward a distinctive mode of living.

Some students who attempt to explain cultural phenomena are so struck by these items that they make them the major, if not the sole, explanatory agencies in the determination of a particular cultural order. From this perspective human beings are little more than robots whose fates are dictated by the nature of the environment. The individual's own life will be caught up in the forces which surround him so that he must conform to them or he will perish. Further, the direction of the society will be guided because its people relate to one another and to other groups in terms of fulfilling the demands of the physical universe. Consequently, if one wishes to understand the determinative factor of culture, he will become conversant with the geography of the land.

This theory is an attractive one. The evidence is quite
readily accessible. The influences of the prevailing conditions upon the nature of life is rather easily identifiable.
It would be impossible to deny the important role which these
factors serve in the composition of culture. Nevertheless, to
use this item as a substantially complete explanation to determine the pattern of human living is an assertion which is
difficult to support. It would appear preferable to think of
these elements as serving their primary function in setting
certain limits in cultural development. The absence of particular geographical conditions will seriously handicap the
creation of a particular type of culture. If a country is
deficient in iron ore and coal, it will be impeded in developing an industrial way of life. A nomadic life-style is
more likely in a desert than in a fertile river valley.[1]

The significance of these feature is largely a negative
one. On the one hand, they seriously restrict what can be
done. Nevertheless, the limitations can be somewhat ameliorated
through human ingenuity. On the other hand, the mere possession of favorable geographical conditions does not guarantee
a culture appropriate to the milieu. A temperate climate with
adequate rainfall does not, in and of itself, produce fine
crops. The American Indians possessed the resources of the
Americas for many centuries. Nevertheless, not all tribes
developed and utilized these assets very successfully. Many
other regions of the world have physical features similar to
those which are present in the United States. But we can speak
of an American culture in the sense that there is a unique
type of life with its own principles.At the the same time, we
recognize that in many respects our way of life differs from
other countries in many of its peculiarities.

In summary, geography has a significant and powerful influence in determining the culture of a society and its people; it
is not, however, a basis for explaining the composition of
the pattern which is followed in the lives of the people. In
several dimensions it contributes valuable ingredients; even
more, it restricts and provides limitations. Other creative
forces operate in the geographical setting to determine the
nature of life for the people.

2. ECONOMICS. One   of the strongest affirmations which is
asserted today is that human life is determined by economic
forces. Any society will devote so much effort to this area
of its experiences that everything else must be seen as con-

forming to the inescapable demands made by the need to provide
for man's physical existence. The more primitive the way of
life, the more insidious are the requirements of human energies
in this area. The difficulties which are experienced in supplying the means for a bare existence are so tremendous that
there is no time for other forces to operate; or, if they do
so, they serve as auxiliaries to the economic forces. Even the
procuring of food, clothing and shelter - the absolute necessities for survival - demand a tremendous amount of effort. Although the coming of civilization and the invention of tools
contributed to a more substantial basis for meeting the demands
of life, the economic forces were still exceedingly powerful.
Even in the present highly technological age, there must still
be expended a tremendous amount of energy in this realm of human operations. Increasing the means for supplying the demands
of life only tend to enlarge the latter. It has been predicted
that in the not too distant future it will require only two
percent of the population to supply the fundamental needs of
people. On the basis of past history, however, it is highly
unlikely that these requirements will become completely satisfied. Actually, with greater leisure time for the operation of
the creative imagination, it is not inconceivable that there
will be a greater gap between supply and demand. Furthermore,
we are now awakening to the realization that our productivity
carries with it a price tage in ecology and other problems.
Moreover, technological expansion demands an ever increasing
array of service industries.

With the importance attached to economic activities, it is
understandable that the explanation of culture and its sources
should be traced back to the material realm. Human beings are
simply caught up in a whirl of economic forces, and they can
only submit to them. Life is determined on the basis of activities which are necessary in order to meet physical needs.
Does this factor really explain patterns of behavior, attitudes,
values, and goals? Again, it is an item which serves more in
a negative capacity than a positive one. Man will be greatly
influenced by the type of economic order in which he partici-
pates. He is certainly not required to be subservient to it.
One of the most interesting features of modern American life
is the not infrequent tendency for a person to move in a direction other than that which he should were he determined by
economics. For example, a challenge has been presented to the
youth in our day to forego entrance upon their business or
professional life in order to serve for a period of time in the
Peace Corps or VISTA. Many of them have responded affirmative-

49

ly. The story was told recently of a young man who had gradu-
ated from Cornell University and was offered an exceptional opportunity with an American corporation. But he rejected the
offer in order to volunteer for the Peace Corps. "You could
be rich by the time you're 30," the executive said. "What,"
asked the young man, "is so special about being rich?"[2] One
can observe here - and the incident in varied forms could
probably be duplicated many times - the suggestion that there
are forces at work in society which are more powerful than
those which are provided by the economic demands of life.

The importance of economic concerns in human living should
not be minimized. They are operative and contribute greatly
in determining what the ultimate cultural pattern will be.
They set limits,and man must be cognizant of them and be willing to respond to them. Nevertheless, the response is made
on the basis of principles which are derived from other creative sources. Within the limits of the economic system, one
can go a long way toward moulding the type of cultural pattern
which he aspires to create - and he will do so! It is at this
point that the Communists make their most serious mistake.
They accept the theory of economic determinism as the fundamental interpretation of history. Then they proceed to draw
the logical conclusion from this premise. If human life is
economically determined, then all members of society will be disposed to set themselves in fulfillment of this goal. A society
will emerge wherein every person achieves his appropriate and
predetermined part by reaching the economic goals. The end result, however, can only be uniformity and sterility. It is
interesting to observe how the program has worked out. First,
in technology it has moved along quite successfully. To have
transformed Russia from a predominantly agrarian society to
its present status as a manufacturing country is remarkable.
In actuality this result has occurred largely in terms of fulfilling what had long been a ccomplished in capitalistic societies. Moreover, the creative work which had been achieved
in the latter was used to guide the operations in other countries. Now there are beginning to be indications that as the
"economic man" is gaining a larger sense of self-awareness
and experiences a lack of fulfillment, restlessness is appearing. Moreover, reports from these countries suggest that this
economic theory was not accepted readily in the agricultural
operations. The farmer was a product of a cultural pattern
which produced values not altogether of a material substance.
In the collective farm structure success has been more limited
than elsewhere. While part of the explanation for this result

can be attributed to the natural tardiness of rustic life to adjust to new perspectives, the basic explanation is the inadequacy of economics as a determinant of life.

In America we see a trend toward the same interpretation of life. To achieve success in life is to be economically successful. The aim of man is to secure whatever has material value. In the last analysis it is to aim toward financial rewards. It does not matter how you get it - but get it! This attitude reminds one of the psychology which appears to predominate in sports, both amateur and professional. Ideally we say that it is not whether you win or lose but how you play the game. One should, however, ask some coach who has been fired because his team did not have a winning season. One well-known coach was quoted as saying that death was preferable to defeat since you had to live with defeat. Is it surprising that we are witnessing an ever increasing amount of violations of athletic codes and that a substantial number of colleges and universities have been placed on probation in recent years?

Economics has a role in culture determination which is both positive and negative. It does contribute to the elements which enter into the formulation of a cultural pattern. But these ingredients provide material which will be used by whatever proves to be the dominant factor in the society. The vital importance cannot be denied; to make economics the essential determinant of the human pattern is not adequate.

3. POLITICS. As human beings enter into social relationships, they find that it is necessary to establish a governing organization. By the very nature of this type of institution, it exerts a tremendous influence on the affairs of the members who compose the group. Consequently, some investigators would argue that the source of culture for both the society and the individual is the political order. The theory is a very attractive one, and considerable evidence can be adduced to support this conclusion. There is a close parallel between the type of government and the way of life which is followed. The latter does seem to proceed from the state. It cannot be denied that government does contribute significantly by guiding the affairs of the people and determining their values.

For the most part this, too, is a negative role. The government proceeds to establish a legalistic basis for the relationships among members of the group and represents the people in their associations with other societies. The role is there but

51

government must be basically in harmony with life of those who are governed. Otherwise there will be continuing turmoil creating an environment wherein a change in the political order will be brought about. There have been many instances when governments have been overthrown or, at least, modified. Not even the most ruthless autocracy can retain its power indefinitely when there is a fundamental incompatibility with the people. Therefore, the successful government will be cognizant of the cultural order and will attempt to relate to it.

Moreover, the laws which are enacted, whereby government will express its will, have limited significance. First, they are primarily negative in statement. Their purpose is to restrict those activities which are deemed to be detrimental to the social order. Only in a rather limited manner can specific human actions be legislated in an affirmative manner. Second, legislation flows out of those goals which have been previously enunciated. Third, laws are primarily products of specific times and circumstances set by the society itself.

On the basis of these consideration, therefore, it would appear that the cultural significance of government is limited. It is a cultural factor whose contributions cannot be denied. It is an especially active agent when it seeks to implement the generally accepted order of life expressed by the group. At the same time its limitations need to be recognized. There are too many other creative forces which are superior to the legal authorities in contributing to human culture.

B. PERSONAL SOURCE

Historians of an earlier period were predisposed to write history in terms of the lives of leading individuals who were considered to be responsible for determining the course of events as they unfolded. From this perspective, therefore, it would be appropriate to say that the nature of a culture, as it will be reflected in the social and personal order, is created by these men and women. Great personalities made history, and culture was described in terms of their contributions. It has been previously emphasized that all persons do contribute to the formation of culture in a society. Moreover, this input will be reflected in the lives of subsequent generations. From this point of view it would be appropriate to deduce that the outstanding personages will exert a tremendously determining influence so that the culture will be greatly enriched by them. There is, therefore no denying

52

the importance of the great saints and heroes of the past and that we owe an indebtedness to those who are creating the present. Without their manifold endeavors, thoughtful ideas, and creative leadership, human experiences would be decidedly inferior. Having enriched society to a very great extent, it seems appropriate to consider some of the different classes and the manner in which each group determines life at any particular time and bequeathes to future generations major values for their lives.

1. TRADITIONALISTS. Some leaders have stood forth to uphold and support the ancient order of things. This type of person is deeply versed in the inheritance of the group and is appreciative of its inherent worth. Consequently, they serve as stalwart defenders of the traditions as they have been transmitted from preceding generations. Their value is immense. They make man aware of these exceptionally worthwhile developments which have come from the forefathers of the society. Were it not for these services, many of the values would be lost; and mankind would be much the poorer because it did not have the guidance which these tested patterns of life could give. Countless errors are not made, and the society is not required to rediscover what had been wrought out in man's earlier confrontation with life. Further, these outlooks serve to impede tendencies to make rash moves on the basis of an inadequate analysis of many areas of life. A lack of historical guidance can oftentimes produce some of the most dismal and disasastrous experiments which man is capable of performing. The traditionalist, therefore, deserves respect and recognition for his valuable role in leading in terms of the past.

2. THEORIST. Some leaders contribute to the cultural order by establishing guidelines for a new society. These individuals begin their work by a careful analysis of the traditional order. While they recognize the worth of these inherited ideas, they are equally convinced that these outlooks are no longer completely suitable. This assessment is based on a thorough analysis of human needs in the present period. This type of study suggests some inadequacies inherent in the received tradition. They begin to project some new directions for human living in order to achieve greater fulfillment. This type of endeavor is a most difficult undertaking since it involves the use of the trained imagination in an effort to conceptualize potentially helpful projections. He is, therefore a most important person in the determination of a cultural pattern.

His creative insights must be taken into account when one is raising the question concerning the sources of culture.

3. REVOLUTIONIST. There will be in any society those who share many ideas with the theorists. They, too, recognize the inadequate status of the present and wish to precipitate changes. But their approach is in the nature of a practical plan. Even their evaluation of affairs will be made from the standpoint of external considerations. Actually, they may not be too certain about the real nature of the conditions which demand modifications. Almost certainly they will not be able to establish any substantial basis for reconstruction. Consequently, there is a likelihood that their efforts will be rather inefficient. Generally there will be a tendency to destroy the heritage of the people simply because it has come from the past. There is the danger that many ideas and institutions will be eradicated in the course of their activities. Fortunately, these groups usually have some theorists in their midst who will exercise a degree of restraint and give a measure of guidance in the creation of the new order.[3]

4. SYNTHESIZER. The real genius of the new cultural age is that individual who can have a sufficiently large enough overview of the situation that he can perceive some grounds for evolving a new order on the basis of both the old and the new. He is certainly no traditionalist although he will have considerable respect for the social institutions and the values incorporated in them. He may, in fact, set forth so much appreciation for the past that he will give an appearance of wishing to maintain the traditional order. He is not basically a destroyer - at least not in any substantial degree. The past can offer assistance to man in the new age. At the same time, he is well aware of the fact that new demands are expressing themselves, and other forms and values must be projected in order to satisfy these needs. This type of person is the real creator insofar as individual leaders do contribute to the establishment of the new order. He has a remarkable capacity to integrate the old and the new.

From the foregoing it is apparent that substantial credit must be given to individual personalities in the creation of culture. The thoughts and actions which each type contributes are of immeasurable worth in the new form of life which will emerge. There is, however, the question concerning one item, the source of the motivation which provides the impetus for the person to fulfill his role in this process. There needs to be that spark which will ignite the inherent creativity in that person. As has been indicated, he is stirred by the state of affairs in his environment at the moment of his emergence on the stage of history. The traditionalist, for example, having been nurtured in the ideas of the past, stands forth to support them vigorously because he is aware of current trends which fail to take fully into account the heritage. Similarly, the other types of persons have their own bases for being activated to engage in their creative endeavors. But there is the awareness that many other individuals have comparable attitudes who do not become stalwart personalities in the period. That fine point which accounts for this distinction must be found in some other element. It is proposed that the real explanation is the religious faith which possesses and stimulates a leader in the society. He has a sense of commitment to those goals and purposes of life so that the needs of the present can no longer be ignored. The firm dedication makes it impossible for him to do other than to take a stand before his peers and to lead them in terms of his religious devotion.

C. RELIGION

We come now to consider that most distinctive area of life as it presents its claim as the preeminent source of human culture. It will not only serve as the primary inspiration for the culture but will also give to it its unique character.

It should be emphasized that religion as the formulating force in creating culture is not isolated and independent. Rather, it is that response within a given social and personal context to all the forces which operate upon the individual and his society. The scholastic theologians were wont to speak of theology as the "queen of the sciences." Today that statement could be rephrased so that it defined religion as the queen of human living in proceeding to give the ultimate status to life. To fulfill this function it must be subservient to the varied experiences of people. It is indebted to all other areas as it issues forth with that overall comprehension of reality so that a genuine loyalty and devotion to that way of life is feasible. Through this type of construction personal and social living can achieve a genuine value because it expresses a correlation among all the particular interests which are expressed in the human domain.

Three considerations should be emphasized in this proposal. First, religion in this setting has to be essentially an indi-

55

vidual, personal discovery. Experiences are so varied that it would be impossible for a genuine religion to be received from outside oneself. The person will receive many contributions from different sources. The fact that one is born within a particular society will mean that he inherits the outlooks of that group. A person who is born in America will inescapably adhere to certain "Christian" points of view. He may be a Jew, Moslem, or an agnostic; but the Christian world view is so deeply imbedded in the social structure that he must reflect this faith to a degree.

Further, those values which are inculcated by parents, schools, church, and other organized bodies will be conveying ingredients to the establishment of his religious faith. These elements, however, prove to be rather impotent unless they genuinely express the religious perceptions of the individual himself. In the final analysis, the only religion which is truly meaningful and active is that which has been wrought by the individual himself. The institutionalized expressions of faith may actually prove to be hindrances in this process. A person may simply accept the stated pronouncements and think that he has a religion. In real life he conforms to other loyalties and devotions and is mystified that religion appears to be inconsequential. Too often organized groups fail to provide encouragement for the individual to engage in a process of growth and development. On the contrary, they may discourage individual thought and determination in this most critical area of life. The person is simply encouraged to give his allegiance to particular formulations provided for him by the organization. It is not surprising that a typical member of a religious society finds it difficult to convey a very adequate expression of his faith.

Second, religion, as conceived in this cultural setting, can never be finalized. It is always in a constant state of flux since human experiences are similarly changing. There is no denying that we generally follow a fairly stable routine in life. But even this mode of existence brings in new ingredients which alter one's thinking and active responses to life in many dimensions. Often we are not particularly conscious of this modifying process.Overall, however, there are constant transformations occurring. It is, therefore, impossible for religion as a force in the individual's life to escape these novel elements. Additionally, it is this situation which may provide a serious problem. A person will be identified with a religious institution whose teachings he accepts as his own.

56

But the organization may present itself as the ultimate form of religious expression, and to deviate from it will cause a loss of faith itself. Pressures will be exerted upon the individual to keep his religion along lines expressed by the group. In some societies failure to conform can result in his being ostracized. Unfortunately the believer finds it increasingly difficult to adhere to this requirement when the religion is no longer true to his life experiences. His anxieties can be greatly enlarged if some leader appears to pronounce a criticism of the old and a presentation of a new position. A person can find himself in a precarious predicament since he does not want to lose the values which have been deeply nurtured in him by his traditional faith. At the same time he will be lured by the new outlooks which are attractive because they express more accurately his own personal discoveries.

Regardless of the nature of the changes, alterations must continually occur in religion notwithstanding the fierce support which is given to a traditional faith. The modifications can come gradually and almost imperceptibly, or there can occur tremendous upheavals. But man cannot stand still. Life moves on, and the religion will inevitably accomodate itself to the perception of reality.

Third, there is always the need for one to consolidate his religious understanding so that he can relate himself with others who have similar outlooks. Further, he wishes to have some basis whereby these discoveries can be transmitted to a larger society. Consequently, it is inevitable that religion will be institutionalized. This step has great value. It reflects the human discovery that correlating efforts with others can be a most fruitful method to achieve success in life. It is difficult to see how a personal religion can be as effective in terms of the individual's own isolated experiences as it can be when carried out in a social context. Even the ascetics have generally found it desirable to establish a society where similar outlooks and goals can be shared. The important consideration, however, is that the institution will function primarily as an association designed to encourage the individual to achieve the most profound fulfillment for himself as it is possible to do so. He will be encouraged to participate in those areas where his own seeking for a responsive order can be most effectively attained. In this context,too, there will be opportunity to share with his fellow religionists aspects of the common quest. The danger which must be avoided is the frequent tendency for institutions to fulfill the religious requirements for the individual. Unfortunately, on the basis of past history, they inevitably move in this direction. They become entrenched in a society, stabilized, and given respect and reverence. In return the organizations do for the believers what they should do for themselves. It may reach a point that the faithful become little more than observers; eventually, not even this type of participation will be required.

The role of religion in contributing to cultural development can be observed from two perspectives. First, it is the product of all other areas. It operates in a geographical environment. The religion must be suitable for this setting. For example, in most Near Eastern religions there is a narrative concerning the god who became angry with humanity and wreaked havoc with a destructive flood. When the same idea was expressed in Artic countries, the punishment was wrought by a great ice age. The story is told of a missionary to the Eskimos who found the idea of eternal punishment by hell fire was not a very effective technique for religious persuasion. The people found the prospect of warmth envisaged by this portrayal to be too attractive.

Economic factors will be given proper consideration. Religion must be germane to the human efforts in seeking for a livelihood. The narrative in the Old Testament which relates the story of Cain killing his brother Abel[4] reflects the nostalgia of certain Hebrews who cherished the good old days when they were shepherds and not farmers. The Book of Deuteronomy seeks to make the requirements of the traditional religion amenable to the demands of an agricultural society. The most pressing problem for the twentieth century is to provide a religion which is adequate for a computerized space age.

The political order will be a contributing factor in the developing of a meaningful religion. As long as the Holy Roman Empire was dominant, the Roman Catholic Church would scarcely be questioned. Given the impetus brought about by the rise of separate states, the concept of national churches became an inescapable necessity. Our democratic society requires a democratic church. Some students in this area have argued that the pattern for our form of government implemented in the political sphere what had already been established in the presbyterian type of church polity.

Great individuals have a significant part in this process.

Someone must arise on the scene to give direction to the religion so that it will elicit a general response and exert influence in the society. At the same time, these individuals must truly embody the spirit of their respective ages. Buddhism required that there be Gautama the Buddha; Methodism had to have its John Wesley. However much these persons may be products of an era, they do genuinely serve by bringing forth concretely and effectively outlooks which can be expressed by the people of their times.

Secondly, it should be emphasized that religion is more than any one of these factors or all of them combined. The latter serve as limiting elements; they establish the framework and provide the raw materials and tools whereby religion is formulated. The resulting religion, however, includes them and is more. It gives an ordered wholeness to the total complex. Man operates as an individual and in group association in the several dimensions of life. Each will serve its appropriate role and make its contribution. Unless, however, there is that entity which is capable of blending these separate items into some unified whole, the person is scarcely a complete being. With this synthesizing and unifying power, he becomes a real person. He achieves that measure of maturity whereby his life becomes directed in its separate forms in terms of a comprehensive pattern and geniune selfhood is attained. This description should not be interpreted to mean that the whole-making operation is ever complete. Even as religion achieves its purpose of creating unification, it must be advancing to new dimensions which are provided by the experiences.

As the faith is established, it assumes the responsibility to direct personal and social living in its subsequent expressions. That is, the process is a two-fold one. The particular units of experience serve as the basis whereby the religion emerges. Once it has been established, then it, in turn, returns to serve in the varied courses of human living as they will transpire. In this interacting process, however, new materials will require a reconstruction of the faith itself. It is a never ending movement. Any faith which is worthwhile will be capable of adjusting to the new age which is constantly aborning. At its best religion elicits the highest expressions in each part of a person's life. It establishes a sense of devotion whereby he makes his best contribution in each field. Moreover, the man of faith can never rest content with the performances which have been accomplished. He endeavors to continue his search for even great values in every area of human experiences. The reconstruction is necessary if the faith is to maintain its relevance.

From the social point of view, it means that a society which has a dynamic religious spirit to give it confidence in the direction it is going will have achieved that cultural autonomy whereby its distinctive areas will be capable of making their appropriate contributions to the group. It will not be necessary to be submissive to the momentary requirements which will arise in the several dimensions of life. A long-range perspective will guide the people in responding to human needs. Geography may be a limiting factor, but it is not necessary to be completely helpless. From the cultural perspective there will flow the motivation to make the most adequate use of the geographical resources which are available. To a considerable extent they can be molded to assist the society. The area may be subject to floods; but dikes, dams, and flood walls can be constructed. Economic needs exert pressures of great magnitude. Through improved methods of farming, an abundance, or even a surplus, can be produced. Society requires laws and enforcement agencies. The determination of them will flow from the overall goals to the people as established by the culture. Great individuals will emerge, but they must be motivated by a creative religious spirit in order for them to be suitable for the level of culture.

In summary, the culture of a people is very complex and includes in its composition a multitude of creative forces. No one of them can be ignored. Neverthless, that which really determines its basic character is religion. Again, it should be emphasized that this term does not necessarily refer to some institutionalized faith. The latter may be completely incapable of serving to determine culture so that personal and social fulfillment is achieved. It must be a religion which possesses the individual and the society and, thereby, directs the course of all life experiences. It will elicit total devotion and commitment. It is the creative spirit which, having responded to the several dimensions of life in attaining its peculiar nature, will mold the lives of the people in the society. As it meets the needs of the group, it will fulfill its true function to be the creator of the culture.

CHAPTER V

CULTURE AND CIVILIZATION

Historical evidence suggests that around six or seven thousand years ago humanity began to arrive at a state which is
called civilization. The term generally implies a settling
down process, the development of new tools for coping with the
demands of life, and types of association which were suitable
for the new endeavors. Once under way it was to proceed toward an ever increasing state of complexity as new means were
employed to meet the needs of the enlarging experiences which
were arising. Progress was more rapid in some areas than in
others. Some groups have not even yet attained to a level
which could properly be called civlization although this assertion has to be taken in relative terms.

Civilization brought many achievements but some severe
problems as well. Basically, the underlying difficulty was
the fact there there was a conflict between the stage of
civilization and the nature of the culture which was present
in the society. The problem is usually referred to as a cultural lag. This gap has always existed to some extent. The
very nature of culture demands that it be coordinated with
the processes of life as expressed by the level of civilization. The problem becomes intensified when a group has been
thoroughly nurtured in an inherited culture and the latter
refuses to adapt to the requirements of civilization when
the latter have become operative in the daily experiences
of the people. The situation becomes clearly evident when
the philosophical and religious perspectives have proven to
be quite inadequate to act under these circumstances. Their
principles have become so thoroughly established in the institutions and the latter have become so inflexible that resistance to change has proven to be quite successful. To
some extent this condition has prevailed throughout the whole
history of civilization. In more recent times the issue has
become even more perplexing since the pace of civilization
has become so accelerated that it has appeared that the integrating process was impossible.

A. TYPES OF SOCIETIES

The extent to which civilization and culture have been
correlated serves as a basis for describing the varied types
of societies. It may be difficult to find pure examples of

61

any one class. Moreover, the peculiar problems of a particular society may be quite unique. Nevertheless, there is in this stratification some pattern which will offer assistance in understanding the fundamental difficulties of human history as it has proceeded from the distant past to the painful conditions as they exist in the world today.

1. UNCIVILIZED CULTURES. Before the emergence of civilization, some forms of group association and identity had taken place. Primitive people had become adept in meeting the demands required for their existence. They utilized whatever was at hand. But they did so in terms of some underlying principles which guided their activities and served as the formative materials for a faith. Most guidelines were rigid offering no substantial basis for any devitation. Consequently, few provisions were made for change. The old order had to be maintained, and it was!

There was a distinctive direction in which the tribe moved; the individual accepted his lot and acted accordingly. There was probably very little inclination to introduce any modifications. Life was too perilous. Experimentation was a luxury which could scarcely be afforded. The guidelines, when they had been established, served almost indefinitely as the bases for confronting the universe and accomplishing it quite satisfactorily. The good and ills were organized into some type of scheme of things which was meaningful. It was only to the extent that there occurred the extraordinary or unexpected that some dissonance would be experienced. This difficulty would arise when the tribe came into relationship with other groups who followed a slightly different cultural pattern. The diversity would generally be in some particular elements rather than in any major area of difference. The similarities among the groups would be considerably greater than the idiosyncracies.

Given the inherent stability of the culture, there is some support for a widely held idea that primitive life was idyllic. From the very restricted vantage point of the people themselves it might be appropriate to apply this term. They did follow their daily pursuits in terms of a meaningful cultural pattern which gave the basis for some satisfactory fulfillment for themselves. This assessment is a far different thing than to say that we could consider it desirable from our later and more sophisticated perspective. Our outlook with its enlarged world view can only make us shudder at the circumscribed and difficult

62

mode of living. On the other hand, we might well recognize the fact that the ancient societies did have the advantage of a cultural orientation which can serve to challenge modern man to seek out that meaningful pattern of life which will do for him what the primitive culture accomplished for the people who followed it.

There are few, if any, primitive groups in existence today who conform to the pattern described. There is scarcely a tribe of people which has not been touched by the hand of some civilized nation of the world.[1] Consequently, we see the distress which is experienced by those societies which are still only on the threshold of modern life. Their experiences have been enlarged so that they have caught a glimpse of a life which is decidedly different than their own. However, much of this novelty has been thrust upon them so rapidly that there is no real understanding concerning the elements of civilization themselves. The story is told of a native woman in the Congo who was seen proudly displaying a refrigerator which she had secured when the white settlers moved out. "Now we can live like the white man," she said, as she took out some rotten fish from the box in which the temperature must have been 150 degrees. Even more tragic is the disruption which has ensued. The old ideals and values no longer exist; or, at least, they have been fractured and are rapidly disintegrating. The individual is being thrown back upon himself with insufficient resources to guide him. These groups are not sufficiently equipped to update their culture through their own assessments. Further, a way of life which might be transmitted to them from a civilized society would be difficult to comprehend. There is a question whether it would be possible to adapt an advanced outlook to meet the needs in this type of society. The gulf would be too great. Therefore, it is probably going to be a long, slow, tedious process of evolution itself which will be required to make possible a meaningful outlook on life as these groups increasingly appropriate ingredients from the existing civilizations. The problem is aggravated by the failure of the more advanced nations to be sensitive to the needs and willing to assist in the struggle. The long history of exploitation has established a pattern which is not easy to overcome. Hopefully, organized religion will be responsive to their cries for aid, and a helping hand will be extended to enable them to make the transition into the modern world.

There is another type of group which falls into this classi-

fication to a limited degree. It partakes of the ingredients
which are found in modern civilization, but it restricts the
extent of its usage. Its course of action has usually been
dictated by a form of isolation. It does not find itself in
the mainstream by the nature of its physical separation. Economic factors may preclude its becoming too deeply imbued
with these activities. But, most importantly, the religious
institutions of the group may set limits. At any rate, its
members live in a world which is severely circumscribed. Yet,
in many ways, it is a cultured existence in that it is based
on an orientation to life which is meaningful and purposeful.
Essentially it is a life directed by faith. The latter gives
solidity and group identity to the individual which proves
to have values which he is reluctant to lose. It is only as
he and, more especially, his children come to be exposed to
civlization in the more comprehensive sense that there is
likely to be tension and the resulting turmoil. The religious
life is built around ideas which preclude his participating
in many of the experiences and is not sufficiently comprehensive to enable him to move into the new dimensions. Given
this potential conflict, there is the basis for a neurosis.
Its external expression may be observed in the inclination
to flail out in all directions. When the number of people
who are affected becomes substantial, a society itself may
become disoriented. Many students of our western world
believe that a situation of this kind is providing the
basic problem of our era. We are trying to ride two horses
which are going in opposite directions. One is civilization
which says to get all you can in wealth, power, physical satisfactions, prestige, and advancements. Further, one should do
so in any way one can. The other approach is the source of
our culture, the Judaeo-Christian heritage. Its advice is
to give all that you can in personal service, possessions, love,
understanding, kindness, and gentleness. In this way the
abundant life, even eternal life, will be achieved. ". . .
no city or house divided against itself will stand."[2]

2. UNCULTURED CIVILIZATION. Civilization is concerned
with the tools, resources, and techniques through which man
carries forward his life. When it was initiated several thousand years ago, it moved forward with great rapidity. It is
quite remarkable what mankind has wrought since the time has
been very short as compared with the long period of primitive
backwardness. Some anthropologists estimate the age of man
at about 1,000,000 years. On the other hand, civilization
has existed a mere 7,000 years approximately. Therefore, it

means that the primitive period covered no less than 993,000 years! Notwithstanding the problem under consideration, this time perspective should enable one to disavow any real note of pessimism or discouragement.

As civilization has developed, there has been the need to create an effective cultural pattern which would be capable of identifying with the civilization. The underlying guidelines for purposeful living, which could serve as the basis for a religious commitment, have not been easily formulated. In part, this deficiency has been due to the propensity of human beings to rely on inherited motifs. Moreover, man has been too busily carving out civilizations to devote much thought or effort to an appropriate cultural pattern. At any rate, the voices have been heard which have attempted to soothe the distraught nature by saying that the traditional faith of the forefathers is adequate and that there is the need only to place confidence in the established modes of cultural orientation, especially as these ingredients have been conveyed by the religious institutions.

Increasingly, however, the bankruptcy of this approach has become obvious. Modern man has experienced an emptiness in his life. He has, indeed, gained the "whole world" but forfeited "his life."[3] The result has been a sense of futility. Both the individual and the society appear to be tossed hither and yon with no realistic affirmation as to any direction. Civilization has provided the "what" but nowhere is there expressed the "why."

3. CULTURED CIVILIZATION. Let us now project the ideal. It should be stated initially that the proposal does not suggest some final attainment. It is inconceivable that the developments in civilization will ever reach a completion. Alexander the Great is supposed to have sat down to weep because there were no more worlds to conquer. He certainly could not have arrived at this attitude in the modern world. The universe is unlimited, not only in spatial terms but, more importantly, in the possibilities for the greater unfolding and enrichment of human experiences. It is interesting to note that the summation of Jesus' teachings concerning the Kingdom of God has the verb in the perfect tense, "The Kingdom of God has drawn near." This statement expresses very effectively a religious perspective. The new order of life is constantly being observed. Yet, it is scarcely possible to think of it as something that is present, complete, and

entire. Therefore, the cultural pattern which is consonant with civilization must always be in the process of being created. As civilization makes its advancement, the integrating religion must do the same.

In this ideal type of society there is a dynamic power at work wherein the people are busily engaged in creating new modes of living and meeting the demands of life. New tools are being invented, new forms of social organization are emerging, new sources of energy are being discovered, and new media for expressing the human interest are developing. But there will be no less an effort on the part of the people to seek for new means to synthesize all of these elements into a unified pattern of life whereby each individual item contributes to a common purpose and meaning. The religion of the people will not be derelict in giving expression to the creative urge. It will be constantly at work seeking to find that direction for the diverse areas of life in the community so that there will be a sense of unity of outlook and a common appreciation for the individuals as each makes his own contribution to the shared ends. The efforts of each person will be made to assist in the fulfillment of life in the whole society. While this activity will result in the establishment of certain religious institutions, the latter can never become so solidified around some patterns that they will cease to be closely identified with the forward movement of the civilization.

In summary, the culture, too, must have that dynamic quality of growth. This process can occur only to the extent that it is very closely and intimately related to the daily activities of the people. It cannot afford to reach a stalemate. Should this occur, it would mean that it would quickly become obsolescent. Since religion is exercising the major role for cultural development, the religious leadership must be so closely associated with the affairs of persons in the society as a whole that the latter individuals will interact at every point of the venture in determining the religious faith. The religious order cannot be shut off from the world. It must be extremely knowledgeable concerning the affairs of everyday life so that it will understand the ingredients of the civilization and do its constructive work in terms of the experiences in the life of the lay persons.

In a very practical way, the religious leadership will serve not only to exercise the prerogatives in creating culture, but it will serve to dispense this understanding to the people as

66

a whole with that degree of effectiveness whereby the latter
will be responsive by giving their dedication and devotion to
it. In performing this service, a great effort should be made
to recocile different groups, and even individuals, in advancing cooperation in society. This operation is particularly required today as a result of the substantial amount of specialization in a highly developed and complex civilization. As a
result of this feature of modern life, different individuals
and groups are predisposed to see their own contributions and
have little appreciation for the values which are provided by
others. Consequently, the society becomes splintered and fragmented. To meet this condition, the religion of the whole person will be greatly concerned to provide thàt measure of understanding for one another whereby it will be seen that the very
success of civilization depends on an interdependence. It may
very well be that the scientist is properly commended for his
discoveries; but his work will be seriously hampered if the
garbage men fail to fulfill their responsibilities. Even
more pointedly, the urban dweller may have an enhanced appreciation for the great machines and their productions. But he
certainly has an inescapable need for the food which is supplied by the farmer. The more intricate the civilization becomes, the greater is there a need for an appreciative attitude toward every segment of society for its contributions.
It is the religion of the society which has the ability to
view the whole picture. It is concerned with all members
of the society both collectively and individually. The continued progress of the civilization will depend ultimately
upon the ability of the religion to provide for this understanding and appreciation one for the other.

B. RELIGION IN AN UNCULTURED CIVILIZATION

The position which has been developed can be most pointedly
expressed, and more clearly illustrated, by observing the status of religion in a society where civilization has advanced
rapidly but religion has not provided a correspondingly developed culture for the group. The problem arises when the
civilization has continued to evolve, but the religion has
failed to maintain a comparable pace. The latter's interest
reflects an earlier stage of civilization. No substantial
effort will have been made to keep step with the continued
enlargement of life. This situation is likely to occur when
the religion has become so fully matured in terms of an earlier civilization that it fulfills its function quite admirably
and successfully in terms of the past. The institutions become

67

organized to sustain these ends. Since the machinery becomes efficient, there is a tendency to lose sight of the reason for the organization. The dominant interest is to preserve the formed structures. Therefore, religion will inevitably lose its perspective and refuse to respond to the newly evolving order. No longer does it ask the appropriate question, How may we serve? Consequently, it becomes a society to be preserved rather than one which is designed to fulfill its essential role in society.

The result is a dichotomy. The vital human interests and attachments are the elements of civilization. New opportunities are observed whereby the expansion of life and the meeting of its needs can be realized. Emphasis is increasingly placed on the attractions found in the new order. This process can result in disaster. There is no genuine value in these things themselves. For example, the progress which has occurred in the medical arts has achieved remarkably in the extension of life and the relief of many pains. How significant is this attainment if life is empty and vain? This type of society and the individuals who compose it have lost heart and soul. Life has become a vacuous pursuit which has no more to it than the adding of one ingredient on to another. It has become a profitless undertaking. The members of the society have busied themselves about that which signifies nothing. Depression becomes common and takes it toll on persons, and they know not why. Pessimism is the most common fruit of this attitude, and it can become very destructive. Suicide is not an unusual end product.

Religion may yet provide a limited service in this situation. Unfortunately, there is an accepted opinion that it is the appropriate task of a faith. The role projected is for it to become a way of escape from civilization. It provides a way out of the dislocation brought on by the complex order confronting human beings. For a short time a person can withdraw into the sacred precinct and commune on the ideal of a meaningful life. It gives temporary rejuvenation and inspiration. It does point to the ideal in the abstract and provides some solace in its contemplation. There is the renewal of confidence in a divine being who is the ultimate determiner of human destiny. It portrays what life could become in terms of a meaningful and purposeful existence. Too often, however, there is only a minimum correlation with the experiences in everyday affairs. The person returns to his daily routine and discovers that the perspectives gained in

68

his spiritual meditation must be disregarded. They are simply
not practicable. Each one must live life in terms of what civilization provides and demands. The dreams portrayed by the religious leader are essentially forgotten.

One further service of religion is available. It can provide
the concept of a future life to which the individual can aspire.
In that order he will not have the problems and cares of life
as he experiences them in the present world. There is an unexpressed expectation that the elements of civilization which
have been painfully created in the course of human history will
not be relevant in the divine order of the future, Somehow - never too clearly spelled out - all meaning of living will be genuinely found in the new existence. This dream has provided contentment for mankind throughout the ages. He has been willing
to entrust himself to a faith which promised the blessings in
the future and set forth the means whereby they could be acquired. But fulfillment in the present state of existence has
not been seen as essentially germane to religion. With this
expressed view of their purpose, most traditional forms of
religion have been characterized as other-worldly.

This conception of religion has resulted in its becoming
formalized in terms of a strictly structured affair wherein
all the requirements are to be met in a carefully established
pattern. Certain requirements must be met. The expert is employed to accept the responsibility that the performances are
properly consummated. Thereby the constituency rests com-
fortably in the confidence that the ideals can be safely sequestered from the disturbing affairs of ordinary living and,
more importantly, be done so that the future bliss can be
assured. The sacrifices will be performed with the regularity
needed to assure the good will of the gods so that they will
not be too severe upon the faithful at the time of the great
judgment. The necessary affirmations will be made. The rituals
which will make the person a part of the anticipated blessed
company of the saints will be carried out with all the minute-
ness and exactitude demanded.

The above picture has been drawn to a somewhat exaggerated
degree. It does, however, indicate how often religion fails
at that most crucial function, the unifying of the elements inherent in civilization into a meaningful cultural pattern.
In reality the ideals of religion have entered into society to
a greater extent than the above description would suggest.

69

Nevertheless, the influence in the mundane affairs has been restricted. Neither the life of the individual nor that of the society has been determined substantially by the ideals upheld in the religious order. Too often in the past religion has become increasingly an appendage. Like the appendix in the physical body, it may, at an earlier period, have exercised a creative role. With the passage of time the function has decreased in its significance. Consequently, just as is the case with the physical organ, there may come a time when it will become so completely incompatible with the dynamic living of the group that surgery will be required. Or it may become so shriveled by uselessness that its services will be inconsequential and valueless. Eventually, it must give way to a new expression of faith which will be required in order to accomplish the task which desperately needs to be accomplished, to provide the basis for an integration of the elements present in civilization.

C. A PROPOSED SOLUTION

The need of society at any time is to have its civilization and its culture consonant one with the other. Every effort needs to be made to avoid disparity both in the state of attainment and the position of importance attached to each one. Both should be coordinated into a common perspective which embraces the totality of living. There is the particular need for the culture to be pervasive among all members of the society. All areas of life which operate from the vantage point of the ingredients in civilization should be inspired by the cultural ideals which will be able to give a sense of direction and meaning.

In terms of what has been developed in the preceding pages, this goal means that the most characteristic feature of culture, the religion of the society, must be dynamically and creatively involved in every facet of human experience. Whatever the cost in terms of established patterns and organization, it must become operative in the course of the daily living which is expressed by the individuals. The famous mystic, Meister Eckhart, expressed it as follows: "As thou art in church or cell, the same frame of mind carry out into the world, into its turmoil and its fitfulness." Man cannot afford the luxury of a religion which holds itself aloof from the daily pursuits in the industrial, business, professional, educational, and social lives of people. Religion must have that capacity to be active in every area which concerns humanity. When this goal is reached, then human affairs will become fulfilling enterprises.

In order to accomplish this objective, the issue of first importance is that of attitude. The religion must be willing to reconstruct itself in terms of the continually changing requirements of a developing civilization. It means, primarily, that there can be no absolutes which are permanent and incapable of change. When there are certain concepts which are basic to a particular faith, they must remain sufficiently flexible so that they will embody that content of meaning which is appropriate to the state of social development attained in a given era. For example, theistic religions may insist upon the reality of God. But this Being must be so conceptualized in the experiences of man that He/It will be adequately related to the processes of the universe with which human beings are most realistically concerned. The God of religion may be "the same yesterday, today, and forevermore;" but, certainly, man must be humble enough to recognize that this Being cannot be fully and finally expressed in any particular or finite terms which are used to describe this reality. In other words, God cannot be too small. As new insights are achieved about reality, religion must be responsive to them in order to permeate the personal and social life. In this way the creative spirit will insure that these new assessments will become a part of the values which are really significant.

In order for this process to occur, the society must have that foresight to dedicate some of its members to the role of providing the required leadership in religion. These individuals must have the usual qualities of character expected of persons who serve in this area - a deep concern for humanity and a sense of commitment to a life of dedicated service. On the other hand, there is, equally, the need for men and women with the intellectual capacity to make religion relevant to an increasingly complex world. The best minds of a society simply cannot be permitted to enter other fields of endeavor - business, science, education, philosophy, etc. Many of these distinguished persons should find their contributing roles in the establishment and furtherance of a dynamic religion. They must be provided with the most thorough preparation which the society can offer. This will include educational opportunities which are broadly inclusive so as to achieve that depth of understanding in the arts of civilization which will provide the competence for the magnitude of tasks confronting them.

71

The quality of the training must be superior so that they can be adequately prepared to meet the demands required by their vocation.[4]

A major problem exists concerning religious leadership. Unfortunately, the principal quality which is often insisted upon is administrative ability. This stipulation may result in the rejection of a thoughtfully creative individual. Aside from the duty to manage the institution, his primary areas of responsibilities arise when he will be called upon to provide the appropriate ceremonies for the several periods in life - birth, marriage, death, etc. These functions are designed to give continuity and stability to the organization. This assessment concerning these areas of clerical life is not meant to suggest that these responsibilities are unimportant. It is tragic when the leader's duties are considered to be coextensive with them. Actually, many of the managerial tasks should not be his but those of the lay membership. The apostle Paul may have been attempting to place this type of role in proper perspective when he wrote the Corinthians: "I am thankful that I baptized none of you except Crispus and Gaius."[5] The first call of the clergy is to serve as a prophet and work creatively through the various areas of human experience so that the interacting of civilization and culture can be promoted. To keep alive a dialogue with the manifold dimensions of human living constitutes his first responsibility. Too often overt recognition is given to this point of view; then, he is overwhelmed by what should be of lesser significance, the sustaining the institution.

A measure of organization undoubtedly is required along with appropriate cultic practices which will embody in visible form certain features of the prophetical ministry. The creation of this part of the faith, however, should be done with great care in order to avoid the temptation to establish the organization as an end rather than a means. Moreover, it must maintain a close relationship with the main steam of the faith as the latter interacts with the issues confronted within the civilization. In particular, the organizational features cannot be finalized. Should this occur, it would lose its ability to challenge the individuals in the society. Too often it simplifies matters so that it scarcely stirs the creative imagination. The person is thought to be a child who still needs milk in a bottle - perhaps canned milk at that! There is an appeal on the lowest level. In reality

72

the person who is being ministered to may be yearning for something more substantial. Thus there is danger of showing the easy way in a faith. Little direction is given to strain after higher ideals.

The cult can serve to provide tools whereby a sense of unity of purpose is achieved. It can elicit a response of an inner, not merely an outward, self to that which will be accepted as the ultimate determiner of life in its entirety. The response will be that of a complete and fervent devotion and loyalty. The unification will be reflected in the life of the individual and in sharing a common faith with his fellow worshippers. In theistic terms, the God of the faith becomes not a far-off possibility but an immanent reality with whom the individual attains a sense of rapport. Flowing from this will be the spirit of brotherhood which begins with his fellow believers and flows out to embrace all mankind. In Christian terminology, there is achieved the one great family of God or, in biblical terms, the Kingdom of God.

CHAPTER VI

CULTURE AND CULTIVATION

No person lives unto himself alone. Nor is he the sole determiner of his being. Personal living is determined in a more or less close justaposition with other individuals and groups. These contacts and associations create, to a substantial degree, his very nature – what he truly is as a human being. His personality is a social product. His ideals and values, his goals and aspirations, are born and developed within him as a part of the social orientation.

The recognition of this dependency on society would be helpful in the development of oneself. It would provide an uncentive to live creatively from the point of view of the social contribution rather than what it might do for the person as an individual. Unfortunately, we have been instilled with the idea that each one is a determiner of his own destiny so that our orientation to life has become almost totally ego-centered. Consequently, we become almost totally oblivious to the social implications of our actions and assess them only in terms of the significance to ourselves. Initially this type of motivation elici s a measurable increase in interpersonal conflicts. Those concerns which have significance to one individual stand, oftentimes, in opposition to those which are valued by others. If this approach is pursued extensively, it will result in many areas where person-to-person contacts become very difficult. The very concept of cooperation may take on a negative label. Were certain social institutions to mediate these disputes not established, society would become impossible.

To live life from this point of view must become frustrating and disappointing. The person's areas of interest will be narrowed. His life will be increasingly circumscribed. The individual is more and more shut up within himself. This mode of existence can only bring disillusionment. Our modern economic operations illustrate this issue. The person who works on the assembly line in one of our giant manufacturing plants is assigned a particular task. As a result of its limited scope, the individual will quickly become very expert at the performance of his operation. Unfortunately, however, he will most likely think of it simply as a job to be done. It is his work; for his performance he receives his reward in the form of a pay check. But his sights are limited to this narrow perspective. There is little recognition of any social consequences in his work. The product is not seen as something to be used by others and, thereby, eliciting a sense of pride in the quality.

Similarly, our educational system has become unsocially organized. Each teacher has a particular job to perform. Learning itself becomes fragmentized. The students become "warm bodies" who are designed to fulfill some quantification scale set up by an impersonal governing body. It is amazing that any education takes place.

In a more detailed analysis, it could be shown that our entire society has been developed along these lines. Sociality as a major factor in human existence has been blurred. It is, therefore, not surprising that we have the amount of social discord which we are currently experiencing. It is remarkable that it is not more extensive. Conflict, tension, hostility, bitterness, and war are the products of the idea that the individual is the determiner of his own destiny.

Fortunately,we do have a greater amount of sociality operating than is immediately apparent. Our basic approach to life is self-realization. When we get actually involved, however, we discover that we must relate to others in our accomplishments. The employee on the assembly line works in a community. Therefore, the major problem is a difference between attitude and practice. A major gain could be achieved if our perspective could be redirected.

Historically, the emergence of civilization greatly accentuated the problem. An enlargement of human interests and concerns rapidly arose. The possibilities of personal enrichment were attractive, and individuals were motivated to seek their own ends. Social institutions were not always available to guide these activities for the enrichment of the group. It would require a long period of time and many experiences to enable the broader social orientation to take place and the requisite social instruments to be created. But civilization moves so rapidly that scarcely has the social reconstruction occurred than new opportunities are appearing. Consequently, it has proved exceptionally difficult for socialization to keep pace with the expanding civilization. No sooner has some adjustments been made than new patterns for living have stared the person in the face. On occasions the modifications were quite radical in nature so that the inherited

76

social instruments simply could not cope with the new directions. The whole world seemed to be turned upside down. It appeared that none of the traditional values were being sustained. A closer examination would probably have indicated that a very considerable amount of the affairs of life did, in fact, continue essentially as they had previously. But novelties attracted so much attention that it became difficult for the person to be aware of these established patterns. Conquently, there was a constant hankering for the "good old days." If the advances which had been wrought by civilization had been seriously considered, that wish could scarcely have been expressed. The real problem revolved around the conflict between individualism and sociality. There was too great a yearning to make the world suit the individual's own desires. Were this goal to be arrived at, many of the new elements of current life would be retained along with what was favored in the earlier stage of history.

Regrettably, life does not proceed in this manner. Civilization is essentially a social product and involves changes which eliminate some of the traditional patterns since they are incongruent with the newer creations. One cannot have the advantages of city life with its closeness in the intermingling among human beings accompanied by the associated noise and turbulence along with the quietness and individual freedoms which are found in the tranquility of a rural environment. The dilemma which confronts the individual is present when one desires the mode of life provided by the latter while enjoying the advantages which are available only in urban living. The "urban sprawl" reflects the problem in American life.

When one observes the relationships which prevail between urban and rural society in America, the potential for conflict becomes more evident. The city dweller is dependent on manufacturing and trade and perceives life from this setting. But the life-style of the farmer provides a substantially different point of view. Neverthless, there is an inescapable interdependence so that life would be essentially impossible for either one without the other. The farmer must supply the food and other raw materials for the urbanite. The latter, on the other hand, offers to the rural dweller goods and services. Machinery, transportation, and chemicals assist the farmer in his work. In order for modern society to prosper, there must be means found to encourage a spirit of cooperation between these two sectors of the economy.

A notable change has occurred during the present century in this urban-rural relationship. Before World War I, the social structure favored the farming community since it controlled a large share of the power structure. In recent years a majority of the people live in the urban areas. Public policies have changed accordingly. They give greater advantages to city dwellers. The only solution for the farmer is to become a part of the urban community; and he has done this at a rapid rate. Technology and big business control of agriculture has added further pressure since the small family operation has become increasingly difficult to sustain. When the farmer moves to the city, he usually is ill at ease in his new environment. He may have difficulty in relating to this type of order. Consequently, he becomes a badly disillusioned individual. Since we live in a society based on the freedom of the person, almost no effort is put forth to make the transition smoother.

Since rapid changes are taking place and no guiding motifs are emerging to direct the course of events, it is not surprising to find the situation developing into general social discord. Increasingly, pressures of life force each person to retreat into his own individual self. It becomes more and more difficult to appreciate the basis for, or even the need of, any genuine relationships with other people. To counteract the inherent loneliness in this type of life, we do try to form some social relationships. But the very fact that our thinking has been molded in terms of separate existences, we find that these groups are very difficult to sustain. Each person will contribute to its functions only to the degree that it makes some contributions to his own personal interests. It must have value for him as a person. When these benefits are no longer adequate, participation ceases altogether; or, at least it becomes severely limited.

Often these societies do as much damage as they do good. They are organizations of small groups of individuals who recognize certain common interests. The group is established for the expressed putpose of advancing the goals set by its membership. The ends have the primary objective to counteract the aims of other societies whose success would be detrimental to them. To meet this threat, the latter respond by expressing a similar attitude of opposition. In the final analysis, the social structures prove to be little more than the separate individuals in larger dimensions and with decidedly greater strength. Instead of the social orientation contributing to the creating of a social consciousness, the real result is the increase in the tensions and stresses of the individuals in society. The group which moves in this direction can only reap the inevitable destruction, not from any   ternal force but as a result of its own inner liabilities.

This very complicated situation generally prevents the unifying power of religion from building a stable culture. The failure rests, in part, with the religion. Its own structure and function has been developed around a traditional order so that its own adjustments are made with great anguish. There is a reluctance to exercise the creativity and to give the directions which are needed. There is, too, the inclination for the religious order to segregate itself from the fulminations of everyday life experiences. As a result, it fails to be very much aware of the new order in society and the need to adjust its own insights and directions. It is this religious factor which makes the society hectic and the life of the individual inchoate.

A great deal of disparity will likely occur in the society. Many cleavages may exist within the social structure. Jesus recognized that this condition would result from his teachings taking hold in the society of his day. "For from now on if there are five people in a house, they will be divided three against two and two against three. Father will be against son, and son against father, mother against daughter and daughter against mother, mother-in-law against daughter-in-law and daughter-in-law against her mother-in-law."[8] If this divisiveness persists, the society will have within itself the seeds of its own destruction. Again, Jesus utilized a figurative statement which conveyed this type of predicament. "And everyone who hears these words of mine and does not do them will be like a foolish man who built his house upon the sand; and the rain fell, and the flood came, and the winds blew aaįnst that house and it fell; and great was the fall of it."[9] It is simply the case that religion lacks the ability to bridge the gap whereby members of a group are separated one from the other.

Thus we have before us the problem of trying to orient ourselves as individuals so that we shall be in a position to relate ourselves more successfully to our fellowmen. The predicament is set for us by our social order wherein there are

the elements of civilization. But these features can serve
their purpose most effectively only when they are geared to
respond to a determining cultural pattern. The latter has as
its major ingredient a creative religion which can coordinate
and direct toward life's fulfillment the varied concerns and
interests which confront persons in life. The individual in
society must be able to move forward within the framework of
the cultural pattern. To the extent he does this provides a
basis for classification into several categories.

B.   TYPES OF INDIVIDUALS

1. UNCULTIVATED UNCULTURED.   This type of person has little
knowledge concerning the modern trends of life. He has been
exposed to the stream of events and the developments in the
varied affairs of the human order; but these experiences have
made only a modest impression upon him. Very definitely he
has not tasted these things very appreciably; they have evoked
little concern on his part. Civilization, in general, has been
either consciously or unconsciously rejected. Even more tragic
is the fact that this type of person does not participate in,
nor reflect, any distinct cultural pattern. There are no guiding motifs which determine the course of his life. Whatever
religious faith he may have been attached to has been all but
discarded. In most instances, there had never been a strong
sense of relating. That is, he had never been substantially
involved in any established religious group. Consequently, it
was very easy for him to become dissociated from it. It would
scarcely have been missed. Growing out of this status, he is
at loose ends in every sense of the term. He simply moves
along in the currents of life regardless of the direction of
movement. Fortunately, there are few persons who could be
unhesitatingly classified in this group. Even the derelicts
of society often have a rather well-established code of behavior. Sometimes it is more carefully formulated and cultivated than is that set of attitudes which is professed by
members of other groups. The expression, "There is honor
among thieves," expresses the idea. In instances of this
nature, external appearances are deceptive. If one were to
probe more deeply into the inner lives of these people, qualities would often be found which could be called distinctive -
even admirable. Insofar as one discovers a person who can be
truly classified in this group, it is questionable as to how
far it is possible to assist him in overcoming his deficiencies
in either dimension herein being considered. It would definite-

ly require a tremendous effort to bring the individual into a
different order of people.[3]

2. UNCULTIVATED BUT CULTURED. In any society it is probably
correct to say that this group is numerically the largest. These
individuals have relatively little knowledge about the currents
of civilization. They have simply not maintained a close and
sustained relationship with the developing of the society.
Their contacts with the world around them are severely restricted,
and they make little effort to expand their associations. Nevertheless, they are not competely isolated from many of the
ordinary affairs whereby the society operates. In modern life
the means of communications are so extensive that people of this
group can scarcely avoid the impact of current events. On the
other hand, the severe lack of preparation to respond to the
social order raises the question as to how much significance
these occurrences have for them. Their knowledge is rather
superficial. As a result, they have great difficulty in understanding the meaning of the activities. To a very considerable
degree the affairs of life are absorbed and comprehended only
to the degree that they have some direct impact on their lives.
They are ill prepared to appreciate the fundamental bases of
the civilization. Consequently, the latter prove to be too
perplexing for their consideration. Seldom will there be an
active seeking to gain an understanding.

On the other hand, this group does have a culture. There
is a unifying force which gives direction and significance to
their lives. They have a group relatedness through which
they participate and share in common outlooks and perspectives.
The affiliation is especially rewarding since it gives a sense
of belonging with others who are imbued with the same orientation toward life. It provides a sense of fulfillment for
their lives which would otherwise be extremely bare and meager.

The item which stands out most prominently in determining
the culture of these people is a religion. Their fundamental
outlooks and values are formed by this feature of their lives.
Most of them will take an active role in the group expression
of the faith. This factor gives an added dimension since the
support from the social relationships will be of immense value
in countering a feeling of helpless in an otherwise isolated
existence. A few of them will go so far as to build their
major activities around the religious community. Their attendance upon corporate service is regular; their contributions

81

to the financial support is substantial;[4] their leisure time
will be utilized in a variety of activities sponsored by the
group. There is a strong predisposition to make this area
superior to every other interest. Naturally, there will the
others who will not be as deeply and extensively involved in
the outward expression of the religion. Neverthless, their
basic orientation to life will be strictly in keeping with
the expectations conveyed by the faith. In terms of everyday
life, one would actually find few differences between the two
groups.

As long as members of this social division are not too deeply
affected by the elements of civilization, their lives will
move forward quite fully and with a considerable measure of
achievement. Even their hardships, pains, and sufferings may
be borne in terms of an accepted plan of the universe to which
they have committed themselves. The important concern is that
they will be kept essentially isolated from the new currents of
knowledge of the universe and the contemporary world order.
Any appreciable relationship with the latter cannot fail to
raise questions concerning the culture founded on a religion
derived from an older civilization. The awareness of the contemporary world and the recognition that there is an incompatibility between it and their own perspectives concerning reality
can bring with it a sense of dislocation and a growing sense
of uncertainty. Life can become terribly frustrating under
these circumstances. It is a particularly tragic affair when
this occurrence takes place after a person has lived life to
a rather advanced age. With proper encouragement and guidance,
younger persons can begin to reconstruct their lives without
major upheavals and, especially, without losing a sense of the
place of religion in their experiences.

3. UNCULTURED BUT CULTIVATED. To a degree, this group represents those persons whose way of life is opposite the preceding.
On the one hand, they know and appreciate the elements of modern
life. They have been trained in the several disciplines through
which the processes of life are unfolded. The physical sciences,
the social sciences, and the humanities have given to them an
understanding of the productive agencies in modern life.
Through a substantial education experience, supplemented by a
continuing interest in the developments of civilization, they
are deeply saturated with an understanding of, and admiration
for, the course of life made possible by the tools and techniques which have been discovered or created. Therefore, this

exposure to the world in all its manifold expressions is not a superficial one. These understandings have been implemented in the experiences wherein they have been involved. There is a genuine approbation concerning what has occurred and are, even now, taking place. Consequently, one thing is assured. There is no turning back. They have recognized that a tremendous universe is available to man and a confidence that he has the ability to relate successfully with it.

But these persons are uncultured. They have a knowledge of many things; they live life in terms of this enlightenment. But the question of the meaning and purpose of life itself has scarcely been faced. There has been the limitation of time. Too often their involvement in the ingredients of their civilization has been so extensive that there has simply been no serious involvement with fundamental questions about reality. As long as they can continue blissfully undisturbed about goals, purposes, human destiny, and ultimate values, they may be able to exist without any real awareness of culture. Usually, however, it is not possible for one to proceed indefinitely without being confronted with disturbing questions. Some major disaster in a person's life may force consideration of them. Even a continuing successful existence may bring one to the point where the inherent worth of the activities may be questioned.⁵ At that strategic moment, a sense of futility or emptiness may emerge. Life may suddenly be experienced as lacking any depth or significance. It is at this juncture that the need for a religious faith may appear most insistently. The traditional cry at these moments has been: What then must I do to be saved? From the jumbled ingredients there is a felt need for a wholeness which is required to provide a solid basis for fulfilling life.

These persons may have been identified in the course of their lives with a religion. But it had been considered little more than an appendage to life with a few perfunctory requirements to be met. As a molding and determining factor of life, there had been no occasion to think in those terms. The individual possessed a religion; the religion did not possess him. Hence, he had listened only half-heartedly to the seers of the ages as they poured forth their challenges to respond to the demands of a creative way of living. There had developed within the individual no real inner spirit of religion. He was too busily partaking of the fruits of life with no effort being made to cultivate roots which were firmly planted whereby the real affirmation of life could be made. Each thing was done for the occasion at hand or for some specific goal in the immediate future. There was no need for a long range perspective and a directing of life toward some profound goal. There was no guiding principle by which the particular aspects of life could be assessed. He had never consciously affirmed the position: Eat, drink and be merry; tomorrow you may die. Had he done so, he would have had to weigh that position in relation to other formulas for a complete life. Nevertheless, the essential ingredients of this philosophy of life did serve that purpose. It was the life of the moment which was operative. Comparable to this ancient prescription is the one which is all too evident in our modern period. It is the concept of speed. There is so much of life to sample that one must move with the greatest amount of acceleration which is possible. The ultimate question is, How long will it take? Hence, life becomes filled - but of what? The characteristic was well expressed sometime ago when it was suggested that "a new type of man is being evolved - one with a full stomach, an empty head, and a hollow heart."

The seriousness of the situation is compounded by the fact that this type of person will generally have a prominent part in determining the course of society itself. He will, in many instances, occupy positions of leadership in a variety of activities. Consequently, he determines not only his own destiny but provides the direction whereby others will follow. He will be accepted as the example to emulate. Consequently, the real sickness of a society, as previously described, may ultimately be his responsbility. The predicament was well expressed in the biblical statement: "Can a blind man lead a blind man? Will they not both fall into a pit?"[6]

It is this group which will be responsible for a growing disenchantment, cynicism, and disillusionment which will prevail. Even worse, it is not unlikely that social chaos will ultimately result. The thin veneer of civilization may not be sufficient to provide staying power for the society.

4. CULTIVATED AND CULTURED. The source of both personal and social fulfillment is to be found only in those individuals who embrace civilization in the context of a well-ordered culture. The richness of society depends on them as was well expressed in the sixteenth century by Martin Luther: "The prosperity of a country depends not on the abundance of its reve-

nue, nor on the strength of its fortifications, nor on the beauty of its public buildings; but it consists in the number of its cultured citizens, in its men of education, enlightenment and character; here are to be found its true interest, its chief strength, its real power." This type of person has an extensive knowledge and understanding of the various facets of life as members of the preceding group. He has drunk deeply of civilization. He has a tremendous appreciation for advancements in human knowledge and the tools designed to make for a more abundant life. Further, there is a passionate search for more knowledge. There is no attempt to downgrade the understanding of the universe as the second group might do. His position on the stage of civilization is second to none.

But he has gone further. He has advanced beyond the examination of the separate and independent elements. He has gained a perspective whereby the discrete parts come together into a significant and meaningful whole. Individual attractions must justify their status in relationship with the course of life to which he is committed. To a very large extent, he controls things rather than being subjected to them. Life is so well-ordered that even his mistakes do not overwhelm him. They are not catastrophes. He does not become disheartened and disillusioned by them. He still has his life organized around an evolved synthesis whereby life continues its onward course even when there are some unfortunate errors. There is an evenness to life. In like manner, the successes of life are not overly estimated as to their worth. Rather, they are maintained in proper relationship with the whole complex of experiences as they come within the province of the person's daily living. Thereby, he can keep on the tried and true course with the need to introduce modifications only to the extent that adjustments appear to be required.

The accomplishment of this status is effected through the achieving of a dynamic faith which is consonant with civilization as it may presently exist and capable of being sustained even in the face of further advances which civilization brings forth. It is this religion which organizes the several parts into a coordinated whole by which the individual moves confidently forward with the achieving of the satisfactions which compose the abundant life. The significance of this type of individual is not only to be found in his own personal attainments. There is, too, the influence which flows from him to infuse the same creativity in the social order and in the lives

of the persons who respond to this influence. Jesus recognized
this remarkable achievement when he described this type of person in his typical metaphors. "You are the salt of the earth.
. . . You are the light of the world. A city set on a hill cannot be hid."7

C. LIMITED NUMBER IN THE LAST GROUP

As in any form of classification, the number of individuals
who would be properly included in each of the four groups
described above is difficult to determine. The process of
actually labeling a particular individual is a rather uncertain one. Nevertheless, in terms of generalizations, the ideal
portrayed in the fourth group would not be attained by a substantial number. That is, those who would be thoroughly acquainted with the trends in modern civilization and sufficiently well identified with its many-sided nature and, at the same
time, would approach these areas of life from the vantage point
of a creative faith would not be substantial. On the contrary,
they would likely be the exception. A number of factors contribute to this state of affairs.

1. TOO MANY INDIVIDUALS HAVE NOT BEEN ENLIGHTENED. There
is a woeful lack of knowledge concerning modern life among most
people. Obviously, this predicament is especially evident in
countries of the world where the literacy rate is very low.
Even more disturbing, however, is the fact that in western
lands, where stupendous efforts have been put forth to overcome this deficiency, there is the depressing recognition that
among the great majority of the citizens the extent of their
knowledge is quite low. This statement is not intended to assert that they are completely ignorant. The modern person has
too many exposures to the many and varied features of modern
life to be totally lacking in an apprehension of elements in
modern citilization. Too often, however, the exposure will be
highly superficial and inconsequential.

This situation exists primarily as a result of the failure
on the part of the people themselves. The opportunities to become informed are extensive. But they have simply failed to
take advantage of the presentations whereby they could achieve
knowledge. Through the printed and spoken word there is no
lack of information. It does, however, require effort and a
creative imagination in order to partake most effectively of
these offerings. They may subscribe to the daily newspaper,

but their reading will be limited to the headlines. Only a few books will be owned, if any; little use will be made of the free libraries; concerts and lectures will not be attended; travel will restricted both in quantity and in quality. In other words, the available means will scarcely be utilized whereby the person could become cognizant of the course being run by civilization.

There is, however, another side to the issue. The amount of knowledge which confronts the individual is so stupendous that he scarcely knows where to begin. It is somewhat like the child on Christmas morning who is so astounded by the gifts of Santa Claus that he does not know which toy should be tried out first. This factor is coming to be an increasing problem due to the rapidity in the increase in knowledge.

Another inhibiting consideration is that too many people underestimate their ability to gain knowledge - or, at least, this is an excuse which is used. One of the most assured results of modern studies is the fact that everyone has greater faculties for gaining knowledge than have been fully utilized. Most individuals have the ability to advance far beyond their present state of understanding. Further, the increasing amount of leisure time provides opportunity for enlarging one's perspective. Unfortunately, there is a counter attraction in the forms of entertainment whereby one can receive satisfactions with only modest effort. The latter receive a higher priority than the requirement to put forth effort to enlarge the grasp of reality in its many dimensions.[8]

An additional factor which hinders the development of this understanding of the universe is a fear of dislocation. That is, the person who lacks this knowledge has developed a cultural relationship which is satisfying. His associates consist of other individuals who have the same level of attainment and perspective. He finds these relationships meaningful. Were he to move away from this stance intellectually, he may well find himself socially ostracized. Consequently, there is mutual reciprocity on the part of the several members of the group whereby no one is willing to make the move toward a larger appropriation of knowledge.[9]

Finally, there is a concern that previously established ideas which have become innate to his very existence will require reconstruction or elimination. For example, why should a person inform himself concerning the findings of cultural anthropology when these insights might serve to upset his theories, expressed or unexpressed, about the inferiorities of certain races. It is much easier and more confortable to keep the mind closed to any truths which could disturb the tranquility of the soul.

2. ORGANIZED RELIGION FOSTERS IGNORANCE. Religious institutions develop wherein only a limited amount of knowledge is required. Very often even this understanding bespeaks another day and age. Hence, it attracts to itself those who are already lacking in intellectual achievements. There follows a cultural identity which is supported by the religious perspective. Under these circumstances, the religious order itself may discourage the enlargement of knowledge. It may even affirm that knowledge of the present world is a detriment to a person's spiritual achievement. The current order is an evil one; there is the need, therefore, to give full attention to those things which the institution values. Faithfulness in these matters will guarantee future salvation. The machinery of the institution becomes well-oiled and adjusted to this arrangement. There is a disinclination toward making any changes in the status of things and in the outlook of its constituency. There is a recognition that to the degree that an individual enlarges his perspective, a concurrent loss of interest in the organization and its teachings may result. Under these circumstances the religious society becomes a follower in the ongoing course of civilization. On the one hand, it condemns the developing civilization. This evaluation may be justified by the failure of the society to relate its advancements to a high sense of meaning and purpose. The religious order will than present an attractive program in terms which are unrelated to the current areas of interest. Under these circumscribed operations it will deny its responsibility to carry out a creative role in the determination of the civilization and its ends.

Through its failure to become involved in the main currents of life, religion does little to give cultural order. The justification for this approach can be easily rationalized. The organized faith does provide a frame of reference wherein the members are happy with the order as it is presently constituted. Why make any changes? To engage in the latter may contribute to the formation of many unpleasantnesses and uncertainties. The prevailing idea is to keep the faith; do not let it be disturbed by modern knowledge. In no way can it be seen that the religion should be the guiding force in organizing the knowledge and making it the effective instrument for human advancement. The organization becomes more important than the purpose for which it exists.

Guided by this perspective, it is understandable that the uncultivated person will be more than glad to follow the advice of the institution. He finds his faith to be adequate in terms of his own understanding. He does not see any particular worth in the task of becoming knowledgeable concerning the world which lies beyond his own narrow province. Moreover, he is much too busy making a living to become really involved. Therefore, he takes his stance and supports the efforts of those who insist that new knowledge is a dangerous thing.

3. THE CULTIVATED PERSON LOSES CONTACT WITH THE SOURCE OF CULTURE. As long as the religious society operates from the vantage point of an outlook and perspective appropriate to a preceding age, the cultivated individual will have difficulty in relating himself to it. His knowledge has been derived from the new order. Consequently, he cannot genuinely correlate it with the perception which serves as the basis for the religion. He may continue to identify with the religious organization; he may even be actively engaged in its affairs. But the religion does little or nothing for him in terms of his status as a cultivated person. His life is lived in its major dimensions without any sense of its having religious implications. In actuality, it may have been so filled with ingredients derived from the new age that he has simply not been aware of the fact that there was anything missing in the fulfillment of the self. He may, perhaps, feel a deep sense of not being particularly appreciative of some ideas expressed by his traditional faith. They may appear to be incongruous with his own outlook. But he does not stop to examine the situation. As a result, the pursuit of civilization is carried out with little concern for evaluating it in terms of a meaningful religious faith.

From this assessment of the situation, the blame must be leveled in two dimensions. On the one hand, the institutional religion has failed in its need to be a creative force in integrating the multifaceted features in the complexities of civilization. At the same time, the failure of the cultivated person to be responsive cannot be neglected. Some individuals in this category have no relationship with the religion or, at

best, only a nominal attachment. Understandably, they can perceive no real values in it. It is essentially incongruent with
their own intellectual development. In its traditional form,
religion has become irrelevant. At any rate, this group ne-
glects its responsibilities. By failing to identify themselves
with the religious societies so as to bring their knowledge
and ability to bear upon the formation of a faith which is appropriate for the present stage of civilization, they do a decided disservice both to themselves and to humanity. They have
major contributions to offer in the way of a broad span of understanding of the universe as disclosed by modern knowledge.

One can appreciate some of the factors which contribute to
this state of affairs. On the one hand, they would feel a
sense of discomfort in the ideas as expressed in the forms of
religion as presently constituted. These perspectives would
appear to be so anachronistic that they would be repellent.
They bespeak a day which has long since passed. Members of
this group see institutionalized religion as it is rather than
as it might become - especially under the influence and direction of their creative efforts.

Moreover, they would meet considerable resistance on the
part of a substantial number of the constituency attached to
the institution. Consequently, they will probably feel a reluctance to suggest modifications in the face of the difficulties which might erupt. Why should one disturb what is appealing to many deeply religious persons? It should be recognized, however, that the continuation of the current state of
religion must eventually lead to an even greater irrelevance
for the society.

There is another factor, too. The cultivated persons are
too often not aware that within the religious societies there
are major currents of change which are taking place. In actuality, there is the need for the men and women who are conversant with modern life in its major dimensions and developments
to lend their strength and energy to an undertaking which is
already well on its way. Fortunately, information concerning
these changes are gradually being brought forth to public disclosure. Sometimes it is being done rather radically. When
a group of theologians bluntly declare that God is dead, the
news makes the headlines. As a matter of fact, however, these
ideas are really "old stuff" to many who have been wrestling
with religious issues in professional settings. While not de-

nying that thoughtful, creative work has been accomplished by these individuals, those who have been trained in the disciplines related to religion will not find startling results in these presentations. The great value will be in informing the educated populace that these trends are taking place in the field of religion.

Closely related to this factor is another problem - and it may be the real source of difficulty. The type of individual who is being described has oftentimes been nurtured in some religious faith. His understanding of religion is what has been engendered in him under these circumstances. Consequently, there has ensued a cultural lag. Understanding has been acquired quite extensively in most areas except religion. In this latter field, there has not been the same exposure and understanding. Especially has there not been a presentation from the standpoint of its challenging potentialities in human experience. The result has been that there has been gained substantial knowledge about many things; in the area of religion it has been microscopic. In other words, the only comprehension of religion which has been acquired has been received through the traditional religious establishments. This situation is especially true in the United States. Its policy of separation between church and state has been especially unfortunate in this matter. It has fostered a nation of religious illiterates. Even more tragic is the fact that this neglect has asserted that religion is a peripheral to life. Its value is minimal.

D. THE SOLUTION

From the analysis of the problem, it is quite apparent what the basic solution of the situation is as it exists today. First, there must be a continuing effort made to enlarge the knowledge which people have concerning the universe. Individuals must be cultivated. As was stated previously, a significant part of this problem is the lack of concern on the part of a substantial number of people to appropriate for themselves an insight into the tremendous potentialities of the universe. It may be necessary for the educational system to redirect its efforts. Conceivably, we are too insistent upon students gaining knowledge of the subject matter instead of its value for human fulfillment. In any field of study no one can gain more than a fraction of the facts which are even now available. Many of them will be forgotten in a short time. Other items will no longer be tenable. But if there were an appreciation for the significance of what was being learned, it may be that the individual would come to have a greater desire for continuing the quest for knowledge. Moreover, it is possible that less would be forgotten by virtue of this more intense interest.

A second factor will be wrought out in the religious institutions as they assume their rightful role as the precursors of life in the society. There is the need to become less concerned to maintain their own interests in order to go out to serve mankind in the age which has its currents needs. They must seek to give direction to the unfolding of the universe as this is brought forth by the developments taking place in civilization. Their role is to be a leader, not a follower. Hence, they must be in the forefront in instilling this desire for an ever enlarging civilization in all of its dimensions. They must present a challenging way of life to their constituencies. Further, the task must be performed within the context of the state of things as they actually are and not in terms of what they might have been in an earlier age when a different civilization was operative. It has been frequently stated that religion must be presented in the language of contemporary man. Perhaps it would be better to say that it must be conveyed in the ideology of contemporary man. This assertion does not mean allowing the civilization to be determinant. It suggests, rather, that religion will determine the nature of civilization but from the vantage point of the latter's own attainment. This process requires a continuing interaction between religion and civilization.

Finally, there is the personal element. The leadership must come from those who are knowledgeable in the things of the present order. It is the cultivated man who must be dynamically associated with the unfolding of the new order as it is created. The professional religious leadership must be trained in the outlook of the modern world; but they need to receive support from the cultivated persons as they take responsible roles in the religious institutions.

CHAPTER VII

THE NATURE OF PHILOSOPHY

With the emergence of that creature whom we call Homo sapiens, there arose that phenomenon which we call "philosophy." As man became conscious of himself and the world around him, he had, perforce, to take some attitude toward the two and their interrelationships. The biblical writer expressed this issue most poignantly when he described the process by which Adam and Eve lost their ethereal status and became human beings. They became aware of a special tree and two possible attitudes which could be taken toward it. On the one hand, they could accept the fact that it meant death; and, therefore, it should be avoided. On the other hand, it might mean proceeding through death unto life. Most importantly, they were confronted with the tree, themselves, and the necessity to respond to the problem of the relationship between the two. When a decision had been made and they had partaken of the fruit from the tree, "then the eyes of both of them were opened, and they knew that they were naked. . ."[1] A simple, forthright statement of man achieving manhood! He had, thereby, become a philosopher. However much we might desire, in the travails of life, to return to that stage of existence where we neither know nor understand, it simply cannot be accomplished. Each person must accept the fact that there is no way whereby one can escape either the world or himself.[2]

This portrayal means that philosophy is a universal phenomenon. Notwithstanding popular opinion, it is not some esoteric ability which is restricted to a small group of persons who dwell in ivory towers. Rather it is a common possession in each of us. Every person must achieve a philosophy for his own living. To a very large extent it may not be one which he has arrived at through his own efforts and searchings. On the contrary, it is likely to be, in considerable measure, the general philosophy of his society. He will have been gradually nurtured in a general position which he will more or less follow through the greater part of his experience. As a matter of fact, it is unlikely that he will depart substantially from the social perspective regardless of the extent of his subsequent quest. Nevertheless, it will be his philosophy and the basis for his everyday living. As a result of the pre-

93

ceding, it is likely that he will have difficulty in giving overt expression to this system of thought. Beyond a few generalities, he will not have probed deeply into the nature of his own point of view and the reasons for his adhering to it. It is in this context that we find one of the tremendous difficulties which is confronting modern man today and is making him uncomfortable. He is being brought face to face with situations wherein, at the very minimum, questions are being raised about his philosophy. His "eyes are being opened" so that he must give some justification for the point of view which he holds. All too often he finds himself woefully inadequate to meet this challenge. As a consequence, he is quite susceptible to a variety of suggestions which can come from those who espouse another philosophy. He has been told by his associates that he cannot partake of another point of view since to do so will bring death, i. e., he will lose his status in the present order of society and, even, jeopardize his future existence. But the tempter comes to him with the promise that he will throw off the shackles of a dead past. He will become a full person; he will achieve freedom; he will arrive at selfhood. The old way is presented as restrictive and defeating. Too frequently modern man does not have the resources to be able to stand forth with any genuine counter arguments.

The pressing need in our day is for man to be able to become a philosopher in the more complete and full sense of the term. The nature of this more technical conception is reflected in the English word "philosophy" which is simply a transliteration of the Greek word which means "love of wisdom." This faculty enables a person to make a more correct determination of the world, himself, and the interrelationship between the two. If the decision is a correct one, then we use the term "truth" to describe it. Hence, our lover of wisdom, our philoser, is basically doing nothing more than seeking for truths. He is reflecting the query which Pilate posed to Jesus, "What is truth?"[3] Very quickly he discovers that this is an elusive phenomenon. It does not make itself available with ease and even less of certitude. Consequently, it behooves one to be very careful in his search. One of the major hindrances is the inclination to be satisfied with the first glimpse. A deeper inquiry, however, discloses that he has not really seen or discovered it at all. What he thought was truth was only a shadow, a reflection, an appearance. From the very earliest stages in man's concentrated efforts to acquire truth, he has drawn attention to the distinction between "appearance" and "reality." It has been insisted that to arrive at the latter requires a careful and concentrated effort. The search requires an understanding - a standing over. This means that there must be a comprehensive grasp of reality. The fundamental question which the philosopher must constantly face is, "What is it?" It has to be kept in the forefront throughout his analysis of the data at his disposal. Beginning with the most ordinary facets of his experience, he proceeds toward the discovery of everything which has a bearing on his understanding of them. His goal is to arrive at the essence of reality itself - to be able to crack the very core of the structure and organization of total existence.

This process may be divided into two complementary procedures. The first is called induction. The method followed is that of moving from the particular to the general, from the individual to the universal. Most simply stated, the process which is followed in this part of the methodology is that of observation. By a careful use of the sense organs, oftentimes augmented by various types of mechanical devices which are aids to these faculties, one is able to collect individual examples of a particular phenomenon. From these carefully observed and described particulars, it may be possible to make some summation which can be utilized as a universal truth. This operation has become quite well-known in the modern period as the procedure which science employs in its investigations. Whether one calls it by its philosophical designation as "induction" or by the modern phrase of "scientific method," the result is the same. This type of inquiry has been very profitable in enabling man to understand himself and his world. Under the impetus of modern science, an additional increment of control over both has been accomplished.

The second part of the operation is that of deduction. It is a reverse of the preceding. One now moves from the general to the particular. What has been learned in the earlier experiences can now be utilized in directing the search toward a greater understanding of the universe. There is present a certain amount of data which can be employed in enabling the person to comprehend the nature of all things. The general conclusions which have been drawn out can be employed in arriving at certain other conclusions in human experiences. The stipulation which must be observed is that the rules of deduction are not to be violated. These guidelines had their origin

among the ancient Greeks. No substantial changes have been made
since Aristotle wrought out the rules of the syllogism.[4]

In this manner philosophy proceeds to carry out its creative
operation. It begins with the particular observations as they
are made in the experiences of life. This function provides
the raw materials whereby conclusions can be drawn. The latter
will be increasingly refined so that they will be recognized
as universal in scope. When these formulations have been
established, it becomes possible to follow their applications
in the particular experiences. Unlike his Greek mentors, however, modern philosophers are not content with a conclusion
which has been drawn notwithstanding the systematic nature of
the operation. Reflecting the tremendous influence of modern
science on his work, he constantly turns to empirical evidence.
In this way there is a continual refurbishing of the materials.
Perhaps, therefore a working definition of philosophy may be
stated somewhat as follows: Philosophy is that discipline
which is concerned to discover the nature of reality in all
its manifestations and relationships. This substance is examined in both its universal and particular natures.

Let us examine this discipline as it carries forward its role
in the gaining of this understanding. It must begin its operation with a receptivity toward all human experiences. There is
no other field of study which is as inclusive in its grasp of
data for exploration. This factor has created a problem of no
mean proportion for the modern philosopher. His predecessors
sought out their own materials, analyzed them, and drew conclusions as defined previously. They had a firm grasp on all
the materials which were available. Even as recently as the
sixteenth century, Francis Bacon is said to have known everything which was available at that time. He was, indeed, in
control with respect to the intellectual realm. This assessment can no longer be made. The amount of knowledge which is
available is so vast that no one can begin to come to grips
with it. Further, it is increasing with such rapidity that
it discourages all inquirers except the most hardy. To attempt a weaving together the staggering amount of materials
which are available into an adequately organized system appears
all but impossible - as it may be. We may have reached the
point where a genuinely definitive philosophy is impractical.
It has been estimated that the total knowledge has been doubled
in the past fifteen years and will be similarly increased in
the next fifteen years. Therefore, the philosopher moves with

much less certainty in our era than he has done in the past.
Being unable to apprehend fully the total realm of human understanding, he works warily with his subject matter. He recognizes that there may be other data which could alter his understanding. Some students in the field have taken what appears to
be a defeatest (they would say realistic) attitude in that they
have proposed that the traditional work of the discipline is to
be discarded. The examination of particulars and drawing conclusions therefrom is strictly the work of the modern scientist.
The latter has developed the tools and the resources for doing
this type of work. Science has proven itself in the course of
its history in the modern period. Consequently, it is quite
inappropriate for philosophy to expect to make any signal contributions. It must, on the contrary, carve out for itself a
decidedly more limited and definitive field for its work. It
would be quite appropriate, and in order, for the field of se-
mantics to be claimed as an area in which philosophy has the
necessary resources for its examinations.

Most philosophers are not willing to delimit their field of
operations to this extent. While not denying the outstanding
progress which has been made in human knowledge by modern
science, they have moved ahead in continuing the great tradition which they have inherited. Quite naturally they have
not denied to science its proper due. But they have insisted
that there are limitations in this discipline. It must be supplemented by other forms of inquiry.[5]

The procedures whereby philosophy does its work have been
altered as a result of modern conditions. Whereas the philosophical scholar in the past has sought out his own materials, made
his own observations, carried out his personal analyses, and,
from these, reached his own conclusions, his modern counterpart
must inescapably rely on others for most of the substance needed
in his investigations. Actually, this state of dependency is
not as much a misfortune as at first glance it might appear.
To be sure, one would feel a greater confidence if the total
operation could be carried forward through his own efforts. On
the other hand, this advantage is counteracted by two considerations. First, the amount of data which can be put at his disposal is so manifestly enlarged that the necessary relationships
with others may enhance the depndability of the results. The
past history of philosophy offers some evidence to support this
observation. Even the greatest minds of the preceding eras have
oftentimes demonstrated an inadequate grasp of reality. One is

97

impressed, for example, how a Plato could be beguiled into accepting some parts of traditional Greek lore and mythology. This inadequacy could have been minimized to some extent if the modes of investigation used in the modern world had been present at that time.

An even greater advantage enjoyed by modern philosophy results from the fact that the resources which are put at his disposal are not only quantitatively greater but the materials have already been subjected to countless evaluations. One of the basic principles which contributes to the success of modern science is the insistence that investigations and their results must be subject to public scrutiny. They cannot be maintained in some form of secrecy if they are to be given any status. Therefore, in the modern fields of knowledge, there is always the effort to discover weaknesses and errors in the inquiries which are made. This principle has become applied to all fields of study. The technique does not guarantee that the philosopher, as he makes use of these materials, can do so with absolute confidence. But it does mean that he has brought into the philosophical enterprise a whole host of additional minds to reflect upon and to assist in assessing the data which come from human inquiry and investigation. One might say, facetiously, that the philosopher has inveigled other individuals to do the grubbing chores which are necessary in any intellectual enterprise. Lest he get too far afield from the level of ordinary experiences whence the data are derived, the philosopher will do well to keep a limited contact with the whole scientific enterprise. Neverthless, in the final analysis, his major responsibility will be to take up the task after the scientist and other observers have done their chores and moved on. It will be his task to formulate the philosophical analysis.

While it is undoubtedly correct to say that no scholar can do the work which must be done in his realm without careful attention being given to the achievements from the past, this position is most assuredly true of the philosopher. The great minds of former years have wrestled long and successfully with the problems and issues as they were presented in terms of the experiences in their times. To follow the intricacies of the evolving patterns of thought is valuable from two points of view. First, one is attracted to the methods of the investigations. To observe the philosophers as they confronted their problems, explored the dimensions of them, studied the results of their predecessors and of their contemporaries, and wove out of these materials their own distinctive understandings of reality is a most fascinating undertaking. Even more importantly, one comes to understand more clearly the procedures which must be followed in his own personal inquiries. Second, there are the results which have been achieved. These accomplishments will provide the starting point for any subsequent investigation. To be able to build upon the foundations of the past is the continuous story of the unfolding human understanding of the universe. He has developed that critical faculty which has enabled him to accept what is profitable and to reject whatever is no longer tenable. With this understanding as a base for further inquiry, he has enlarged his perspective so as to include the new discoveries and apperceptions which have come under his own observations as well as those of his associates who have been involved in his labor.

This study of the past has been carried forward in terms of certain types of classifications. Previous philosophers have set forth their ideas so that some general areas of common positions have been recognized. As a consequence, it has been customary to identify certain schools of thought and to provide suitable identifications for each of them. This process, undoubtedly, facilitates the considerations which are given to the past - actually, it would probably be impossible to make any systematic study otherwise. Notwithstanding this gain, it does need to be recognized that this method of consideration must be used with caution. Any particular philosopher will be classified in terms of the several types of philosophy only in part. Each makes his own unique contributions. Too frequently there appears to be a propensity to set up the classifications in a rigid pattern. Then the particular individuals will be forced into these classes. Sometimes a considerable measure of obfuscation occurs with the employment of this process.

It is at this point that the distinctive contributions of the investigators will begin to manifest themselves. Gradually, there will appear certain conclusions which the evidence discloses. The perspectives which have been gleaned from the past will be brought into the formulation. But they will be utilized in the context of the total discoveries which have been made in the present experiences. It is now that the cooperative intellectual enterprise begins to show itself in a distinctive way. The persons who have worked in the other disciplines will enable the philosopher to offer a more cogent and competent analysis of the concerns as they are brought to bear on the individual's experiences. That is, he can proceed with a considerable measure of confidence to assert that the most fitting conception concerning the nature of reality is at hand. From the total accumulation of carefully analyzed data, certain general ideas or principles can be presented. While he will not assert that these conclusions can be depended upon with a sense of absolute confidence, he can, nonetheless, assuredly establish his position that the evidence does point in a certain direction. Insofar as the studies have been made with care and fullness, the results will stand the light of scrutiny which will be directed to them by his peers. While they may, and undoubtedly will, disagree with his presentations, they will do so on the basis of a difference in the assessment of the evidence and the individuality of perspectives which are present. Although differences and disagreements cannot be resolved, there will be no less a high appreciation for the thoroughness and thoughtfulness which will have gone into the analytical process. One of the characteristic features of the intellectual enterprise is the fact that scholars reach diverse positions; but there is no diminution of respect for the contributions which have been made by those with whom they disagree. Debate may become heated; but, upon the cessation of the battle, each will be able to express appreciation for the efforts which have been contributed by the others. Perhaps it should be observed at this point that no one is immune from this type of opposition. Rather, it is probably correct to say that the more highly honored and respected is the scholar and the more influential his results, the more extensively will he be scrutinized and subjected to rebuttal. Actually, this type of controvery contributes substantially to the enhancement of different points of view. Even more importantly, it sets the stage for additional developments in the intellectual enterprise.

Were the scholar's conclusions not subjected to counter ideas from other individuals, his own considerations would bring about reassessments. The philosopher formulates his conclusions; but, in the actual course of placing himself in the continuing stream of life, he recognizes some difficulties with the answers which he has stated. The inductive operation must always be followed by the deductive. Therefore, the general ideas must be tested in the concrete experiences of life itself. As a matter of fact, he will probably be anxious to point the direction wherein the application might be made. Basically,

100

he must receive his finest satisfactions in the realm of the human enterprise itself. The most distinctive theoretician will reach the ultimate culmination of his endeavors as he enters into the area of the ordinary human living and finds therein the basis for the utilization of his own creation. He does not hesitate to act while recognizing the dangers confronting the ability of his own system to maintain itself in the face of the application. Naturally, he is quite pleased if the ideas can be shown to be appropriate and operative in the concrete issues of experience. Should failure result, however, it will serve as a stimulus to reexamine his contributions to discover the weaknesses.

A particular philosophy, for example, might suggest that certain implications will emerge in the realm of the political life in society. Some form of government will appear to express the developed thesis. If it were adopted, the fulfillment of human experiences would be greatly enhanced. Should implementation take place and the organizational machinery be formed, it is not inconceivable that it would prove to be more or less ineffective. Further, the fact that the theory did not work successfully in this form of its expression could very well point up some more basic weakness of the notions themselves. At any rate, some new studies would be required so that the system would be realigned, corrected, or discarded. The fact of major moment, however, is that the process by which the general principles become established in concrete situations makes substantial contribution to the work by the philosopher. His value to human society receives its real impetus at this point.

The philosopher is always the investigator, ever bringing to bear the acumen whereby his work can stand forth firmly. He does not withdraw from the most thoroughgoing analysis. He will not become so enmeshed in a certain position that he himself will not be willing to take a critical view of it. He will, also, be quite receptive to the dissections which will be made by others. Whatever insights are forthcoming will be welcomed. He will scarcely have reached the point where his philosophy will have been formulated before the time will have arrived for his turning back to begin the consideration again. In our modern world, the situation is made more demanding because of the constant flow of new evidence relating to any issue. Sometimes the new data will require a radical reconstruction. If this is necessary, it will almost assurredly be necessary to make some adjustments. The extent of the impact on any set of ideas will vary. On occasions considerably more elements should be admitted as worthy of revision than the proponent will concede. Were he psychologically able to give full weight to the new discoveries and insights, he might become a more effective contributor to human knowledge than actually occurs. Unfortunately, human weakness may impede the intellectual quest. Even in this field, where a full openness and receptivity should be the normal order, individual philosophers are frequently too blinded by their own systems to be able to look clearly at the new evidence. The commitment and assuredness is so complete that an adequate reappraisal is not possible. In theory, it is recognized by all philosophers that their work is never complete. There is always the sense of dissatisfaction because inadequacies are present in the areas which have been formulated in their systems of ideas. In the crunch of real life, however, there may be a deficiency in forthrightness and admission of failure in the quest for truth.

It should be noted that one of the perplexities which confronts the later student as he examines the work of an earlier philosopher is the lack of complete consistency in the latter's position. One can often trace chronologically the course of development as the ideas have been reformulated. A point of view which will have been asserted in his first writings will be substantially modified in his later works. A philosopher usually becomes become conservative in his mature years. In his first efforts to present his views, a person may do so quite rashly - partly because he is so thoroughly convinced that his analysis is correct, partly because of a general youthful enthusiasm. In his later years his outlook will have broadened; he will have been exposed to more extensive studies; his own position will have by that time been exposed to assessment by his colleagues; and limitations of his work will have been stated. Most importantly, his perspective will have been greatly enlarged so that he can do a more effective job in synthesizing diverse positions and providing a place for philosophers whose work he would have been opposed to in his earlier examinations. He will have become more truly a wise man because he will have correlated his understanding of reality with the wisdom of the ages.

This factor warns further against the attempt to classify

102

a particular thinker within a stated school of thought. The more intently he is engrossed in the intellectual process, the more difficult it becomes to find that unity in his point of view which will enable one to work out a mark of identification.

For the sake of emphasis a sixth item should be included in the philosophical methodology. It is the process of constantly reconstructing ideas and restating them so that they will convey, in a positive manner, an understanding concerning the nature of things. No person can really live in the negative. One may find inadequacies, criticize, and reject. In the final analysis, however, some affirmative position must be discovered. Over the centuries wherein philosophical speculation has developed, there have been many schools which have expressed themselves in an essentially negative vein. They have asserted the impossibility of making any concrete statements concerning the nature of the universe. A close examination of these systems of ideas would reveal that they are not altogether devoid of certain insights into the conceptualization of existence, however limited they may be. The more common position of philosophy is to use the critical methodology in order to remove those impediments to a philosophical point of view which can give clear and forceful insight into the comprehending of reality. Too frequently the casual observer is impressed so strongly by the controversies which are carried forward among the various schools of thought that he is prone to conclude that the very essence of philosophy is to support a negative position. The philosophers themselves have been partially responsible for this assessment of their efforts. They do engage in a substantial amount of critical evaluation regarding opposing points of view. This form of response is not inappropriate, but the proper goal should be kept in mind. The genuine purpose of philosophy is to scrutinize varied positions not simply for purposes of raising questions about the correctness of them but to elicit elements which are of positive worth in the comprehension of the very nature of reality itself. However inadequate and incomplete a position may be, it will have more merit than will be evident when only the weaknesses are emphasized. Therefore, the philosopher who is primarily concerned with the task of pointing up the negative will do his discipline a major disservice. To state the proper task of philosophy in a succinct formulation is simply to say that its essential work is to discover truths. To bring to light unacceptable points of view is primarily an ancillary operation, a necessary one, to be sure, but not the major business at hand. To conclude, it is philosophy's business to seek out and to present that comprehension of reality which will give to human beings a basis whereby a relationship with that universe can be implemented. There is no denial that all positions lack a finalization of the theoretical understanding concerning reality. Every conclusion will suggest new directions for examination. But, at any particular moment, there will be some solutions to the problems which have been raised. There will be bases which will serve until new discoveries are brought forth.

CHAPTER VIII

PAST RELATIONSHIP OF PHILOSOPHY AND RELIGION

Since philosophy and religion are concerned with many of the
same problems and examine the same data in seeking solutions, it
is sometimes difficult to draw a very exact distinction between
them. Theology and philosophy, in particular, have similar interests concerning their search for an understanding of reality.
It is at this point that the difficulty becomes most evident.
Too often theology is considered synonymous with religion. If
this were an accurate equation, the mistaken notion that there
is no significant distinction between religion and philosophy
would be more in order. But theology is actually only one area
of religion. It is most unfortunate that through the centuries
it has occupied a major position.

Both philosophy and religion draw upon the same raw materials
in making their investigations. They examine those elements
which are apprehended by men. For theology it will be stated
as an inquiry into God or the gods. But this is a comprehensive term which ultimately encompasses the totality of existence. And it is this latter that is the province of philosophy.

There may be differences in method between the two disciplines. Philosophy has inisted that the ascertaining of the
nature of reality must be performed by the mind. Theology may
agree to a greater or lesser extent. Some schools of theology
would even suggest that what enters into man's religious formulation must be achieved in precisely the same manner as any
other apprehensions. In this case it is recognized that the
distinction between it and philosophy is virtually non-existent. About all that could be said, in the way of separating
the two, is that theology may be somewhat more specialized or,
at least, that it gives greater attention to certain facets
of reality. Other schools of theology would propose that human reason should be employed as far as it can. At that point,
other resources must be drawn upon to provide a supplement for
understanding and guidance. There is a conviction that these
resources are available. They have come from the past through
various means of disclosure. The general term to describe the

105

supplement is revelation. Man proceeds to seek for God with
all the resources at his disposal and with all the faculties
he possesses. He may study nature, he may examine past history, he may utilize his rational capacities. All of these
exercises will be supremely useful, and he will not minimize
their significance. But, in his seeking after the understanding of God,he finds that the latter has made some disclosures
of himself. These unveilings do not contradict the true rational analyses since ultimately human faculties are themselves
God-given. Hence, should there be any conflict, it is necessary to seek for reconciliation. These revelations have already been subjected to a careful sifting so that a firm col-
lecton of dependable data is at hand. They provide resources
for man which are essential for his full apprehension about
the nature of things. Obviously, this value which has been
given to this body of materials leads rather naturally to the
conclusion that they constitute the real concatenation of
data for human understanding. That is, some schools of theology give little of no place to other forms of disclosure
or discovery. As a consequence, theology and philosophy may
be poles apart in their comprehensions of reality.

In the genuine formulation of religion, the relationship
it holds with philosophy may be very close. It can be illustrated by a comparison between the Hebrews and the Greeks.

We are fortunate in having a wealth of materials concerning
the life of the Hebrew people. Evidence of substantial quantity enables us to trace the course of their history through
many ages. These resources focus upon those things which were
of primary importance to this people, namely, their religion.
They are reflections about the religious life. But for the
Hebrews, perhaps above all peoples of the earth, the distinction between religion and the remainder of life was scarcely
discernible. Therefore, as one examines the course of their
history from ancient times to the present, he is aware of a
continuing interrelationship between religion and philosophy.
The common elements for the inquiry consists of experiences
derived from living and its issues. That is, neither philosophy nor religion is constructed out of the abstractions of
human thought. Rather, both must devote their attention to
everyday realities. In a general way, it can be said that
the Jews never achieved notice because of any outstanding
philosophy in the technical sense. This assessment does not

deny full credit to the occasional philosopher who has come from this heritage.

But the discipline of philosophy has not been a medium of understanding for the people as a whole or for a significant group of their scholars. Neverthless, they were philosophers. They produced a comprehension of reality which was woven out of the fabric of daily experiences. It was a popular type of philosophy. For example, Wisdom and the Wise Man are frequent themes. But an examination of the literature wherein this type of material is found discloses a concreteness and earthiness to it. In an earlier period Wisdom was concerned with the ability to distinguish between the useful and the harmful. Later, its major interest was to make possible a correct selection in the realm of moral actions. In its highest exemplifications it was to seen as the "fear of the LORD." Hence, even when that which might be referred to as the love of wisdom was considered, it was quite empirical in scope. Further, there was always the religious perspective. It is not, therefore, surprising to find that the most profound examinations concerning the nature of things are cast in the symbolic. Partly this approach may have been due to the general predilection of people in the Middle East toward the use of picturesque language, partly due to the early date assigned to a substantial part of the materials created before abstract language was generally available. But in the final analysis it occurred because the Hebrews or Jews remained in close contextual relationship with earth and things earthly.

The result of this development is most interesting. As the Hebrews underwent changing experiences in the course of their living in different environments and under changing conditions, their thinking kept pace. They could modify their positions about realities. This operation did not come easily. The sources indicate that it was often a painful process. But they did change. New ideas were accepted. Other influences were not excluded completely. At the same time their religion was changing in accord with their thinking. New understandings about the nature and character of the supernatural forces of the universe were accepted. Broadly speaking, therefore, at no time was there any real conflict between what would be their philosophy — if it may be called that — and their religion. They were woven out of the same fabric, the same experiences of life. For this reason they never became renown in the field of philosophy. There was never any need for a discipline which was separate and apart from their religion. The latter met their needs in providing a comprehensive understanding of the universe.

When one turns to the Greeks, however, a somewhat different phenomenon confronts one. These people were by no means devoid of religion. The assertion made by St. Paul in his sermon on Mars Hill in Athens presented a description which could have been applied to them throughout their existence. He said, "I perceive that in every way you are very religious."[1] From the most primitive period through the days of the ascendency and decline of this country the same evaluation could be made. At no time were they lacking in religion. The problem arose because their developments in the field of religion did not keep pace with their enlarging experiences. While the mind was being stimulated by vast new panoramas as the Greeks carried forward their relationships with the larger world and its inhabitants, their faith was not similarly affected by a more realistic appraisal concerning the divine powers. Either they kept their own gods and goddesses untainted by any essential modification in their nature, or they appropriated the supernatural beings of other people and imported them to their own country. But the basic essence of religion remained unchanged. To be sure, the epic writers, especially Homer, attempted to give a reformulation of the Olympian religion. In many ways they did a commendable job. Homer's descriptions of the divine powers and the organization which he made of their relationships one with the other were very appealing. But his writings reflected too much of the poetical artificiality. The ordinary person might find aesthetic value in his presentations. But the artistry was recognized for what it was, a human construction designed to fulfill the need for a unified religion. In other words, the form was imposed on old materials. But the underlying structure and essence remained unaltered. It did not spring out of man's seeking for a religion which would challenge his life and move him to aspire to the nobler fulfillment which was being proposed.

In some respects the epic writers degraded religion. Their presentation of the gods and goddesses often left much to be desired in their personal decorum. Their moral status was scarcely higher than that of human beings. On occasions they actually deported themselves in a manner which would be contrary to the morality exhibited by the ordinary person. One almost gets the impression that Homer was seeking to convey a bit of levity in his descriptions. As a consequence of these developments, the more serious-minded individual would not be particularly inspired by the faith. Although he continued to participate in its performances, he did so more from custom than anything else. Or he may have feared the consequences of his heretical behavior. But it should be emphasized that there was never any general revolt against the religion and its traditions. For the general populace the Olympian faith or the other cults proved to be satisfactory. After all, they knew no better.

But there appeared on the scene some individuals who unconsciously moved in other directions. The descriptive word "unconscious" is used since they did, for the most part, conform to the traditional faiths. When they turned into another direction to seek an understanding concerning the nature of things, it was not accompanied by an overt rejection of the established order. Rather their approach would be essentially to engage in their investigation with no open conflict with religion. It is probably correct to say that they may not have been aware of any discord.

Therefore, in its initial phase, philosophy may be considered as having an independent status with no concern for religion. In its development there would very quickly emerge those ideas which would have tremendous consequences for religion. In reality it meant that the status of the gods was undermined. Men were finding ways to account for things essentially outside the context of divine operations. Should one be able to discover some primordial matter, an inherent energy, and the laws of change, he would have the necessary ingredients to produce a cosmology. Where would there be a place for the supernatural forces in this scheme of things? It is not surprising that those who upheld the traditional ways sometimes recognized what was occurring. More than one of the early philosophers came in conflict with the law and suffered the consequences of his disturbing ideas.

But the philosophers were not genuinely concerned to uproot religion. They would simply assert that they were proceeding to make their own inquiries without regard for any religious disruption. They would agree with Socrates that they were appreciative of religion and its values for mankind. They were completely loyal to the traditions of their fathers. It was appropriate for the philosophers to pursue their interest while religion was proceeding on its course. Each would contribute its part in the on-going course of human experience. It would be their hope that they would leave religion undisturbed, and the latter would not be affected by their pursuits.

Eventually there appeared those who proceeded to advance their inquiries to the extent that philosophy must concern itself with religion. The very nature of the philosophical analysis led to the disclosure that something more than human was required in order the complete the philosophy itself. When this realization appeared, the philosopher discovered that he must come to grips with the traditons which had been formulated in the concept of religion. The examination proved that many of the established traditions were completely unacceptable Philosophy itself pointed out the total inadequacy of the popular faith. These investigators brought serious accusations against the ordinary forms of religious expression.

The next step set forth the results of philosophical inquiries in relationship to religion. The eventual outcome was the production of a religion by philosophy. If then religion was derived from philosophy, did it not mean that the latter was superior to the former? This assertion was not presented this bluntly; it seemed to be the direction in which ideas were evolving. That which was acceptable in the field of religion would be that which had been arrived at through, and as a result of, philosophical analysis. It must be part of man's total understanding concerning the nature of the universe. Religion would be scarcely more than the capstone of the philosophy. It was required to bring the inquiry to a proper conclusion. For example, Aristotle worked out his philosophy so that he could give an overall explanation of the universe. But the problem of gradation in the realm of existence seemd to be inexplicable by means of purely "naturalistic" considerations. As a result, he turned to religion with God as the "pure form" which could serve as the final cause. It provided an explanation for the teleological structure of the universe.

Similarly, in the realm of morality the general basis for for living was to follow reason. Seemingly, it was not neces-

sary to take religion into account in making moral decisions.
But Aristotle did conclude that when man had reached that highest peak of excellence in the field of ethics,he would find
himself in a realm whereby he could be related to God. In
this area, too, religion served to give completion to the philosophical quest. Throughout these inquiries, however, Aristotle - and other philosophers of the time would have agreed - was
giving the higher position to philosophy as the discipline which
must be followed in order to arrive at the understanding of reality.

More or less as a natural conclusion to the preceding position, there was the point of view that philosophy was a religion. One gets this impression especially in the development
of the Platonic position. As his school of thought advanced,
there was the growing recognition that the conclusions were
to be given that degree of commitment which is the very essence
of faith. One result of this development was the attraction
which Platonism had for Christianity. The philosophy stressed
that the transcendent realm was the true area of being, and
this conception paralleled the world view of the newly emerging
faith. Throughout the whole Hellenistic period there appeared
an ever increasing amalgamation between philosophy and religion. For some, the philsophy was expressed in essentially
religious terminology; for others, religion was portrayed
through philosophical concepts. It became increasingly difficult to draw a clear-cut line of distinction between the
two realms.

As Christianity developed, it attracted individuals who had
been trained in the philosophical schools. When they became
converts, they did not at that point put aside their whole
past and start de novo in reconstructing their whole world
view. They brought with them their questions and answers as
they had been wrought out through the rigorous discipline of
their past training. At the same time, they found that the
new faith had its questions and answers which had been formulated in terms of the more ordinary experiences of life. But
with some effort, these two positions could be reconstructed
so that they would be essentially in agreement and would meet
the needs of two classes of individuals. On the one hand,
they would serve to satisfy the speculative approach of philosophy; on the other hand, they would meet the everday needs of
a person in his quest for salvation. This development con-

tributes toward explaining the cause for the emergence of Christianity as victorious in competition with other faiths of that period.

This point of view is illustrated by the development of the creedal expression which eventuated in the doctrine of the Trinity. In Greek philosophy God had been portrayed from two perspectives. On the one hand, he was the only true metaphysical reality; other existences derived their status by participation in the ultimate being. In the case of Neo-platonism, the human predicament sounded almost like the cry as depicted by religion, What, then, must I do to be saved? Plotinus had portrayed man as being caught up in the realm of matter which meant negation. He had lost his status in the realm of True Being because he had turned from his appropriate position as an emanation or overflow from God. He had proceeded to follow an independent mode of action by exercising his own creativity. Consequently, he had become enmeshed in matter, the realm of non-Being. Nevertheless, he did have a spark of genuine reality still within him which made it possible to deny the negative and to turn back to that which was truly the real. If he did so, he would become absorbed again into Being, that is God.[2]

On the other hand, Greek philosophy had ascribed to God a more creative role in the making of the universe. There was an energizing nature which had to come to expression by attempting to bring to realization the Ideas or Forms. As far back as Heraclitus the idea of the Logos, as a formative influence in the production of the universe, had been introduced. It was the rational principle whereby the course of events could be guided in a more appropriate and desirable fashion.

Likewise, Hebrew thought had presented God from two perspectives. He was the creator of the universe and of the regulations by which it was directed. He was its architect both in terms of its natural and moral nature. From this point of view man was depicted as dependent on this Being for his very existence. In order to be a recipient of this power of God, however, it was required that he be obedient to his will. Man must determine his requirements and conform to them. Therefore, the function of religion for this society had been determined to meet human needs in this area. Sometimes these requirements were construed as ritualistic; at

112

other times, they were thought to be moral. In every instance
there was the recognition that man was subservient to the creator God of the universe.

The evidence was unmistakable, however, that man did not
meet the demands of the deity. His conduct did not conform
to the divine expectations. As a matter of fact, it would not
be too rash to say that he, more often than not, found himself
in a life situation which he would evaluate as undesirable. He
had failed to measure up to the standards which had been stipu-
lated. Were God's nature entirely that of the creator and law-
giver, there would scarcely be any hope for man. But the Hebrews
never felt that they were completely cut off from their God.
He was always present and could be propitiated. Experience
had suggested that he was not only holy and righteous but merci-
ful as well. He was attentive to man's plea for compassion.
He was a redeemer in the sense that man could be restored to a
proper relationship with his creator.

When Christianity moved out of the Jewish environment into
the Gentile world, these several influences demanded resolution
so that they would constitute a coherent system. Gradually, as
the religion expressed its own points of view more concretely,
these several positions began to consolidate. It was seen that
the Hebrew and Greek understandings, in each instance, were
basically two sides of the same coin. The difference would be
one of perspective. If one looked at life from the standpoint
of philosophical analysis, one form of interpretation would
be present. If, however, he saw it from the frame of reference
of a personal relationship with the deity, another side came
into view. Slowly a fusion occurred. It was not a carefully
planned and consummated operation. Rather, it was the gradual
unfolding of what was evident to anyone who had the capacity
to appreciate the real natue of the two thought patterns. In
other words, the doctrine was created out of the experiences of
the church. God, the Father, expressed the Greek idea of deity
as ultimate reality and the Hebrew perspective of personal creator; God, the Son, portrayed the more direct personal concerns
of the divine nature for the particulars of the universe whether in terms of created entities or redeemed individuals. As
the church itself became accepted as the embodiment of the
normative pattern of faith, God, the Holy Spirit, would become
an additional element. Moreover, the traditional Christian
idea of monotheism could be maintained by utilizing the con-

113

cept of one substance expressing itself in three persons appropriate to the respective areas.

But the ultimate solution did not come about without great internal struggle and dissension. The history of Christianity from about the beginning of the second century reflects these controversies. The most vigorous was the Arian-Athanasian debate in the fourth century. That is, there emerged two forms of the religion and each had been created through the utilization of the philosophical methodology. It was evident, therefore that following reason could not be used as a basis for the establishment of a strong institution. There was the need for some more ultimate authority which had the ability to resolve these difficulties.

The solution which emerged asserted that religion was superior to philosophy and should take precedence whenever there was conflict. In theory this methodology did not eliminate philosophy as a valuable tool for arriving at an understanding of things. In practice it did not work out in this fashion. When it became apparent that the conclusions which were reached by the philosophers were acceptable only to the extent that they agreed with the teachings of the church, the value of them was severely questioned. They were scarcely more than duplications.

St. Augustine (354-430) appeared at this very strategic moment in the history of the church. He was eminently qualified to make a signal contribution in meeting the needs of the time. He was well-trained in the classical traditions as a result of his father's striving to procure for him the best education which was available. Consequently, he appreciated Greek philosophy. When he was converted to Christianity, he carried with him this mode of thinking. Nevertheless, as he became involved in the controversies of his day, he saw the value of a strong, authoritarian church which would be adhered to in instances of dispute. Therefore, on the one hand, he did not minimize the significance of philosophy. He made substantial use of it in evolving and expressing his own theology. The methodology which he used in formulating his own statement of religion followed the method which was described above - religion was the product of philosophical analysis. But in the ensuing conflict, with positions which were at variance with his own, the priority for the authoritarian approach became more evident. His own experiences seemed to justify this point of view. The transformation of his life had been effected under the influence of that faith which was espoused by the church. Hence, the latter must have a status greater than that of philosophy. While his own system of theology reflected Greek thought, especially Neoplatonism, nothing could be accepted which ran counter to the dogmas of the Christian church. Essentially Augustine's basic position could be succinctly state, I believe what the church proclaims.

After Augustine the authority of the church became increasingly entrenched. Philosophy declined and withered. It was appropriately recognized that there was no need for it. Truth had been established and promulgated. Nothing could be permitted to gainsay it. To a very great extent classical knowledge disappeared. Only here and there in Western Europe were there feeble glimmers of the light from the past. Fortunately, the Muslim centers succeeded in maintaining the intellectual approach. In time they would serve to reintroduce to Christian Europe this method whereby the search for truth could be reawakened. This renewal would emerge slowly, and only with considerable reluctance was it accepted. Initially, it would be limited to a rather negative role. One might eliminate items of religion when philosophy could demonstrate conclusively that they were false. Or one might accept the teachings of the faith and then proceed to seek rational bases for them. The former did not apply to certain ideas which were construed to be beyond the realm where reason was properly equipped to operate; the latter was unacceptable should it reach a point of questioning the teachings of the religion.

This feeble revival of the philosophical approach did bring some individuals to recognize the potentialities of philosophy. Eventually some status had to be given to it as a means to search for truth. But its position was quite limited. The church was still insisting that its tenets were to be accepted and that it had the authority to make the final determination concerning truth. Reluctantly it recognized that the voice of philosophy could not be entirely silenced. It offered too many insights to be dismissed by the strong hand of authority.

Some solution to the conflict had to be devised. The course which gradually appeared to offer some promise was that of fol-

lowing a two-fold way to truth. In certain areas religion
would be allowed to voice its truths; in others, reason would
be permitted to utilize its canons. Thereby human understanding would be completed by two complementing approaches. Philosophical analysis would be allowed a free hand so long as it
did not conflict with religion; the latter would not intrude
into that province which was the special prerogative of philosophy. In other words, there was to be a division made in the
area of knowledge. Let philosophy be philosophy; let religion
be religion. This perspective was certainly a very appealing
answer to the situation which existed. It provided a solution
to what was rapidly become an impasse. Additionally, it was
an attractive proposal since it provided a measure of specialization. By limiting one's efforts to a particular discipline
one would do a more adequate job than by overlapping into the
other domain. It was a very attractive scheme - in theory.
In practice, however, it proved to be much less successful than
had been hoped. It failed to reckon with a basic factor which
underlies all life. We do live in a universe. Hence, there
is a oneness to things which makes such a division artificial.
One might attempt by a forced effort to keep his thinking
focused upon some part of the whole; but there is ever the
felt need to break through the accepted boundaries. One
must inevitably follow where his rational analysis leads him.
Consequently, there was the unavoidable invasion into the domain of that which had been restricted to faith. Philosophy
was probably most guilty of this violation, especially since
it began to call into question many of the hallowed conclusions set forth by religion. But the latter, on its part,
was to find it desirable to make greater use of reason. This
need would be particularly recognized when it was appropriate
to present the teachings of the faith to those who did not
accept its authority and could not be persuaded in this manner.
Since everyone possessed the common faculty of reason, it
could be appealed to in order to justify the truths embodied
in the religion. Moreover, there was the   disclosure
that the authoritative sources of the religion were not always in agreement. In order to resolve these conflicts, there
seemed to be no alternative except to utilize rational analysis.
As so often happens, what appears to be a stand-off compromise
does not work out very well. It means giving up too much by
each of the two parties. Sooner or later the conflict will be
revived.

It was against this background, with the issue still rather sharply drawn, that it was evident that the problem required some other approach. A methodology was needed whereby the interrelating of philosophy and religion could be achieved. A coordination of efforts was required; reason and revelation should be considered as essentially cooperating enterprises. Religion without having been philosophically examined and evaluated lacked total assurance. Philosophy was sorely lacking without the outlooks and perspectives which religion could provide. These conclusions are based on the fact that we do live in a universe wherein no element can be properly observed in isolation.

CHAPTER IX

COORDINATION OF PHILOSOPHY AND RELIGION

The past history of the relationship between philosophy and religion has shown that the two have failed too often to recognize a state of interdependence. Each has demonstrated a predisposition either to ignore the other or to consider itself superior to the other. In the latter case, there has been a proclivity to exercise a right of domination. The ultimate result has been that whichever happened to be in the inferior position was usually shifted off to a sideline and given no significant role in determining human experience and destiny. Man has been the poorer as a result of this attitude. For example, it appears not at all improbable that Greek civilization could have been substantially strengthened if the philosophers could have exercised a more creative role in the religious life of the people. It is even more obvious how the darkness of the Middle Ages could have been lessened had Christianity been more responsive to a continuing philosophical examination of its credentials. Consequently, we should like to make some tentative proposals concerning the interrelationship between the two aspects of man's apprehension of, and reaction to, the universe.

A. PHILOSOPHY NEEDS RELIGION

In the pursuit of its inquiry into the nature of the universe, philosophy can be greatly assisted if it is responsive to religion and recognizes the tremendous range of materials which can be derived therefrom. The very nature of religion puts man at the heart of the universe in his seeking to discover that which will serve as the basis for the total orientation of his life and commitment to that which is recognized as ultimate Being. Its concerns and interests are those which philosophy needs to take under advisement as data for its own inquiry.

To a degree this process has been carried on in philosophical inquiry. Many philosophical treatises bear close resemblance to theological studies. But, to a very considerable degree, there is an inadequacy at this very point. Philosophy

119

has too often considered that its major responsibility in this dimension was an investigation of religious beliefs. Additionally, the latter have usually been ideas about the nature of transcendental reality. The principal elements of religion have been considered to be those associated with the supernatural. In brief, religion has been examined from the standpoint of the nature and character of God or gods and the resulting status of man in association with divinity whereby his own everlasting existence in a realm beyond the present could be guaranteed. Consequently, philosophical analysis has been directed toward theoretical considerations pertaining to the evidence for or against certain beliefs which were either affirmed or rejected.

It cannot be denied that these elements have been major considerations for religions in the past. Moreover, for many faiths they provide the essence of religion today. This perspective is based on a rather rigid dualistic conceptualization which has dominated human thought, especially in the West. For decades, however, a substantial thrust in western religion has been strikingly different. It has been caught up in the transformation of civilization which modern science has effected. As a consequence, it has turned its attention to people in their present habitat with all the issues and concerns which beset them at this point. It has sought to come to grips with man as he finds the operations of religion in the confluence of his daily experiences. Religion must be seen as a historical phenomenon. Efforts are made to analyze the social elements of religion in the context of the sociology of religion. Personal involvement in religion is seen from the viewpoint of the psychology of religion. This analysis does not deny that in the immanental theory there may emerge, and probably will, a transcendental element. Only the more or less pure humanists restrict religion to the mundane. But the supernatural is not arrived at in a sequestered experience but in the confluence of daily affairs. His acceptance of a future life is based on the incompleteness of his present existence.

Even those who have become disillusioned with the above described form of religion and have formulated a neo-orthodoxy have not denied altogether the empirical avenues for the religious life. It has been an effort to give greater balance to the relationship of man with a supernaturally organized and governed universe. This movement has performed a service by

drawing man away from his inclination to give so much weight
to a dependency on himself that he has neglected a more substantial basis for his life built in terms of responsiveness
to some undergirding divine power. But the point of major
emphasis is that those in this school have not veered too
sharply from the empirical basis for the religious life.

It is at this point that philosophers need to enlarge their
perspective. It has done so in respect to the ordinary metaphysical problems. Philosophy would not erect a system of
thought based on sheer speculation and rationalization. It
begins with the empirical evidence derived from the sciences.
Its metaphysics cannot contradict the evidence furnished and
supported by the latter. Instead, it must assume the results
of this discipline in order to proceed to formulate a philosophical position. The same adjustment must be made with respect to religion. Philosophy must begin with the religious
life as it is expressed and its meaning is discovered in daily
life. It is in the market place, in the home, in the social
experiences, that real religion is present. The sanctuary
is at the end, not the beginning, of the faith. One attends
church because he is religious, not in order to become religious. The worship experience has become what the word
basically means. It is a value seeking participation in which
a person, both as an individual and as a part of a group,
aspires toward a greater fulfillment of his religious living.
He expects to be nurtured, to be encouraged, to be educated,
to be emotionally renewed, and, most importantly, to be brought
to rededicate himself to the faith. It may be that this is
the source of a difficulty for our present church institutions.
Man may be failing to find that which he is seeking in the operations of these organizations. Voices are expressing the idea
that the church, as presently constituted, is doomed. Should
that occur it is difficult to see the failure of new forms of
religious societies emerging. Man does need that which symbolizes his basic yearnings and aspirations in this area of life.
It should not be overlooked, too, that there are varied forms
of experimentation taking place within the present groups.

In a similar fashion, God is not the beginning of religion
buts its culmination. He is that Being who embodies those
qualities and values which stand at the highest pitch of excellence. He is that Being who already is what man is seeking
to become. Thus the conceptualization of God is not a static

121

one. Rather, it is quite as dynamic as human experiences. Man discovers Him in an ever more comprehensiveness as his own living becomes more complete. As man attains to a higher basis for his own life, he sees the divine from this enlarged perspective. God becomes the attainable, but the unattained reality. Jesus expressed this when he said, "You, therefore, must be perfect as your heavenly Father is perfect."[1] God's perfection is meaningful only in terms of human perfection. Otherwise and too often this has occurred - the supernatural becomes simply an unknown quantity to whom man gives lip service in terms of devotion and adoration.

By the same token the future life is projected from the vantage of mundane realities. Man rises to higher levels of achievements but attains no final realization on this earth. Consequently, he can only conclude that man's brief sojourn in this life can be meaningful only in terms of some more complete fulfillment. For some there is the requirement that provisions must be made for the individual person to do his own completing. Others would see it in a more social frame of reference just as his present creativity is embodied in human society. His own fulfillment is not so much as an individual but as a part of the total structure of human living. From this point of view personal immortality might not be considered as the most appropriate expression for him. Rather, he bequeathes to his successors what has expressed genuine value during his lifetime. This increment will continue on in the later unfolding of the society.

The major point of emphasis is the need for philosophy to become more conversant with the nature of religion as seen in the context of modern life. When it does so, it will recognize that there is a major source which will be profitable to take into account as the questions of philosophy are analyzed and answers are promulgated. Religion is at the very heart of all reality. To ignore it is to do a disservice to both religion and philsophy. Ultimately, it is man who is deprived of a philosophy which is adequate to give some understanding and perspective for his personal relationship with the universe.

B. RELIGION NEEDS PHILOSOPHY

Historically, religion has been quite wary of philosophy and disinclined to be responsive to its analyses of religious

phenomena. A major factor in this attitude is the perception
of philosophy as negative in its examination of religion.
There is some basis for this observation since the very nature
of philosophy is to exhibit inadequacies in any system of ideas.
Since adherents to religion have a very strong conviction in
its correctness, they have difficulty in accepting this methodology
when it is employed in this area. Religion has failed to recognize the full scope of philosophical examination which includes
a constructive side. Altogether religion has been the poorer
insofar as it has not taken into consideration the significant
contributions made available by philosophy. It has been subject to retaining errors in its nature and operations which
could have been eradicated by a closer, cooperative relationship with this discipline.

Furthermore, religion has too often thought of itself as
primarily concerned with the supramundane whereas philosophy
is a pursuit of worldly interests. Having established this
dichotomy, it has insisted that a person must make a decision.
He must follow the disclosures of philosophy or commit himself to a religious faith. He could not utilize both simultaneously. With the advance of knowledge which discloses a
universe of tremendous scope and the necessity for man to
respond to it, there is an increasing awareness that he can
ill afford to ignore any discipline which will serve to bring
understanding and direction. Somehow philosophy and religion
must discover a viable relationship one with the other. It
has been indicated that philosophy can draw upon the vital
disclosures of religion and be enriched by the process. Similarly, it should be insisted that religion must recognize the
possibilities for using rational analysis in the determination
of its own nature.

1. Religion needs to have an understanding of the philosophical method. When there is a realization that the genuine
philosophical approach is concerned to search for the true
understanding of the universe as this may be discovered with
whatever evidence is obtainable, religion will have no grounds
for distrusting the approach. It must remain alert so that
attention can be called to any propensity to limit the materials
which are studied. There is always the possibility that some
individual students and even schools which will be predisposed
to restrict the areas of their inquiries so that they do in

fact approach religion from a negative position or place limitations upon the nature of the evidence which is brought under
surveillance. When this unprofessional attitude appears, it
will simply require that the dereliction be made apparent. It
does not mean that philsophy itself will be rejected. Actually,
the true spirit of philosophy will be quite congenial to the
rejoinders of religion and will seek to modify its position
whenever circumstances and evidence requires this action.

2. Religion needs to have a comprehensive understanding of
the results which have been achieved through philosophical
inquiry. On the one hand, this study of the history of philosophy will elicit a greater appreciation of the tremendous
scope of this discipline. Further, it will set forth an awareness of the very considerable diversity of results which has
been achieved. It will be seen that philosophy has often reflected a great appreciation for religion and its role as affording a distinctive understanding concerning the nature of
reality. Moreover, there will be a recognition that the advancement of man has been aided substantially by the contributions of this methodology. It has laid the ground plan for
the modern world. This knowledge should enable religion to
become more aware of its own responsibilities in the present
age to a greater extent than is otherwise possible. There
is probably no more profitable way to achieve an understanding of present realities than to trace their unfolding through
the pages of philosophical research. Our indebtedness to it
cannot be overestimated.

It will be observed, too, that religion itself has achieved
its status at various periods largely as it has been amenable
to the philosophical comprehension of reality. On this basis
it will welcome whatever light philosophy can offer as it seeks
to continue to fulfill its own responsibilities based on the
understanding of the universe as understood in terms of the
philosophical perception.

3. Religion needs the philosophical spirit of tolerance.
One often thinks of religion as being by its very nature charac-
terized by a lack of sympathetic appreciation for contrary views.
From a certain vantage point this is a correct assessment.
If one's faith centers around a certain specific element of
belief in, or of loyalty to, certain forms of institutional or-

der or of the acceptance of certain modes of action, it cannot
fail to reject any and everything which run counter to them.
The history of religion substantiates this perspective. Philosophy cannot, by its very nature, develop this attitude. It
does not mean, of course, that a particular individual may not
express a scurrilous estimate of an opposing position. When
he does this, however, he is really doing the very thing which
religion has too often done and, thereby, is rejecting the
spirit of his tradition.

It should be categorically asserted, on the other hand, that
religion can be as tolerant as any other aspect of life. Moreover, on occasions it has been. It should, by its very nature,
be more appreciative of diverse points of view. Religion reflects a perspective wherein man is always seen as incomplete.
He has not attained his goal. If this perception is true, then
it scarcely behooves an adherent of a particular faith to be
overly opposed to other points of view. One of the most effective ways to accomplish this outlook is to achieve a genuinely philosophical spirit. The latter is a type of inquiry which
never attains the goal of its search. Hence, the philosopher
is appreciative of all different strains of ideas even though
he may ultimately reject them. He will examine and evaluate
points of view; he will not deny their existence. When a person has committed himself to a distinctive faith, he will react negatively to expressions of religion which are contrary
to his own. But he will reject them only after he has completed a thoughtful examination. This methodology will bring
a recognition about the bases for the divergent points of view,
the values which they offer to their adherents, and their
overall part in man's religious adventure. He may find that
other faiths can make some contributions to his own. Certainly the broadening outlook of philosophical inquiry and its approach to divergent points of view will be a severely temper-
ing force in religion.

4. Religion will encourage philosophy to analyze and evaluate its nature and character. Since religion counts substantially in the life of man, it would be most appropriate for
it to be subjected to the most severe analysis which is possible. A faith which has not been exposed to careful study
and exposure can scarcely be relied upon with that degree of
certainty which would convey a feeling of confidence in its

dependability. One senses that the reason why religion has too often refused to submit itself to this type of evaluation is an underlying fear that it would not survive if this were carried out. Therefore, it has attempted to keep itself insulated from all forms of assessment which are made outside its constituency. It has become one of the major problems which has emerged, especially in the modern period. Religion has attempted to hold on to its traditional ideas, values, and forms simply on the basis of their historical authority. As its membership has been exposed to knowledge which has been produced by other disciplines, adherence to the faith has become difficult to maintain. Had there not been this obstinacy of the established faiths as they resisted this exposure to the enlarging thoughts and outlooks which were proceeding, the transition could possibly have been made easier and many of the old conflicts have been obviated. No religion worth its salt will be other than delighted to have every form of thoughtful examination carried out.

5. Not only will religion encourage philosophy to explore its nature and character, it will also be responsive to the assessments. It will not be reluctant to reject some feature when it has been shown to be lacking in any genuinely tenable support. More importantly, it will incorporate whatever may have been projected as having value for a faith concerning man's relationship to the universe. These adjustments need not be radical in nature or require a major reconstruction of the faith. Through a continuing and cooperative association, the results of philosophical analysis can be introduced almost imperceptibly into the religion. But the latter must be constantly reviewing itself. From a historical perspective the difficulty has arisen whenever religion has been adamant in refusing to expose itself to analysis until a new world view has emerged and it found itself woefully unprepared to cope with it. Under these conditions a traumatic response may be expected. What is generally needed is simply a restatement and enlargement of previously established ideas.

6. Finally, when the preceding procedures have been achieved, religion will be able to present itself without fear of embarrassment. It will go forth with the confidence that it has survived a most careful examination. Its positions remain intact following upon the most severe testing by philosophy.

Thereby its very spirit should be greatly empowered. It will have no fear that some serious errors in its presentation will emerge. Its adherents should reflect a greater confidence in their following the faith. They can meet others who might be brought under its influence with greater assuredness. It cannot but be an impressive demonstration of a religion which is solidly grounded in its affirmation and in its empirical demonstrations. Should there be some indications of an unacceptable point of view, it will not be disturbing even if it has to be modified or eliminated. In other words, the religion will be able to stand firmly and resolutely. It will have become a religion through which man can confidently stand and build his life.

C. PATTERN FOR EFFECTING THIS COORDINATION

In this cooperative enterprise, as proposed above, it will be necessary for the philosophical tools to be carefully employed with the materials supplied by religion. This procedure will necessarily enlarge the content of faith. No longer can it be confined to certain major concepts as these have been found in the stated components of particular religions. Man's commitment will no longer be limited to these items except as they are operative in the totality of human experience.

1. Religious experience, therefore, is the only legitimate place to begin. Even as metaphysics must start with the disclosures of empirical science, the same approach must be followed in religion. It must be seen as a dynamic and active way of life which involves the whole realm of human experiences as they occur in the daily affairs of mankind. That is, the philosopher must not seek out some segregated aspect of life which he will designate as religion. He must be willing to explore the total fabric of living and discover the interaction of the many areas of human involvement with the universe. As he does this, there will be seen some indications of the interspersing of the religious faith through which the particular facets of man's being and acting are determined. From this total picture will emerge the ingredients which, taken together, will constitute the commitment of the individual, his religion.

In the course of this examination, one may observe a rather

127

interesting feature of the individual or group. It may be recognized that religion is on two different levels. On the one hand, certain affirmations are made about the content of the faith. These assertions will be those items which are usually expressed in the formally stated positions of the religious group with which he is affiliated and to which he gives a measure of loyalty especially on stated occasions. As a general rule, they have been transmitted through the institutional orders of the society. On the other hand, there may be only a partial expression of these items in the more ordinary affairs of life. A substantial difference may exist between the so-called sacred and secular dimensions. It means that profession and confession of religion fall into separate categories. The latter constitutes the genuine elements and serve as a meaningful basis for devotion. The former is little more than a superficial and external form. One would not deny altogether the possibility it may have limited influence. When this differentiation occurs, however, the stated religion has become another item separate and apart from the genuinely operating faith. The latter will be woven out of the total complex of the human confrontation with the universe including some features from the professed religion. The only genuine expression of faith is formed either consciously or unconsciously out of the multiplicty of human experiences in a vital relationship with the universe.

2. Then philosophy will examine the religion which has been identified and described. The initial task will be to direct attention to whatever incongruities there are between the two dimensions of faith, the professed and the confessed. For example, one may state a belief in a personal God. It would appear to imply that there is accepted a Being in whóm are conceived the ideal forms of personal qualities. Supposedly one worships the Being with these attributes. This same person, however, might consider these features when found in a finite expression to be negligible. The individual or group senses no inconsistency when there is the exploiting and degrading of human personality whether in oneself or another. This form of action would appear to be a denial of what had been asserted in worship, the sacredness of personality. Usually, the denigration of human beings is done for the purpose of securing other items - for example, material goods - which would become the actual objects of worship.

In a more comprehensive field of operation, the philosopher would be interested in attempting to formulate a religion which would achieve a consistency. He has the resources to examine the wide ranges of human life in order to see the possibilities for a faith which can be meaningful and operable in all areas. In this task he should have the full and enthusiastic support of those who have a vital concern for religion. This undergirding of his efforts should come especially from those who have the practical task of developing and expanding religion in the membership of religious institutions. Were the participants given an understanding of their faith in terms appropriate to their daily affairs, it could be discovered as affording the opportunity for developing a genuinely creative role in personal and social fulfillment. The unification of life both individually and collectively could be accomplished so that the whole-making undertaking was realized. It would mark a distinct advance in this regard over the bifurcation of life as presently construed. Philosophy, therefore, would assist in providing the intellectual formulation for a dynamic faith which would be more than a mere appendage to life.

3. Philosophy will need to discover the foundations of the religion. What are its bases? What are the premises which are accepted? These are crucial questions. Answers will disclose the principles which the religion is seeking to express overtly. A genuine service will be performed for religion since some of the major difficulties are found at this point. Either the assumptions are not recognized, or there is a lack of clarity concerning their meaning and significance. For example, one who follows the traditional Christian faith will start with the premise that the Bible is the infallible word of God. But several problems arise. First, there is the textual difficulty. The original manuscripts do not exist, and extant texts differ in their readings. What did God disclose to the original authors? Second, for most readers there is the necessity to rely on translations. But these are interpretations and the translators have varied understandings. Third, there is reflected in the Bible the world view appropriate for the occasions when the Bible was revealed. Usually, there is little effort expended to differentiate between the ancient and modern world.

The greatest difficulty lies in the fact that the tradi-

tional Christian will usually assume not only that he accepts
this foundational principle but that others to whom he address-
es himself do likewise. He may actually be at a loss to understand why the other person is not in accord with his point of
view. To him it is unquestionable that the Bible clearly states
and supports his position. Obviously the real difficulty,which
had not been faced in the beginning, is the fact that the other
person has a different assessment concerning the Bible. Essentially the same problem arises in the dialogue between Protestants and Roman Catholics. Both groups accept the Bible as
the authoritative source of the Christian faith. But for the
former it is the Protestant interpretation which expresses
the true meaning of the sacred scriptures while for the latter
they have been formulated in the traditions of their church.
It is at least conceivable that a recognition that there are
the two diverse bases for the individual positions will open
the door for a more meaningful and successful dialogue in that
some more common grounds for religion can be found. In the
rise of the Schoolmen, one of the factors contributing to the
employment of reason in religion arose at this point. It was
discovered that Christians and non-Christians had different
sources of authority. Each one was responsive to whatever
came from his own heritage. But, so it was argued, all persons possess reason. Therefore, if we start with this assumption, we shall be able to arrive at a religion which will be
established adequately for all men. Unfortunately, reason
was too often used to support a particular religion or, at
least, to lay the foundation for a faith which would require
an authoritative revelation which had come in a particular
form. It did, however, confirm a matter of real importance,
namely, that conflicting premises do not offer much hope for
a universally accepted religion.

In our day, it is probable that,as an outgrowth of the
scientific method, it would be appropriate to accept as a
basic assumption that man is a religious being because of
the experiences of life. Faith, therefore, should be examined from the standpoint of its relationship to life and
life's values. If this premises were accepted, there would
undoubtedly remain large areas of disagreements. It does
offer the promise that some common concerns might be discovered.
It would provide areas of cooperation. But it would require
the philosoher to bring vividly to the forefront the new prem-

130

ises so that they could be employed successfully in seeking for a common implementation in the fulfillment of them.

4. Once the varied possibilities were formulated concerning the premises, religion would proceed toward the construction of its order along the lines projected. It would include theological statements, moral objectives, and institutional practices and organizations. This approach might appear to require a thoroughgoing abandonment of the past with its traditions. On the contrary, the latter would provide a mighty reservoir of materials for thoughtful consideration. Of greater importance is the fact that it would open the door to an examination of materials from all other forms of religion with the expectation that they might offer some valuable insights into human experiences. New techniques to meet human needs might be revealed. For example, if western religions were more open and responsive, they could be assisted by the oriental faiths. The latter would be able to disclose the nature and worth of mysticism as a means for developing a greater spirit of serenity in the hectic pace of modern society. Western religions could guide their constituencies by encouraging them to devote some time in reflections upon life's meanings and relating themselves more harmoniously with the underlying foundations of the universe. The eastern religions, on their part, might be brought to a greater involvement with the distressful social issues. The interacting thus initiated could lead to the finding of common grouns among the world's religions.

5. As the modifications are being made, the philosopher will maintain a constant vigilance to observe the results. His tools will enable him to be more aware of failures to interpret the foundations and purposes and to call attention to incongruities and conflicts. He is able to maintain greater objectivity as the reconstruction occurred. Further, and most importantly, he is in a position to state categorically the need to return to reassess the bases for the faith. This evaluation could eventually cause him to reassess his own philosophical faculties to see that they had performed their proper role. This need would become especially evident if the philsopher had little sympathy for religion. If he did not accept the possibility that faith was a major dimension of life and provided materials for philosophical explora-

131

tion. Furthermore, his awareness of other areas of inquiry and their achievements will provide continuing grounds for reassessments of religion in its total formulation.

6. It is quite obvious that the course being proposed never arrives at a point of finality. The work of philosophy in its relationship with religion is a never ending process. The latter needs to be continuing its adaptation to the constantly changing order of the universe and, especially, of mankind. Only stagnation and deterioration can result when a permanent order is set forth and supported as the ultimate object of human devotion. Every day and age requires its own statement of faith which is adequate to the experiences engaged in. Tomorrow will bring forth new responsibilities for establishing a basis for commitment which is germane to the human needs of that time. Continuing interaction between philosophy and religion should result in a more viable and functioning arrangement for each.

CHAPTER X

NATURE OF ETHICS

A. INTRODUCTION

From a comprehensive view it can be said that philosophy has two major concerns. First, it must discover the nature of reality. Second, it will evaluate that reality so that man can derive the most appropriate and adequate values from it. A major part of the value system is ethics. No better expression of the nature of this discipline is to be found than in the Chinese word for it, li. This term is composed of two symbols. One is the word for man; the other, two. It suggests that at the moment when one person relates himself to another individual, he has entered into the field of ethics. At that point man is no longer a solitary individual who is seeking to achieve value as a separate person. Rather, he must accomplish this goal in terms of another human being. Consequently, some concern must be present to discover how this relationship can be achieved. In other words, ethics exists only in a social context.

A similar perspective is expressed semantically. The origin of the two English words, ethics and morality, brings this out. The former comes to us from the Greek word, ethos; the Latin term, mos, gives us the other. The latter is seen more clearly in the plural form, mores, which has been anglicized. In both instances the literal meaning is custom. Therefore, it can be said that, etymologically, the understanding of the concept is that which has to do with the customary things. This meaning would be appropriate only in a social context where the accumulated experiences would be transmitted from one generation to another.

It is not to be denied that what an individual does may have moral significance even though he may be very much alone. The results of his conduct affect him in some way which has repercussions in the social context. For example, an individual might lock himself in a room and overindulge

133

in the use of alcohol. Were there no social consequences of
his action, ethical meaning would be lacking. But it does
have significance since he will emerge from the bout to become a part of the social order. Or, to take another example,
one may withdraw from society and become a hermit. In establishing this life-style, assuming no direct impact on his fellowman, there would be no moral meaning to his act. But the
failure to fulfill certain duties or to make some contribution
to society may create a moral situation. Therefore, since
most human activity involves some measure of interpersonal
relationships, moral judgment becomes a major consideration.

Thus from the most ancient times man has not been able to
escape the fact that he is a moral creature. It is one distinguishing quality of his humanity. He has found it necessary to examine his actions in order to find bases for social
community. He has not been able or willing to live alone as
a solitary individual. The full value of existence is discovered in relationships with other human beings. Some
schools of psychology have spoken of this drive as the gregar-
ious instinct. But it may be that this psychological theory
reflects one of the problems in regard to man's sense of
moral responsibility. If it can be argued that his sociality
is the result of an inborn quality, then his social grouping
is the product of it. Consequently, morality would be construed
as that which would be designed to foster his own personal
values. The only support for moral behavior would be that
which would be accepted as personally valuable.

On the other hand, if man were considered as inherently
a social being, it would mean that his own nature was incomplete in his solitariness. Consequently, morality would be
recognized as that which would guide man to reach his personal fulfillment as a social animal. The developed ethical
system would have to be that which would be designed to achieve
group fulfillment. For example, killing another person would
be justifiable from the instinct point of view insofar as
the murderer was convinced that it would fulfill his own being
better than not committing the act. In like manner, he would
refrain if it would contribute to his personal needs. He
might not murder in his own group since he would recognize that
it would be detrimental to the group relationships wherein he
derived value. He would not, however, hesitate to kill in war

since he would not sense a dependency on the enemy for his own achievement. Actually, he would convince himself that the enemy was opposed to his group in which he did find personal satisfactions.

From the social ethics point of view, however, this line of reasoning would not follow. He must recognize his human status as a part of a group. But it could not be limited to a particular society since he would have to consider himself as a part of all humanity as the finalizing of all group associations. The only way murder could be justified would be to disassociate the other individual or group from the human family. This type of rationalization is operative on occasions. There are materials in the Old Testament where there seems to have been an underlying point of view that anyone who was not a part of the covenant community really lacked status as being strictly human. God had imposed a curse on him which made it not only appropriate to kill, but it was in accord with the divine will. Fortunately, there was a considerable measure of opposition to this point of view. In modern society, during times of war, efforts are made to depict the enemy as being so atrocious that they are basically outside the human sphere. Similarly, the vicious criminal will be referred to as one who deserves to be shot down like a mad dog.

In this regard a rather interesting development may be taking place. The recent war in Vietnam was really the first conflict in which we have been engaged that the television camera brought the daily engagements into our living room. Almost unconsciously we become involved in the operation itself. Suddenly we have become aware of the fact that the members of the opposing armies were men, too - or, perhaps, we should say men and boys. It was amazing how young many of the prisoners of war appeared to be! There is a streak of compassion in most of us which causes us to recoil when a realization of this nature begins to be evident. These individuals were husbands and fathers, sons and brothers, just as our soldiers were. It may be that this new communication medium will help to develop a repugnance to war that has not been achieved in any other way. That is, unless our government recognizes it and demands that war scenes not be shown. It is highly probable that many of the atrocities committed by our forces were not permitted to be photographed and transmitted to the American public. How much censorship was imposed?

It is proposed that morality is an inherent part of the social order and human beings follow it as members of society. Therefore, the need is to bring man to an awareness of his essentially social nature. When this understanding has been attained, his moral response will be unlimited.

The history of ethics suggests that there has been an evolution in this dimension which is equivalent to that in the physical nature. In a broad sweep it is proposed to trace it through three major stages.

B. PRIMITIVE ETHICS

In the dawn of human living there began this process of social relationships. The foundations for it may have been laid in the subhuman period. But it could achieve its full stature only when man had arrived at his manhood. As stated previously, he made certain observations. He became aware of himself in relationship to the universe. But, in terms of the theory proposed above, it was not as a solitary individual that he arrived at this perception. It was as a part of a group. In other words, he became self-conscious as a social animal. It was from this point of view that his moral situation confronted him.

Obviously his ethical perspective at this stage was extremely limited. It applied only to his immediate associates whether this would be in the context of a family or a tribe. It probably began at the former level. Then, more or less quickly,he grew into the larger order. The Old Testament narrative of Abraham suggests this type of process. First, we see the patriarch leaving the land of his ancestors accompanied by a group which could be described as a family. But, in time, there is the expansion so that a larger society was created. Then his nephew Lot breaks away to form another family or tribe. Throughout the Old Testament it is difficult to draw a clear-cut distinction between the two types of organized bodies. They blend together into a blurred picture. In either case, however, there is a society and the need for moral considerations as a response to the formation.

Several striking characteristics of ethics at this stage are evident.

1. Primitive ethics is applied to the small group. It is a natural and understandable feature since the individual lives in terms of a very limited social environment. His relationships with those outside his own society are very circumscribed. The opportunities for sociality beyond the immediate associates are few. It is partly caused by the very considerable amount of time which has to be devoted to the struggle for survival. Leisure time is simply not present. This same factor creates competition with the outsider. The latter becomes the enemy even as the animal which destroys food or even the lives of the people. The result is that there is difficulty for the human beings who are beyond the pale of his own tribe to be considered as strictly human in the same way he would consider his fellow tribesmen. The rules of conduct are based on a value system which defines the social context in terms only of those who are directly related to the individual in the daily pursuits incidental to his own survival. There is no interest beyond this point.

Morality must be formulated for the group itself in order to provide direction for behavior and to sustain the tribal order for the common good.

Another side of this same issue is that the focus in formulating the ethics does not take into account the individual as such. The latter is rather blurred as a distinct entity. The attention is directed toward the group as a whole. The person is important not in himself but as a segment of the community. Consequently, the regulatory directives are seen as contributing to the group life. This characteristic is illustrated by two well-known factors in many primitive groups. First, there is the totalitarian nature of the tribal government. The tribal chieftain or patriarch will usually be granted absolute authority over members of the group. He symbolizes the will of the whole, and all powers are granted to him to maintain this wholeness. Further, punishment will frequently be carried out by death sentences.[1]

2. Primitive ethics are generally negative. The concern is to restrain the individual from the antisocial actions which

137

adversely affect the group. It should be noted, however, that
negative ethics do have an indirect positive effect. When
something is not done, the consequence will be that there is
brought about some concrete reaction. It may be nothing more
than the noninterruption of what has been present heretofore.
For example, if one does not steal, the result is that the
original possessor will continue to hold his property. But
the weakness, as will be noted later, is that ethics of this
nature is concerned with the static situation rather than a
dynamic one. It preserves rather than creates. It has a
severe limitation in terms of being a powerful factor in
helping to bring about the unfolding of the full stature of
man. It is rather discouraging how much of present day ethics
is still couched in this vein; perhaps it is necessary but
still distressing. There is a great need to try to break
down the idea that morality is found essentially in these
terms. For example, we who are in the academic world too
often appear to be more concerned with failing students than
in directing our efforts toward a creative educational role.
We must punish rather than see ourselves as having a prime
responsibility in instilling an appreciation for all the
things which enter into education. Administratively, this
negative approach is easier to measure and to control. If
one does not know, then he will be failed. If he fails
a sufficient number of courses, he will be denied his degree. A dean from a midwestern university recently stated
that about one-third of entering students failed the first
year. It is probable that this percentage would not be
unusual. If a manufacturer were to have this much spoilage
in his production, he would most certainly try to remedy
the situation.Evidently our ethics have not grown sufficiently
to seek for improvement in the educational realm. We are content to blame the students and let them suffer the consequences
of what might be failures in the institutional order due to
the fact that we have not asked ourselves if we have the right
goals in mind.

Therefore, the usual statements in this area are expressed
in the well-known phraseology, Thou shalt not. Certain parts
of life are set aside and one is prohibited from entering. A
Polynesian word is applicable here as in some other areas of
primitive life. It is the word "tabu." Something is untouch-
able. Eventually the prohibitions become so numerous that life

is completely circumscribed and, thereby, becomes exceedingly cumbersome. It can reach a point whereby moral obligations expressed in the law become rather superficial. The laws are taken lightly and obeyed to the extent that they seem to suit one's interests. They may be supported by fear of great risks were one caught by the enforcing authorities.

The major deficiency in this form of moral expression is the lack of provisions for the major goals and objectives in life. The rules state what is not to be done; they are silent in terms of what can be performed and how these acts can be effected most effectively. As a result, man directs his attention, morally speaking, to the areas which are closed, seeks to avoid them - at least when there is a danger that he will be caught - and develops a sense of peace in his inner conscience. In the main course of life he moves as his own ingenuity dictates until, finally, some laws further restrict his activities.

One of the disturbing facts in history is the extent that popular ethics has persisted in this negativistic frame of reference.Even in the current era it is supposed to solve all human problems - and, apparently, many individuals believe that it will. But there is some question about its efficacy. Let us set up an extremely hypothetical situation. Suppose all the laws pertaining to murder were removed from the criminal codes. How many additional murders would be committed? Undoubtedly there would be some. But would the number be substantially increased? Consider a less radical case. Suppose a college or university would cease giving grades or other forms of academic punishment. What effect would this action have on the educational process? Immediately, the repercussions would be traumatic. But in a longer period of time there is considerable uncertainty that this policy would prove to be detrimental. The positive result would likely be a substantial change in the teaching process which could conceivably create a better educational system.

The above digression simply suggests that the negativistic approach in ethics has continued to be very influential although it may have long since lost its value as a primary basis for human living. Primitive man, in his groping with the elementary relationships in the universe, did find some

139

areas which had to be sealed off. But we have given up many of his physical tabus; should we not begin to rid ourselves of some of his moral restrictions?

3. Primitive ethics usually employs a religious sanction. Human life is very precarious. Man is aware of forces outside himself which can be very dangerous if their machinations are not safeguarded against. This consideration is involved, too, in matters pertaining to morality. The rules can be seriously damaging to the group if they are broken. They must, therefore, have their origin in the supernatural order of things. Consequently, it is appropriate to make man aware that punishment can come from either of two sources - possibly from both simultaneously. There is certainly no reason to congratulate oneself should detection by human instrumentalities fail. The supernatural order cannot be escaped.

This factor gives a powerful arm to the moral arbiters of the society. On the one hand, what they do is accomplished not simply from the standpoint of human resources. They are really serving as the instrument through which the divine order is maintained. The ordinary person, therefore, would be inclined toward subordination before this awesome magistrate. On the other hand, this type of psychological perspective would aid in detection. Why should one deny the act? The deed must be discovered. It is even conceivable that innocent people have confessed some misdeed since they had become convinced that they had committed the act.

4. Morality, at this stage, is largely static. There is limited opportunity for an enlargement of outlook for several reasons. Contacts with other people are restricted, and this is almost a necessary ingredient for any modifications of established patterns. Moreover, these associations would be mainly with people who shared the same level of personal and social development. There would be little challenge to the established lines of human interaction. Furthermore, life itself would change only modestly. No expressed need for revising the moral perspectives and standards would be recognized. The most serious difficulty would be found in the precariousness of life itself which would make groups quite wary of altering the basic rules which had provided for survival.

It is not to be understood, however, that no transformations
occurred. Obviously, if this were the case, man would still be
living according to a primitive level of ethics. But the variations were made so slowly that they were scarcely perceptible.
Partly, the new outlooks would be formulated in the actual performance of the established mores. Slightly different imple-
mentations would occur. Occasionally, new situations would
arise which would demand facing up to forms of actions which
had not previously been met and standards provided. Interactions among different people would make some impact on the
course of human living.

C. TRANSITIONAL ETHICS

But the substantial changes would be introduced by certain
individuals. A variety of factors would contribute toward
this movement. A particular person may feel that his own position was not sufficiently recognized under the traditional
order. Hence, he must carve out new paths for his own personal
advancement. Quite often the motivation will be selfishness.
Not infrequently the effort will fail as far as that individual
is concerned. But he may have formulated some way of action
which will be taken up by others until it is incorporated into
the morality of the group.

On other occasions, the individual will be confronted with
a definite areas of responsbility and find that the traditional
pattern imposes some difficulty in fulfilling his role in society. He may break with the past not necessarily with the
idea of formulating some new mode of living but simply as an
expediency. In the Old Testament there is the story of Saul
and his war with the Philistines. On one occasion he went
forth to battle only to discover that Samuel was not there
to offer the required sacrifice. Rather than see his men dis-
sipated by delay, he took upon himself the responsbility of
performing the priestly task.[2] In the subsequent periods one
observes that the king assumed an increasing part of the religious realm.

On a more constructive level, however, stand the great
persons of history who have introduced changes into the society for the expressed purpose of enlarging the sense of group

values. They have observed some of the limitations imposed by
the traditional morality especially as it proved to be detrimental to many of the inhabitants. The break with the heritage
was not motivated by personal gains. As a matter of fact, they
may have incurred substantial opposition and suffering. But
the vision was there and could not be denied. They moved forward to create a system of ethics - or some changes in the
perception of values - so that they might bring to fruition
the aspirations for the more abundant life for their fellowmen. As a rule, the resulting patterns of life are depicted
in more positive terms. There is a search for guiding motifs
which will lead to appropriate values which will offer some
goals to be achieved rather than simply dangers to be avoided.

Both types of individuals may suffer considerably for their
willingness to deviate from the inherited courses of action.
It is almost inevitable that some price will have to be paid.
Should the individual not become a victim of the established
order, the fears and trepidations which beset him can scarcely
be eliminated. But this approach is the only way whereby
progress can be made, especially in areas which affect so
vitally the entire scope of human existence. Were it not for
the daring of these transitional figures in the moral history
of man, the subsequent life would be poorer. One can observe
this situation on occasions. There have been periods in history when life settled down to a quietude which brought
sterility and ennui. Once this condition has occurred, it is
difficult to renew the march toward a more meaningful life.

D. ADVANCED ETHICS

The conclusion to the quest creates ethics in its most significant form. The emphasis is placed decreasingly on the negation of human actions and the effort to restrict life itself.
The older controls will be retained only to the degree that
persons fail to achieve that sense of individual responsibility
so that restraint is required. Ideally, the time will come
when these forms of moral direction can be eliminated entirely.
There is considerable uncertainty concerning the value of this
type of morality and the social control which is associated with
it. They accomplish very little in making possible a genuine
fulfillment of human life. Further, to the extent that sig-

142

nificant attention is directed toward these rules, there is a
danger that they will instill an attractiveness. It is especially true for individuals who are naturally adventurous.
There is the possibility that the deed will go undetected and
a sense of achievement will be realized. Too often, also, a
society which relies on the policy of restraint may devote
so much of its energy and resources to this form of morality
that it will assume little responsibility toward developing
more creative approaches to life. The most destructive fact
is that these rules and regulations develop a smugness or con-
ceit in those who are not guilty of infractions even though
they accomplish very little otherwise to warrant this attitude.
It may even draw attention away from persons who perform more
socially destructive acts which are not condemned. It occurs
in modern society when there is the exploitation of persons
for economic advantages. What are the characteristics of the
higher ethics?

1. Advanced ethics are positive in nature. They are designed to give direction to human living. They are based on
goals which are desired to be fulfilled. They will provide
guidance in achieving these ends. The outlook is expressed
in terms of the living of life rather than the denying of it.
Since this approach can be accomplished primarily in social
relationships, the lives of individuals interacting one with
the other become the primary interests and the fulfillment
of these associations are projected as the goal.

2. The ethics are applied to a larger group. It is recognized that basically human beings, wherever found and whatever
may be their particular physical characteristics and social
status, have the same inherent worth. It becomes increasingly difficult to construe morality as applicable to a discrete
group of individuals. It becomes particularly evident as people
from various situations in life associate together. The ordinary differentiations lose their meaning and relevance. The
life of a person, or of a group, is so intertwined with that
of others that moral rules which apply to everyone become
prerequisites for all those who are in that form of relationship. Were a person to see his own achievements in life properly , he would recognize that to the extent there is a failure in the life of others, his own experiences are thereby

143

limited. For example, one man kills another. What are the consequences? On the one hand, a person who has contributed to society, or might have done so, is removed and with it his creativity. The person who is the murderer is incarcerated. Additional tax burdens are put on the rest of the people. The act of murder must cause a measure of uneasiness on the part of all others. The positive approach has greater values to offer. Through it successful efforts are made to involve all men in personal fulfillment and direction. Society is enriched.

3. Advanced ethics are dynamic. This characteristic is its most essential feature. The very process of reaching out toward greater participation in life constantly brings human beings into new forms of interpersonal relationships. When morality works at its best, there is a persistent search for increasing both the fullness and meaningfulness of associations. Unlike the negativeness of the more traditional forms of ethics, there is a major concern not to restrict or to impose limitations upon the contacts being wrought between individuals and groups but to promote them. The increasing complexity of life brings about new problems which require solutions. Even as the issues are arising, there is the opportunity to extend the horizon of one's life so that it is no longer the narrowly restricted form which might have been. There is simply no basis for a static mode of existence nor of the moral procedures which are designed to give guidance to it. The interests of the various individuals broaden, and they are consistently reaching out for the fulfillment of new potentialities. At their best, these new interests stimulate each one to find the most successful modes of relationships among the individuals involved. One of the great values of public education is the fact that it brings each child into contact with children from widely different backgrounds and with uniquely varied personalities. Each one is an entity requiring that there be developed the basis for comradeship if enmity is not to occur. The great value which should emerge from the policy of school integration is that there will be associations which will evolve a moral understanding of children from many traditions. It should pave the way for an enriched society as the development of a common morality will be operative at the level of adulthood.

4. Finally, the primary goal of advanced ethics will be to

set up broad, general principles which can be made applicable to varied situations and among different people. It should provide for greater freedom so that each individual and group will have an opportunity to implement these ideals in the process of actual life situations. It should limit the extent to which specific rules would have to be enacted. There should be a definite effort made to move away from an overly emphasized concern for prohibitions and the punishments which would be inflicted whenever these regulations were broken. Different individuals would have the opportunity to make applicable the principles in terms of varying circumstances as they arise. Furthermore, there would be a more lasting quality. One of the unfortunate aspects of precise rules is that they are limited in application. New situations demand a continual examination of the regulations to see how they can be made operative. But ideals are unlimited in guiding the wide ramifications of human relationships.

Morality at this stage should challenge man as he is presented with tremendous opportunities to move his own life toward a more exalted level of performance. The zest with which he directs himself toward the realization of these ideals can scarcely fail to make his own life more exciting and intriguing. His fellowman is seen as one not to be used but as a basis for cooperative association whereby mutual enrichment is achieved.

This way of life demands that it be closely related to religion which will serve to give the necessary premises, the goals and purposes of life. and essence of value itself. As will be suggested later, it is probably correct to say that advanced ethics is inconceivable aside from a religion which can provide the foundation for it. The scientist would not be able to perform his work were he not convinced that there is an orderliness about the universe. Similarly, moral man would not be able to move very far in human relationships were he not convinced that there are conditions in the universe which support ethical goals. These elements can come only from a religion working carefully with the moral aspirations of mankind.

CHAPTER XI

PAST RELATIONSHIP OF RELIGION AND ETHICS

The very nature of both ethics and religion necessitates a relationship of one type or another. Both have the essential essence of a concern for persons. Apart from homo sapiens there would be no place for either. Given this underlying premise, it is not surprising that a significant problem has been to effect a working relationship between the two. More often than otherwise religion has been so constructed that it has promised to provide for human needs and has relegated morality to a distinctly inferior status. This situation can work effectively so long as the pattern of religion operates with individuals whose moral background has precluded the rise of serious ethical problems. Difficulties begin emerge, however, when the ethical considerations lose their force, when new problems of human relationships arise, and when the religious order becomes lethargic. The result will be a decline in moral responsibility so that a revolution begins to be formulated which will be designed to discard the traditional religious order and life. In its place will emerge concerns for human behavior which will subordinate a distinctly religious formulation. The thrust will be to form a pattern of life with ethical responsibility being paramount. But the remnant of a traditional religious pattern will be present to reassert itself. Furthermore, those who become involved in the new order will carry with them a zeal for life's activities which reflect the religious spirit.

As the moral emphases face up to serious difficulties, meeting both direct opposition and a more invidious undermining of its concerns, then the need will express itself to reconstruct the order so that a substantial part of the traditional religion will again be brought into the picture.

Furthermore, there is considerable question whether a system of morality apart from a religious context can be supported to any great extent or for a substantial period of time. It, too, begins to lose its creative power and becomes embodied in

a set of legalisms which remove much of life from the guides
designed for human behavior. Several problems of this relationship have appeared in the course of past history.

A. RELIGION AS A SANCTION OF ETHICS

As was stated in the preceding chapter, the most common role
for the relationship of religion and ethics has been for the
former to serve as that which enforces the moral regulations
of a society. This position has been found continually and in
many groups. The basis for this association has been the idea
that the group has derived its identity from a divine power.
There is a commonality by virtue of divine origin, divine
guidance, and divine assistance. Therefore, the maintenance
of the society depends upon proper relationship with the supernatural powers. All human activities must be carried forward
with the recognition that they are in accord with the gods of
the people. An important part of these affairs concerns the
relationship existing among the members of the group and with
those outside their society. Careful attention must be given
to moral regulations which will achieve these ends. As they
are drawn up and become operative in the society, they are
not accepted as products of human effort to achieve relationship with others. On the contrary, they are set forth, or
come to be considered, as divine regulations. Since they
are expressions of supernatural demands, there is an un-
usually strong force which supports them. Moreover, they
are expressed in terms of rigid requirements, even as legisla-
tive. That is, they are finalized into a permanent set of
rules which must be explicitly obeyed. There is, theoretically,
no basis for change. The only pattern open for alterations
is either through interpretations, as the laws are applied,
or by the additions of subsequent disclosures.

In the enforcement of the moral regulations, the guardians
of the group have a very strong weapon at their command. They
fulfill their responsibilities as representatives of the supernatural overseers of the society. They operate not in the name
of the group but under the aegis of the group's gods.There is,
consequently, an almost impregnable power in the enforcement
of the rules. The rituals and ceremonial procedures surrounding the operation of the ethical order are not essentially
different than those which are present when man's relation-

148

ship with the divine powers themselves are being carried out..
Further, the same sense of awe prevails; one is doing that
which will, in the final analysis, affect not only his association with his fellowman but also with the supernatural
beings. Of more importance, however, is the fact that the
successful operation of the moral standards will preserve intact the proper status of the group with the divine powers.
Oftentimes moral derelictions will actually contaminate the
tribe so that it will not be able to carry on successfully
its normal functions and, in some cases, will not be capable
of survival.

The full story of this form of connection between morality
and religion would demonstrate the extent to which human interactions were governed and determined by supernatural considerations. Further, it would show how strongly entrenched and
how incapable of being changed this system was. As a matter
of fact, this type of ethics is still a substantial part of
man's way of life, both in theory and in practice. The legislation in our western society is often based on the biblical
laws even though the enforcement is carried out by a secular
state. Moreover, there is still an effort to surround the
arbiters of justice with a sanctity which harks back to the
time when the church was the enforcing arm of the law as well
as the source of the legislation. Practices in the court
room, such as oaths and swearing in of witnesses, reflect
this background. The garb of the presiding official, the
title of address, and the honor accorded him have the same
significance. It may be that some of the rebellion against
the social order is, in effect, an effort to say that laws,
the legal system, and the inherent power of the divine order
are being questioned as the basis for social morality. The
latter must be reexamined with the idea of discovering what
will reflect the ethics of a democratic society wherein the
regulations must depict an inherent worth.

B. METAPHYSICAL SYSTEMS AND ETHICS

When man had advanced to a stage where he had an increase
in leisure time, he began to work out a more systematic analysis
of the universe. He examined the nature of reality itself.
From a very early time, these observations suggested that there
was a considerable diversity in the nature of things. Some

things experienced reflected one feature while other items
which he surveyed suggested something different. This diversity was especially noted when man observed himself. There
appeared to be one component which was physical and solid.
But another part was less capable of being grasped and was
more incomprehensible. Since he was already acquainted with
beings who were similarly devoid of ordinary reality, it was
easy to formulate a view of the world which provided two
realms. He became a dualist. There was the physical; there
was the non-physical. Since the latter was already occupying
a substantial part of his concerns, it continued to do so.
Whatever he might do with the physical, the spiritual must
be kept separate. It operated in its own realm according to
its own procedures.

Out of this type of analysis there emerged a religion expressed in terms which gave it a firmer base. Even the nature
of the universe provided grounds for religion. The latter was
written in the very essence of things.

This exaltation of religion, however, denigrated morality.
The nature of man as a being like unto the divine powers meant
that it would be to his advantage to pay more attention to his
connections with these beings. The forms of actions and responsibilities which had been made operative would now achieve
a higher place in his estimation. It may be questionable whether other considerations would retain much importance at all,
except as they might have some subsidiary consequence in the
realm of religious obligations. The duties of man to his fellows would be construed as demanded insofar as they would
contribute to his associations with the powers of the divine
realm. The independent status and value would be minimal.
They would certainly lose those real force as a creative basis
for human experiences and social interactions. It is likely
that they would have diminished even further had there not
been the necessity for morality to serve as a basis for continuing group life. But the real strength came as the religious establishment incorporated it into the system of
faith.

An additional development in the metaphysics, however,
would have an increased impact on the diminution of the
role ascribed to morality. In some religions a position

has been projected wherein the deity is considered as a completely omnipotent being. He is the creative source and sustainer of everything which exists. Every activity is determined by him. Man, in particular, thinks of his own life as controlled by this supreme being. When one asserts this theological belief, it is difficult to find a genuine place for ethics. In theory, it makes moral responsibility impossible. If events occur because they must, there is the elimination of alternatives and freedom of choice which are the prerequisites for morality. Man does not have the right of self-determination. He acts by virtue of a directing power which causes him to do whatever actually occurs.

This conception in the field of religion and ethics has caused religious thinkers a considerable amount of difficulty. On the one hand, there is a great reluctance to deny supremacy to deity. He would be less than a god if he were contrued in this manner. The very nature of a divine power suggests that which is sufficiently great to be relied upon. Surely man would be reluctant to place his confidence in a being with less than complete power. It would even suggest something greater exists. If this position is taken, however, what is the motivation for man to seek an independent course of action in striving for moral goals? The latter will be those ends which have been established by the divinity; and, in turn, man is so controlled that he will move toward them. But the decision to act in a certain manner will not belong to him. Man becomes a puppet who responds to the activity induced by the arbiter of the universe.

A somewhat less extreme idea is that of predestination. This theology does not establish direct control of individual acts. Rather, it is concerned to say that his ultimate destiny has been determined by the God of the universe. It does leave some ground for emphasis being placed on morality. But it is greatly weakened by the fact that man's major concern is his ultimate fate. The present life is minimized. If he is able to anticipate a blessed reward that has been prepared for him, why should he be concerned with doing his duty in the present life except as it may be a part of his religious obligations? It is in this manner that morality has been kept partially in the picture. In certain forms of Christianity, for example, the very proof of being among the elect will be

151

shown by one living a highly moral life. The latter is a part
of the holiness which the chosen one will demonstrate.

But the motivation for morality is greatly weakened by this
theology. Ethics relates to the present life. The elect person is so obsessed with the hopes for the future that he can
scarcely be overly concerned with the present life. Fortunately, religions with this point of view usually have a rich ethical tradition. The moral ideals which have been transmitted
provide considerable guidance for the believers. But adherence
to the inheritance can easily become perfunctory and fail to
generate much enthusiasm. The most unfortunate result is the
fact that there is little incentive to engage in a creative
search for a more vital and dynamic morality. Whatever has
been commanded will be obeyed. But it will be done simply
because the rules have come from the past and are considered
to be divine commands. The grounds for a genuine concern
for one's fellowman, for the establishment of a more wholesome society, and for the achieving a richer and fuller personal life are sadly lacking. The religious organizations
often have to exert tremendous pressure in order to achieve
a reasonably orderly society. In other instances, the political machinery will be requeathed divine powers so that
it can exert the necessary force to maintain some orderliness within the state.

The ultimate result can be a very deadening form of experience. Morality increasingly is conceived negatively;
few provisions are made for change; and the punishments which
are inflicted for violations can be extremely brutal. The
United States is finally on the threshold of eliminating
capital punishment as a means of enforcing morality in our
society,[1] and many individuals are horrified at the anticipated results of this occurrence. In fact, there is probably
no area of our western society which is as archaic as the
area of morality in all its varied ramifications. To effect
the necessary changes will involve some tremendously traumatic
experiences and much injury will result on the part of individuals and social instruments. But the reconstrction is
long overdue and must be accomplished notwithstanding the
cost.

In the transformation which has resulted in the gradual

discarding of the metaphysics which established the spiritual power as supreme, there is now appearing another form of the dualism which is having an equally devastating impact on morality. This type of philosophy places the emphasis on the material values and considers man to be a product of forces which achieve a fulfillment of his economic needs. Consequently, there is the same determinism which scarcely provides for freedom of choice. Man moves inexorably toward his goal which is to achieve physical rewards. The moral rules are those which will contribute toward this end.

In capitalism this perspective has been set forth in regulations which will provide those who own the instruments of production and distribution the means to reach the fulfillment of their desire to make a profit. Given this objective, ethics emphasizes those features which will contribute to this result. One of the most obvious expression has been the exploitation of human beings for economic goals. Often there has been slavery, the "sweat shop," long hours of employment, child labor, low wages, unsafe working conditions, and many other practices. Slowly some of the most reprehensibile forms of oppression are being eliminated. Some religious organizations have made significant contributions toward this end. In becoming involved they have incurred substantial criticism. The general attitude is that religion should have no role in the economic order.[2]

Now this same type of economic determinism is being presented from another standpoint. The theory is that the worm should turn, and the workers should rise up to throw off the shackles of bondage and assert their own economic aspirations. But this process is not considered to be a matter of freedom of choice. Rather, it is a philosophy of history based originally on the general theory of Friedrich Hegel. Following this perspective it is contended that the course of events has moved so that the pendulum is now swinging toward the time when the laborers will be able to respond to those affirmative forces which are now on his side. Just as the capitalistic system has not hesitated to use forms of human behavior which would contribute toward its ends, communism asserts it is the duty of the workers of the world to do the same. They are actually acting morally when these activities will serve to contribute toward the transformation of the economic system. Thereby a new society will be created.

153

C. RELIGION AND ETHICS INDEPENDENT

On occasions religion and ethics have been considered to be independent of each other. Each should fulfill its own particular role in human experience with little or no concern for the other. It is a perspective which is closely related to the preceding. In many respects, it is a more honest position. It takes seriously the dual nature of human living. On the one hand, man lives in the realm of the spirit; but, on the other, he is involved in mundane affairs including personal associations with his fellows. The requirement for the first mode of existence is a proper fellowship with the divine; when he turns to the second area of life, he must relate himself with a different creature. The requirements are essentially separate and distinct in each of the two cases. What he does to assure proper rapport with the supernatural power has little or no significance in determining his moral responsibility. Similarly, it is not considered essential for his religious fulfillment to give any considerations to moral stipulations. Usually, the position is not stated quite this pointedly; but the results point clearly in this direction.[3]

Given this point of view, the individual will be inclined to give his allegiance to that which is of greatest concern to him. Some will be most deeply committed to religion. Consequently, the demands of the faith will be most assertive; and he will put forth effort for their fulfillment. Normally, these requirements have been formulated within the context of an institution. The organized patterns of action which express the dedication will be insisted upon. They are construed as the mediums through which the relationship with the higher powers can be most effectively achieved. These stipulations have developed over a considerable period of time with the result that their antiquity will have enhanced their status. Ultimately, they will be considered to have been received from the divinity and thereby cannot be ignored except at one's peril. They have been carefully structured so that there is a simplicty to them. It makes for ease in performance. Oftentimes, a considerable part of the activity will be done for the communicant by a special class of individuals who have been set aside for this purpose. The ordinary layman has only to support the institution through membership, monetary contributions, and attendance. For the remainder he can rest assured that the professional personnel will maintain the congeniality of the universal powers.

An example can be found in the history of the ancient Hebrews. Their religion appears to have maintained through its existence an emphasis on moral responsibility. While the elaborate codes of law in the Old Testament reflect many centuries required for their development, there was an elementary ethical requirement expressed in the Sinai Covenant. When they entered into Palestine and became associated with the Canaanites, they had to come to terms with the religion of the latter. It appears to have had an ethical dimension of considerably less force. Moral obligations did not constitute the essential item. Man fulfilled his religious duties when he offered regularly the required sacrifices. Throughout the Old Testament one observes a persistent concern on the part of those who reflected the desert environment for the moral impetus which was associated with the traditional faith. They simply could not understand how the Hebrews could be considered faithful when there was a manifest failure in the elementary appreciation for members of their society. Their opposition to the Ba'al religion was not simply, probably not primarily, due to the apostasy, the turning to the worship of another deity. The real evil was the fact that it turned man away from his moral responsibilities. This resulted in an acceptance of the fact that he could be loyal to his own God by engaging in the same type of activities required in the Canaanite religion. In this respect there came to be little difference between the two religions.

The tension grew until there was a showdown between those who supported the institutional form of religion and those who had developed an attitude which could not rest content with this external show of religiosity. The latter's power base was weak since they represented the disadvantaged. Their credentials could be seriously questioned because they had no professional identification. But these handicaps did not deter them from forcing the issue and confronting the establishment. It was a precarious undertaking since the religious and political orders seemed to be working together very smoothly. The sincerity and the conviction which they manifested that they were expressing the divine will could not be dismissed. One could remove the individual, but the seeds he had planted could not be uprooted. They never achieved complete maturity in the sense of becoming the way of life followed by the Hebrews. Neither would they ever be destroyed. Historical events, especially the periods of exile, contributed to the firming up of the position. But there was enough of the moralized religion in the traditional heritage that the words of the prophets would have been heard even without this course of history.

This association of religion and ethics is always on the defensive since the requirements are more stringent than those in a faith whose demands are forms, customs, and rituals. The latter can be performed rather perfunctorily; it is more difficult to do so in activities where man is relating himself to other individuals. Therefore, the ethical emphasis must be continually renewed. Dynamic and creative leaders, who dare to contest the institutional order, are always required.

Early in the history of Christianity, essentially the same phenomenon is seen. It appears against the background of the Gentile environment and the religions which had been operative. These faiths set forth their requirements primarily in terms of relating oneself with the deity or the lord of the cult through ceremonial and initiating stipulations. In some of them, appropriate relationship could be achieved and maintained through offering the required sacrifices. In the mystery cults there was an emphasis on initiation whereby one became a possessor of a new nature. Only limited attention was paid to moral obligations. A notable exception to this general picture is found in the Orphic cult where there developed an increasing emphasis on various types of ethical conduct which could supplement the mystical practices. Even here, however, these regulations took the form of various ascetic practices.

This assessment does not mean that these religions were completely devoid of any ethical concern. They did accept and encourage the common morality of the community. But the real insistence was that the one who aspired to membership must accede to the rituals whereby he could be assured of immortality by divesting himself of his mortal nature so that he became one with the lord.

When Christianity moved into this world through its ever expanding mission activities, there were those who saw in this

new religion features which scarcely differentiated it from
the older faiths, especially the mystery cults. Since there
was as yet no carefully structured organization with the power
to determine the content of the religion and to enforce its
will upon the constituency, the door was left open to considerable freedom of interpretation and action. Consequently,
there were those who took the position that once they had been
baptized into the faith, their salvation was assured. Through
this act they had put on the Lord Jesus Christ and had become
"spiritual." Therefore, they felt no particular necessity to
live according to any specific moral standards. Some asserted
that the new status which they had achieved relieved them altogether of these obligations. They had gained a new freedom
since they had moved beyond the realm of ordinary living with
respect to the things of this world. Their transformed nature
made them part of a new order. It might even be said that it
would be inconsistent with their faith to accept moral responsibilities. Had not Christ saved them from this? To demonstrate their new status they lived a life of license. They
did as they pleased because they were "in Christ."

Paul, who had been responsbile for converting these individuals,was horrified. His Jewish heritage made it impossible
to conceive of religion which was deficient in ethical living
on the highest plane. He would insist that he could demonstrate his spiritual status as effectively as anyone. But,
at the same time, he manifested a constant concern to fulfill
the most stringent forms of human living both in terms of his
personal life and in relationship with others.[4]

A modification of this position appears in the later writings
of the New Testament. By that time Christianity had become a
more carefully conceptualized and organized religion with the
result that the special stipulations were caught up in the
phrase, "the faith." In the earlier stages the use of the
definite article was seldom used. Now the religion had become
something to be accepted rather than a total confrontation
with life and its varied experiences including those in the
area of ethics. Increasingly, the emphasis was placed on
orthodoxy which meant conforming to institutional demands.
Whatever ethical requirements existed depended on the leadership at a given time. Too often they were minimal. The major
expectations were to be found in maintaining loyalty to the

institution in its more formal representations. It meant agree-
ing with the dogma, accepting the rituals, recognizing the
hierarchical authorities, sustaining the institution through
financial contributions, and, in general, being loyal to the
whole operation. The ethical requirements were there but not
as a major or an essential part of the institutional order itself.

A particular form of this position has expressed itself in
the various perfectionist groups which have appeared in the
history of Christianity. The ordinary believer might be subjected to some rigid moral requirements. The societies usually
supported a very carefully articulated moral code. Confessions
were required at intervals. But the ultimate goal was to reach
that stage of development when the adherent would be "perfect"
and, therefore, beyond the pale of ordinary ethical considerations. Members who had attained this status were supposed to
live completely holy lives so that there was no need to be concerned about ethics. The latter would be for those who had
not attained this stage. Hence, there was implied an essential bifurcation. Ethics and religion went together until
the latter became the individual's total way of life. It is
probable that these groups would have gone to even greater ex-
tremes than they actually did had there not been the restraint
stemming from the Hebrew heritage conveyed through the Bible
and, especially, through the teachings of Jesus. It is rather
amazing how often Christian societies have been so devoted to
the grace of God conveyed through the death of Jesus that the
power of God to lead man to a life of moral nobility has become side-tracked. In Protestant circles there has been an
overwhelming concern to avoid the emphasis on "good works"
lest the adherents be taken as following Roman Catholicism
too closely. The Pauline theology has been exploited on this
point. Ephesians 1.8f. has become the key passage - one
could almost say the Bible -for this position: "For by grace
you have been saved through faith, and this is not your own
doing, it is the gift of God - not because of works, lest any
man should boast." It is amazing how the groups fail to recognize the extent to which Paul urged upon his readers to be
responsive to the "fruits of the spirit." In every letter
except the one addressed to the churches in Galatia, he was
at great pains to set forth, at considerable length, his concern that his converts would accept a most comprehensive and

extensive statement of ethics. It is difficult to see Paul
making religion and ethics into two separate and independent
areas of faith.

D. PREEMINENCE OF ETHICS

A final form of the relationship between religion and ethics
has become especially evident in our day. It has emerged with
the rise of modern science and the considerable impact which
this discipline has had on western civilization. This methodology, which has been developed to gain an understanding of the
universe, focuses upon experience and empirical evidence.
When it is directed toward persons, the primary interests are
those things which reflect man's relationship with the universe.
Among the major items examined are those which concern themselves with man in association with his fellowman, that is,
morality. Consequently, ethics takes priority over all other
facets of human life including religion. There is, moreover,
a tendency to see the latter as inconsequential since it regularly appears to relate itself with that which transcends the
present order and has little concern with mundane experiences.
Religion itself must bear a goodly share of the blame for this
representation of itself. As discussed previously, there has
been a trend in religion to become so absorbed in the relationship between the human and the divine that the association of
man with his fellow creatures has been, for the most part, subordinated or disregarded. Obviously, this denial of a major
role concerning ethical responsibility in traditional religious
societies does not commend the faith to those who are vigorously exploring the whole realm of human living to find those
bases for the most successful personal fulfillment.

As this development moves in the direction of even greater
attention being paid to morality, there is a corresponding
diminution of traditional religion. The admonition is for
man to follow the scientific approach and to develop a system
of morality which will be a more reliable guide for human living. It will have been derived from the concrete areas of
personal and social contacts. Therefore, it will have been
substantiated in the same manner as the great discoveries in
the realm of the natural sciences.[5]

The most influential school of thought which has appeared

159

in the western world in this context has been pragmatism. In keeping with its major thesis, the grounds for determining the good life is its effectiveness in human experience. The question is asked, "Does it work?" An affirmative answer suggests that the quality in question is to be accorded acceptance as an appropriate ingredient in human living. Thereby, man gains a repertoire of moral resources which he can rely upon for guidance in his personal experiences. But there is nothing which is necessarily permanent about the moral affirmations which are made. Given changing conditions, it may be, and quite probably will be, necessary to educe a new set of moral principles.

Some proponents of the position which asserts the preeminence of ethics go one step further. After a system of morality has been formulated, it is appropriate to create a religion which will give greater impetus to this area of human experiences and relationships. That is, the religion which is created is derived from and dependent upon morality. It is recognized that religion can give susbstantial force and dedication to a way of life. While man's foremost concern is moral responsibility, he can utilize the expression of religion to reinforce these values. A society can be organized which will seek to make more viable and vigorous the human concern for his fellow creatures. Many of the instruments which are appropriate to a religious institution can be employed for this purpose.

The problem with this approach is the fact that it becomes so absorbed in giving concrete expression to achieving ethical values that it becomes bogged down in the deadening routine of accomplishing particular goals. For example, concern for some social problem will be seen and considered from the vantage point of an ethical issue, and major efforts will be directed toward meeting that particular goal. With mounting opposition which usually emerges in a situation of this type, however, the project can drag on interminably. Consequently, one may easily lose the initial enthusiasm. On the other hand, were he committed to a religion which was based on a comprehensive philosophy, theology, and anthropology, then the ethical ideals would be seen in the context of the larger world view and become a part of a continuing basis for living. One would not lose his perspective so easily as he dealt with the

160

"nuts and bolts" issues of life. He would have the capacity
to rejuvenate himself in terms of a comprehensive commitment.
It would serve as a reservoir to replenish his flagging energies.

CHAPTER XII

COORDINATION OF RELIGION AND ETHICS

The preceding chapter has described some distinctive patterns concerning the past associations of religion and ethics. One basic trend has been the perennial proclivity for the two to be separated. The primary factor which has contributed to this state of affairs has been the dualistic perspective which has dominated much of human history, especially in the western world. The two realms of existence, the secular and the sacred, have appeared to be so disparate that it has been difficult to give appropriate responses to the two-fold responsibilities set forth. Since the preeminence of religion has dominated western civilization, there has generally been very little room for moral considerations. The latter were recognized, but they were of lesser importance than those which were required to maintain a right relationship with the divine realm. Consequently, as religion has flourished, morality has all too often floundered and has become weak and insignificant. The pendulum may be swinging in the opposite direction at the present time. With the rise of modern science, there has been a focusing of attention on the human realm and a corresponding diminution in the concern for the sacred. This assessment does not mean that the majority of people have become anti-religious. Even in nations where there has been a deliberate attempt to destroy religion, it is doubtful that the effort has been too successful. The growing trend is simply to recognize that religion no longer occupies the signal role which it has had in the past. Religion has been relegated to a subordinate position and its counsel largely ignored.

The factor which has contributed to this situation, both in the past and in the modern period, is the separation of religion from the daily concerns of people. The sacred organizations have had a sanctity attached to them so that they have disdained any close relationship with the secular realm. They have been confronted with a tremendous task to perform in relating man with divinity; they developed the appropriate instruments and techniques for accomplishing this end; and, thereby, they performed their role most successfully. To have

reached down into the ordinary affairs of life could have con-
taminated and lessened their exalted status. Furthermore, they
had so many far-reaching responsibilities in the area of the
sacred that they could scarcely have provided the resources
for any other concerns. Even today, it is often difficult for
the ordinary individual to see his religious institutions relating themselves to mundane interests. It has become a cliche
to say, Let the church be the church. It would be most unbe-
coming and improper to probe into the economic, political and
social interests and to set forth moral considerations in these
areas.

   In the past, the situation reached so low a state that some
individuals, who were morally sensitive, could no longer remain quiescent about the state of affairs. Religion was still
the most dominant power in human life. It was controlled by
a very special group of persons. Hence, it would not be possible to have ordinary individuals assume prerogatives in
this domain. Consequently, a different order of religious
personnel has arisen to combat the established institution
and to challenge man to recognize that religion without ethics
was impotent. The contrast between this type of individual and
those whom he opposed was most impressive. The priests, who
represented the established religious society, were professional leaders whose credentials had become certified. They
had a long and ancient heritage which was manifested in the
institutions whose history was of ancient lineage. They
could call upon the great traditions of the people to whom they
ministered to indicate that they were, indeed, men who owed
their positions to the deity. Their role was to serve as
mediators whereby man could be sustained in his relationship
with the supernatural realm. They had been adequately trained
and given sufficient knowledge so that their efforts would not
be futile. Quite often they were closely related to the state,
and additional support could be gained through this association. This class of leaders transmitted the values which had
been finalized in the past history of the group; they would
preserve this inheritance; they would bequeath it to the generations which were to follow. They saw their role primarily
as that of bringing men into the desired relationship with the
gods so that their lives would be long upon the land and safeguarded from all evils. It was a powerful order whose credentials would scarcely be challenged.

The other group of religious spokesmen has dared to confront the established order and to proclaim the need for a new direction in human living. The rise of these persons can seldom take place unless there is a sense of disenchantment and distrust with the order. As history repeatedly emphasizes, the time makes leaders as much as the latter determine the course of events. This individual is sensitive to the conditions of the society, has some deeply rooted convictions, and possesses the courage to speak openly against the authorities. It is highly probable that many revolutionary figures have appeared only to be destroyed by the power structure. They left no appreciable mark on the pages of history, and their work has not been maintained in the written records. Even their names have been effaced. They appeared anterior to the time when a sufficient weakening of the social structure had taken place to permit new voices to be heard. Even those who did succeed in restructuring the outlook generally paid a terrific price for their boldness. An entrenched social system can repond harshly against one who is seeking to move in new directions; and it usually does so.

Fortunately for mankind, there has been that individual known as the prophet who has entered upon the stage of history to dispute the social system and,especially, that part of it formulated in terms of the religious institutions. He has done so with a conviction that mankind has reached a level of degradation which, if not reversed, would make it impossible for humanity to survive. This belief has been affirmed from an awareness that the religious order was moribund and no longer able to provide for its constituency the leadership necessary to effect a significant fulfillment. The appraisal has emerged with an intensity so that it could only be said to have come from the deity. The prophets, therefore, have declared their message with that formula which expressed their innermost conviction, "Thus saith the Lord." The words which they have uttered have carried with them their own authority supported by the depth of earnestness manifested by these individuals. While they themselves were convinced that their message was not their own, the impression which was conveyed to their listeners was the authority sprang from within the depths of the hearts of the spokesmen. Their message, their voice, their whole being portrayed a realism which was inescapable. Further, the

message had within it the ring of truth which elicited from
members of the audience a response out of their own nature.
The prophets issued forth a clarion call for a moral rearma-
ment as grounds for a genuinely held religious faith.

These seers have regularly been laymen rather than profes-
sionals, although some notable exceptions have appeared. Generally, the creative leaders of mankind have been those who
have had no particular institutional attachments and dependency.
This factor is one of the reasons why a democratic society has
a basis for strong commendations; it provides the means, when
these are not blocked by carefully fabricated obstruction,
whereby laymen can enter into positions of leadership and bring
with them the deep yearnings of their background to bear upon
the issues which cry out in their day for resolution.

The prophets, too, have not been particularly interested in
soothing a distraught society. On the contrary, they have
wished to challenge their hearers to recognize a higher calling
whereby they could creatively achieve a personal fulfillment
for themselves and a more effective society for their people.
The effort has appeared to be destructive to those who were
committed to the traditional ways. Too often the latter have
been so blinded by their attachments that they have been unable to see where the new way was leading.

The prophets do not ordinarily have any goals capable of
being formalized as a basis for social stability. Instead,
their messages have seemed only to "disturb the land." Therefore, confrontation has been inevitable. Too often the prophet
has been eliminated. But his words have lived on after him.
They have been planted in the minds of the people so that the
social order could never again rest contentedly with its established patterns. The people were not necessarily transformed. It was often difficult to see any perceptible changes,
but the long sweep of history has indicated that alterations
had taken place. Living was never the same again. At the very
least, the prophetical words remained to prick men's consciences
and to make them aware that there had been a "prophet in Israel." Almost without being aware of it, human character had
changed. The spirit of these men occasionally was reflected
in the new leadership. Their ideals may have become incorporated into the governing principles or laws of the society.

166

It is in this context that human history has portrayed the preservation and correlation of ethics and religion. Even as the latter has minimized, or even ignored, the ethical implications of faith, the former has continually reasserted itself as an essential part in the total order of human living. The religion of man as the source of culture cannot evade the need for moral aspirations as a requisite ingredient. We do live in a universe; a religion which purports to concern itself with man in his total relationship with this entity cannot evade its consideration of morality since the latter is an integral part of the whole. Therefore, there is the need to recognize certain aspects of the relationship whereby the potential dichotomy can be overcome.

A. RELIGION AND ETHICS HAVE BEEN RELATED IN

THE PAST

From the earliest period of human existence, a primary source of morality has been religion. The tabus of primitve societies were initial efforts to guide human conduct so that intercourse could be maintained both with the spirits and with mortal men. Subsequently, the need for developments in this latter realm became obvious and the religions had to give consideration to them. Some traditional rules might be eliminated and others would be reinterpreted; but the need for new insights, also became apparent.

In more highly developed societies, however, the most powerful motivation for ethical advancements has come from the sensitivities of individuals. They have insisted that the traditional religion of the people had become so totally unresponsive to the living of life in human associations that a strong and dynamic stand had to be made to call man back to his moral obligations. The primary responsibility of the faith was to assure man's proper relationship with the universe; therefore, there was no need to give any serious attention to his attitudes and actions in relationship with his fellowmen. Consequently, these individuals stood forth against this interpretation, not as moralists but as persons with fiery convictions stemming from a religious faith whose purpose was to direct man to high ideals and noble actions. However, they never doubted that these oracle came from a divine source.

In numerous instances these new directions took place when there existed a powerful religious institution which was concerned about its own position as mediator between man and the divine powers and resisted these innovations. They were concerned lest their own leadership be brought into question and their status diminished. It is very difficult, if not impossible, for institutions which have been established for a considerable period of time and have been encrusted with prestige stemming from an ancient tradition to permit themselves to be too thoroughly examined and proposals made for new directions. The emphasis is constantly made that their status has resulted from having some sort of divine commission. Therefore, any revision would not only mean that their position would be altered but also that the unchangeable source of their origin would be called into question. One rather suspects, too, that an institution which boasts of its ancient heritage has come to rely on the supportive power rather than on its own contributions in guiding human destiny. Conflict between the ancient order and the needs of the new society would be inevitable.

Furthermore, there was no effective method for resolving the contest; both were claiming that they derived their positions from the ultimate power of the universe. On occasions, each attempted to employ common grounds of support for the position. For example, miracles have often been tools in the hands of each side of this type of conflict. Ultimately, the established order attempted to eliminate its adversary. Failing this, the two groups could only go their separate ways. Therefore, the beginnings of many new religions have grown out of situations of this nature.

These insurgencies on the religious scene have almost uniformly reaffirmed the close relationship which ought to prevail between religion and morality. The claim has regularly been made that they were not being disloyal to the faith. Rather, the assertions have been stated that it was the organized religious society which had failed in some of its fundamental responsibilities. Many of them have said, or implied, that many of the operations performed under the aegis of the order were not really germane to the faith in its genuine form. Rather, they were later accretions which should be discarded. The true religion must insist on personal and social morality

168

as the items of first importance. Therefore, instead of being
departures from the ancient ways, they were actually proclaiming anew those fundamental principles which had been established
originally. This extreme statement of the case may be questioned. Nevertheless, it cannot be denied that ethical considerations have always been a concern of religion. The failure of
religion at this critical point will inevitably result in a de-
generation of it and the society which it is attempting to
serve.

B. A UNION OF RELIGION AND ETHICS HAS CONTRIBUTED MANY

NOTABLE INSIGHTS IN MORALITY

Moral ideals and principles have originated from individuals
who have looked at this area of human experience from the point
of view of a deeply imbedded religious faith. Have there been
any significant contributions to this field by persons who had
no religious identities? It is doubtful. A distinction should
be made here between two types of individuals. On the one hand,
there are those who have made their contributions, as far as
possible, within the established system. They have certain ap-
preciations for the organizations but have recognized the incompleteness of them. Consequently, they have dedicated themselves to a renewal of the moral vigor which, they were convinced, the religion has had historically. Moreover, they have
appreciated the importance of an instrument which can be used
as a medium for the promulgation of their convictions concerning interpersonal relationships. Therefore, they have attempted
to operate within the organizational structure. This endeavor
was often done in the face of continuing opposition; and, all
too frequently, they were rejected. But it should be emphasized that they made considerable effort to remain since they
had a deep emotional attachment to the institution. The process of being ostracized has brought profound sorrow to them.
They could not surrender their conviction that the true nature
of religion is to foster and to encourage moral emphases. But
there was a deeper tragedy in that they perforce had to remove themselves from the society which had a profound place
in their lives. How many tears they must have shed because
of this turn of events!

The second group has been composed of those individuals

169

who have not had that emotional attachment to the institutions.
Nevertheless, they have been identified with them, have been
nurtured in their ethical teachings, and have imbibed the spirit
of the religious orders, especially as they have emphasized the
worth and dignity of man. But they have not been reluctant to
separate themselves from these societies when they have recognized their failures in the realm of moral values. At the same
time, they have taken the genuine spirit of the faith with them
as they have gone forth to formulate a more definitive ethical
system. The latter may appear to the ordinary person to have
been developed without religious connotations and associations.
A careful analysis, however, will disclose many features which
will have been derived from the religious traditions. The most
significant factor, however, is the fact that they have lived
under their influence and their own character has been molded
by the religious environment. The ethical values which they
have promulgated were drawn largely from their heritage which
has been creative in forming their own character. Their sensitivities to these values were so much a part of themselves
that they were incapable of looking at matters from a radically different perspective. They were amazed to see how their
own past had contributed to the development of their ethical
perspective.

C. MANY OF THESE IDEALS ARE STILL CHALLENGING

One of the genuinely rewarding experiences received by in-
vestigating the past in the fields of religion and morality
is a discovery of lasting qualities in both areas. The great
truths from previous eras still present their challenges to
subsequent generations. This observation is made with the
full realization that, in specific areas of human life and
conduct, there are many crudities which a later generation
has had to discard. He has to extract the principle and find
new modes of presentation and application. A wider world view
and an enlarged conception of humanity will demand a revamp-
ing of the earlier insights concerning human responsibilities.
This task, however, is very rewarding since it places one in
a great tradition wherein his forefathers struggled mightily
in the light of their own day. It gives him a sense of being
a part of the task advanced by the great persons of the past.

One is made particularly conscious of the evolution in religion and ethics through a study of the Judaeo-Christian Scriptures. Herein is disclosed an exceedingly long period wherein man has engaged in his search for moral and spiritual values. The story opens with primitive expressions not unlike those which are found among other people at this level of development. But the moral earnestness which prevailed at every stage of the unfolding story dictates that the pursuit for those ideals must continue. An ever enlarging sense of responsibility must be the goal.

There is, of course, no denying the fact that man can sink to an exceedingly low level. The Bible repeatedly substantiates this occurrence. It is no glamorized picture of humanity; it tells it like it is. At the same time, the goals and aspirations are there to draw human beings to their true destiny. When the story stands complete, insofar as the records carry it, one is overwhelmed by the remarkable insights into moral values. Many of them have not been realized even yet.

These principles were proclaimed, like all the ethical perspectives through the ages, as constituting divine imperatives, since the source of all goodness was considered to be the basis for their exposition. Moreover, it was understood that man would be motivated to work toward the realization of these ideals only in terms of a religious commitment. It would be in the service of God in his own personhood and in that of his neighbor. Given this sense of dedication, he could not but seek for the realization of a high sense of fulfillment as a human being. The moral guidance was there, and he must live in accord with its principles. In subsequent periods, the same moral attitude has emerged for man to live in keeping with these ideals. The precepts possess that permanent nature which makes them still vital and worthy of human response. The sensitive person will feel that sense of guilt when he fails to measure up to these expectations.

D. RELIGION SHOULD SUPPLY THE CONTEXT WITHIN WHICH

A VALID ETHIC IS SOUGHT

Past history, therefore, suggests that religion provides the only appropriate context within which an adequate ethical pattern can be created. It is the area of human living which

171

is concerned with the whole person. Other sectors which relate to the human scene direct their attention to only a part
of the story. They look at ethics from the more limited perspective of their own particular interests. Political morality
is concerned with standards which relate to the governmental
order; economic ethics provides guidance for the appropriate
performances in the business world; educational standards
classifies individuals into different groups and assign appropriate relationships. But religion categorically asserts
that human beings constitute a unique species. A moral system
must be concerned with this wholistic status. Theistic religions add an additional dimension by saying that a person is
a child of God, and the moral principles must be established
on the basis of this divine origin.

When ethical ideals are created, they must be indicative
of the uniqueness of humanity. Every area of relationship
with one's fellowmen must be considered as involving the highest level of moral responsibility. The moral guidance must
be inclusive. There is a wholeness to it. From these fundamental principles will flow particular applications for the
different segments of human experiences. But at no time will
the nature and significance of man be forgotten.

Without this undergirding, morality too often moves quickly into a matter of expediency. Some form of manipulation
becomes evident. When religion determines the nature of
ethics, there can be no compromising in order to arrive at
immediate goals. There is ever present the insistent voice
which states that the person is a human being.

E. PHILOSOPHICAL ETHICS WILL BE CONSIDERED

The religious person does not reject any source of goodness
or resources for guidance toward reaching this objective. He
is a seeker. Ever yearning for a more complete comprehension
concerning the nature of moral attributes, he examines every
area of life which can offer assistance.

He will be especially responsive to the disclosures which
have come from all the thoughtful men of wisdom who have engaged in an intensive examination of human experiences in order
to find a basis for human conduct. The interaction can have

172

major importance. The philosopher has probed the fabric of
reality in order to find the ultimate nature of existence. In
the course of this perusal, he has produced some profound insights which have made it possible to project ethical ideals
with which to challenge mankind. These perceptions can prove
to be most useful for the man of faith as he yearns for the
most complete attainment of human relationships at their highest point of excellence. They serve to give him additional
insights for fulfilling his basic goals. They provide support
for an expanded devotion based on his religious perspectives.
The philosophical ethics may even serve to renew and to stimulate religious persons to be more truly responsible in this
area of life. This occurrence will eventuate particularly
when a religion moves so far toward a way of life which is
devoid of ethical emphasis. Then the philosopher will restore
this dimension of religion to its proper place.

This source of moral ideals and guidance is made more valuable for religion since many of the philosophers have been persons who have been nurtured in a tradition of faith. Oftentimes, they have turned to philosophy simply because the organized religious society, with which they were identified,
failed to give sufficient expression to the ethical precepts
which were a part of its heritage. Moreover, since philosophy
does have a very close relationship with religion, as was
indicated previously, this discipline would attract them. It
would afford a more significant basis for achieving what the
religion should have done and failed. These individuals can
scarcely reject their past. On the contrary, it will have
provided a reservoir of principles which will become integrated into their philosophical system. Especially will the
moral teachings continue to serve as influences in the formation of their intellectual position.

Under these circumstances, it will be impossible for a religion, which has a strong sense of human values, to ignore
the contributions of philosophers. The interaction will be
most healthy and helpful. Difficulties may emerge in trying
to integrate the rational analysis of human relationships
into the previously formed sacred traditions. But, in the
final analysis, the results of this undertaking can have immense signifiance in enriching the faith by providing incre-
ments for a more profound morality which can renew the total

basis for human living. Thereby personal and social fulfillment can be more adequately achieved.

F. ETHICS CAN ACHIEVE ITS BEST EXPRESSION ONLY

IN THE SPIRIT OF RELIGION

When all resources have been utilized for moral consideration, it is questionable whether it is possible to have a viable pattern for an ethical life outside religion. Without a
dynamic setting in this dimension, ethics may become one of
several things.

First, it may be simply an intellectual system. This danger
is exhibited in philosophical ethics. When the philosopher has
completed his investigation, he can scarcely go further from
the standpoint of his discipline. The latter has no real power
to make any system of thought a vital one through its own efforts. Actually, it would be contrary to its purpose to attempt an implementation. This form of inquiry can be concerned
only with a rational examination of the many facets in the
universe. When it has moved beyond this stage, it has become
something other than philosophy. Within limits, other disciplines may seek to implement its conclusions. For example,
the politician can demonstrate and seek to utilize them in
the affairs of state. But in terms of fudamental relationships, there can be only one thing which can give full force
and direction to morality. It is religion.

Second, it may become a formalized system. Not only can
a system of moral principles be developed, but also they can
be constructed so that they provide a unified pattern for life.
The philosopher can make a substantial contribution at this
point. But he can only suggest the application. A very con-
sistent and coherent pattern can be established, but the real
test in the field of ethics is the direction that life is
lived in terms of this proposal. If the perspectives go no
further, they become as inept as a highly institutionalized
religion which has lost its vitality in terms of genuine
religious experiences. Both do have great strength in terms
of careful correlations of the elements derived from the respective areas. But they constitute lifeless orders with
little or no meaning in the furtherance of their appropriate

174

functions by their participating members. Invigoration must come
from some other source.

Third, a system of ethics may find some limited application
if it is translated into a set of legal precepts. As noted previously, however, casuistry is characterized essentially by negation. It serves a partial role in human living, especially
in a social context, since it excludes areas which have proven
to be detrimental to the group. Its significance in guiding
human life is quite limited. It may prevent a society from
disintegrating into a state of disorder and chaos. Its positive
values are very inadequate.

Therefore, in conclusion, when morality is embodied in a
dynamic faith, it can become a way of life and capable of attaining the highest exemplification. The principles begin to
take on a life-giving, not a life-denying, quality. A partnership is formed which is mutually advantageous each to the
other. Morality becomes implemented in life instead of existing as a set of principles; religion is transformed vitally from a set of theological ideas to a way of life for its
adherents.

CHAPTER XIII

NATURE OF ECONOMICS

Economics is concerned with the issues relative to the production and distribution of goods and services. It is associated with the basic requirements for human living. Therefore, everyone is involved in this area of human experience. The fulfillment of these activities is the result of man's work. The latter is universally required; no one can escape some form of participation. It is not surprising, therefore, that scarcely any human problem is devoid of an economic factor. The tracing out of history can be accomplished from this perspective. It is understandably that a commonly held theory today is that this factor is a major, probably the sole, determinant of history. Even if one does not accept totally this idea, he cannot deny the substantial impact which economic affairs have upon man and his society.

Through the greater part of human history people have borne what appeared to be an impossible burden since the ability to meet economic needs has required a major effort on their part, and the results have been most uncertain. Their dreams, therefore, have frequently projected the ideal society wherein these efforts were no longer required. The fulfillment of all their material aspirations was the goal which they deeply desired. Or they dreamed of an existence wherein these needs were no longer present. That is, another form of being was anticipated - usually called a spiritual existence. In either case, the most vivid aspirations were expressed in these terms.

Since these ideals occupied a prominent part in their thoughts, it has inevitably required some type of explanation to account for the presence of labor in their present state. In some way they have felt that not only would there be a satisfaction of their needs without labor in the future; but they have, in like manner, perceived in their deepest and most profound thoughts that there had been a period when labor was not required to meet their wants. The golden age of the future seemed to require a similar period in the past. Consequently, they have concluded that the intervening age has been the re-

sult of deviation from some ideal order introduced by that
which is evil. In oriental society evil is frequently construed as an illusory form of existence. But the same basic
explanation is present. Some power or force from the super-
human realm has brought on this predicament. This explanation
would be necessary in order to make it possible for the establishment of some way of extricating themselves from the unde-
cired order.

In our modern society, especially in the western world,
there is beginning to appear a glimmer of an idea that this
earlier conception may not be entirely correct. Many factors
in our society suggest that human nature is so constructed
that labor is required for fulfillment. Either man engages
in productive endeavors or he moves into a meaningless existence. Usually, the alternative to constructive participation in the order of life is to engage in some deviant form
of behavior. It is not a question of whether one labors or
not. Rather, it is to determine what the nature of the activity
is to be. One may thoroughly hate his job, but he would be
even more unhappy in a state of idleness. He would find some
way to achieve a mode of action which would provide some measure of satisfaction by participating in other types of work.

This situation can be illustrated by an examination of
several types of persons. In an earlier period of history
productive activity was required for survival from a young
age. Scarcely had the child learned to toddle before he had
some duties to perform. Very quickly he grew up to take a
significant part in the activities of his elders. In our
society, this mode of life is no longer necessary. One might
say that it is not even possible. But the need of the child
is still there. The failure to meet it has created a tremendous problem. It is seen in the growth of deviant behavior
which we call juvenile delinquency. In actuality, it is simply
another form of productivity.

Some of the efforts which have been made to cope with this
issue have been far from successful. A variety of forms of
play activity has been introduced. As a form of recreation
there has been tremendous value found in this activity. As
an auxiliary form of labor, it offers rewards which provide
value to people. The difficulty is that play is productive

only in an essentially inward manner. The goal is to win for oneself or a group. After the score has been achieved, there is no additional expression of creativity. It does not extend out beyond itself to become rewarding in a continuum. This characteristic is observed sometimes among professional athletes for whom it is their employment. Even winners express frustration; others seem to have a sense of futility.

Our educational system has not succeeded in coping with this problem. The additional leisure time created by our modern economic order provides greater opportunity to become knowledgeable. But one of the discouraging features of the teaching profession is the difficulty in developing within the students what has been called the "joy of study." There are many causes for this situation. One of them, quite possibly, is the tremendous emphasis which is given to a tangible return for the performance. If one does the assigned work, he is rewarded with a good grade; if he fails to do so, he is punished. The effort is seldom made to develop a sense of creativity in the endeavor itself. One of the greatest indictments of the teaching profession is the failure to convey the understanding of value to be received from the intellectual inquiry for its own sake. In part, this problem may be due to the fact that the teachers themselves have little enthusiasm for it. When one observes the type of student who is to be employed as a teacher in our public schools, one ponders the course of the future. Too many display only the most meager appreciation for their own course work. It is difficult to believe they will be able to convey any appreciation for their subject to their students. Another factor, which will be discussed in a subsequent chapter, is that we are reflecting society's value in thinking that motivation comes primarily from some external reward or punishment. The laborer simply receives his wage whether in some form of monetary return or through another kind of compensation.

The indications are, therefore, that modern society has a monumental problem which will probably increase rather than diminish. It is not geared to utilize juvenile labor, and neither recreation nor education provides a very adequate substitute. The issue does, however, illustrate very impressively that the traditional idea that work is evil should be questioned.

At the other end of life stands the person in our society who has had an active life of productivity. He may have developed very negative attitudes about his employment. Then he arrives at the time of retirement. This experience can be very traumatic. Initially, he may anticipate having the opportunity to engage in many activities which had not heretofore been possible. But very quickly many of these interests lose their attractiveness. They simply fail to satisfy as a regular basis for living. Consequently, there is often considerable effort expended to secure some form of work. Agencies which concern themselves with this segment of mankind have utilized their resources to attempt placement in some economic order. While there is an element of monetary consideration, there appears to be a much greater need to provide a basis for usefulness.

Among the disadvantaged people in our society, this issue is met in another way. These persons are oftentimes individuals who have few if any marketable skills in the modern economic society. This situation is particularly apparent today since the number of jobs for the unskilled has diminished significantly and is expected to continue to decline even more drastically. Enough of the humanitarian spirit is present in our affluent society that we can easily provide for the primary needs of this group. From a physical standpoint there is no major problem. The deprivation is not especially acute in the basic necessities. While their physical well-being could be substantially improved, the most pressing issue relates to a negation of the spirit. They become so completely deprived of the opportunity to make a genuine contribution to themselves and to society that they become simply parasites. The result is an incomplete life. Children born in this environment scarcely have the opportunity to develop any meaningful understanding about the possibilities for personal fulfillment. They cannot be blamed since their surroundings are not conducive to any broad perspective concerning the meaning of achievement. Very often, therefore, they will perpetuate the inertness of their parents. This status may continue in the family for generations. It has been suggested that the only way to break this cycle is to remove the children from this type of environment. In the United States an experimental program known as the Job Corps has been developed to make this type of response. It appears to have produced some positive results.

The entire problem concerning the role of work has arisen
because economics has been limited to the materials having to
do with the production and distribution of goods and services.
The dominating goal has been to produce a larger amount with
less effort. All evaluations of the economic agencies have
been made from this point of view.

The goods and services have been classified into two groups.
First, there is the production which is designed to meet primary needs. For the greater part of human history this area
has been the most demanding. Efforts have generally been directed toward this goal. Throughout the past ages the quest
for food, clothing, and shelter has occupied an inordinately
high percentage of time and effort. This commitment was necessary since the economy was one of scarcity. It was difficult
to provide a sufficiency in the basic requirements for life.
In the greater part of the world, and for most people, this
condition still prevails. Hunger and deprivation are all too
common. Assuming, as we must if there is to be the survival
of humanity, that population controls and continued improvement in technology will solve these problems, a new day will
arrive wherein there will be a greater participation in the
economic order. A major hindrance toward meeting these needs
even today is the inability to find ways of distributing the
productivity. A part of this problem occurs because methods
of distribution, as now employed, upset the economies of
those countries to which goods are shipped.

In the affluent countries, however, the difficulties
in producing and distributing goods which meet primary needs
are relatively minor. This assessment is made with the full
awareness of dire needs among some parts of the population
in these lands. But these necessities can be responded to whenever we are sufficiently aroused about them. Comparatively
speaking, the poor in the developed countries would scarcely
be considered deprived in the other countries.

Consequently, the economic problem in western societies
arises primarily in the matter of secondary needs. Fantastic
advances have been made in developing creature comforts. They
have become so extensively used that we take them for granted
and consider them as important as the essentials of life. Our
desires have been developed through a highly organized adver-

181

tising machine which attempts to convince everyone that they would be considered poverty stricken if they did not possess the latest gadget which has been invented. But our economic system performs very poorly in making possible a wide distribution of these products. As a result, conflicts inevitable arise.

Throughout history, therefore, attention has been primarily focused on the goods and services received as a result of productivity. There has been a failure to recognize that there is another form of value. It consists of the non-material rewards which result through people being involved in the economic operation. There is still only a limited appreciation of this feature. The material well-being is the major interest in the society.

Increasingly, the personal factor in this domain is forcing itself upon society. When any attention has been given to it in the past, it has been related very closely to the material area. Some restrictions have been placed on the exploitation of human resources. It was insisted that appropriate working conditions were provided. Modest attempts have been undertaken to assure a more equitable distribution of the goods and services. These interests have led to the organization of the several segments in society to insist on their interests being protected.

Two additional personal interests have come to the forefront in recent years, and considerable effort is being expended to resolve problems related to them. One is the involvement of minority groups in a more substantial manner as participants in the rewards of the system. The other is a more general concern, the ecological issue.

The human problem which must be given the highest priority if the economic order is to be properly operated is the inherent creativity of people. Through the persistent attempts to improve the material factor, vast technologies have been installed. Their success has been unbelievably substantial, and there is the promise of even greater abundance. But the question is being posed, How large has been the price? Its cost in the depersonalization of individuals has not yet been assessed. Labor in all areas is becoming so routine that the very personality of employees is being altered. The task which is performed develops tensions so that personal attitudes and outlooks affect adversely social relationships. The evidence is most apparent in the health problems which pervade our western society. The heavy toll taken by diseases of the heart is devastating. Mental disorders are widespread. It is estimated that at least one in five persons will require psychiatric services during the course of a lifetime. The number of suicides is appalling.

A great many social issues are equally disturbing. The rapid polarization among the classes reflects economic dissatisfaction to a considerable degree. The inability to maintain full employment is evident. It is not only the unskilled laborers who are affected; even highly trained individuals and professionally educated people find the job market closed to them.

These problems and similar ones suggest that increasingly a considerable amount of planning will be required to achieve a fully adequate economic order. First, we shall continue to require the material results of the economy although we may be rapidly approaching the point when some radical reorientation in this area will be required. Already, in the area of food, a considerable change has taken place. The United States has essentially accepted the proposition that no citizen will be deprived of ingredients which are necessary for a healthy diet. But for the vast majority of the people, it has become necessary to limit the amount of food which is consumed. For those persons who do not follow a prescribed diet, there is a normal effort to restrict the intake of food. The human capacity is limited; desires must inevitably decline.

In the area of clothing, there is no problem in meeting the needs. As a matter of fact, the clothing industry has probably been able to maintain its operations by high-powered salesmanship more than by the real requirements of its customers. The fashion dictators have attempted to build an obsolescence by a continuing change in the styles. A mild revolt may be erupting. It is highly conceivable that the resistance on the part of the consumers to the flow of new patterns may encourage the manufacturers to create a more basic type of clothing.

Shelter is probably the most serious problem in providing the basic material requirements for people. The technology in this area has not advanced to the point that the meeting of needs can be achieved. A major barrier is space and the attendant environmental conditions. Water resources are limited, and the amount of this commodity used in the modern household places considerable strain on the supply. Water levels have been falling at an alarming rate, and cities and towns have had to transport it from great distances. It would appear that some new type of sewage equipment will be required in the not too distant future. The very considerable amount of water used in industry and in some types of farming where extensive irrigation is required further depletes the supply.

In the area of secondary needs some major transformations may be required. For example, how long can we continue to increase the number of motor vehicles and the highways over which they run? The destruction wrought to the environment by this one item, which we consider essential to modern life, is beginning to be recognized. The pollution of the air by the car itself, the damage inflicted on land and water by the extracting of petroleum, and the elimination of land from other productive use by the construction of roads are slowly arousing people to the dangers inherent in these items of modern life. The vast chemical enterprises pose major threats to human survival. Human ingenuity will, undoubtedly, discover means to combat many of the ills which have accompanied modern technology. Nevertheless, a crisis is approaching when some more radical reordering of priorities will be forced upon us.

The entire thrust of our consideration has been to observe the transformation of economic issues and concerns as they have emerged from the past and attained their present status. The production and distribution of goods and services can no longer absorb the entire attention of the economist. The scope of this area will have to be enlarged so that there will be a wider participation in reaching decisions. The issue which must receive the greatest attention is the involvement of people in the toal process.

First, a new attitude about work must be developed. The

184

idea that it is evil must be eliminated. It must be seen as a medium through which humanity can achieve its most significant fulfillment. Second, economic operations have to be considered not only from the standpoint of the goods which are produced and distributed but, also, the extent to which they provide opportunities for people. An industry, for example, should be evaluated not only from its ordinary economic assets but also from the standpoint of its capacity to utilize personal services. It may even be necessary to alter our outlook concerning "labor-saving" gadgets and machines. They may be too expensive by destroying productive opportunities.

A. FOOD GATHERING STAGE

Let us examine, briefly, the course of economic history to see how man has arrived at the present atage. From this perspective the prospects for the future can be observed and the direction which will lead to it.

The initial efforts were directed toward the achieving of survival. They were limited to the securing the necessities of life. Evidence suggests that the results were not too substantial. Notwithstanding stupendous efforts, he was fortunate to obtain a sufficient amount of the essentials to provide for the continuation of life itself. In this endeavor he was in constant conflict with myriad forces and competing with other living creatures for these resources. While he had certain advantages including the use of his hands and an upright position, the presence of other creatures like himself, other animals, and the ordinary vagaries of nature made his existence a precarious one.

One of the most limiting factors was the necessity to live on a day-by-day basis. There was almost no opportunity to secure more than was required for present needs. Even if he were to obtain a surplus, it would be extremely difficult to preserve it so that it would contribute to a longer period whereby plans could be made. It meant that he was always involved in meeting the recurring requirements of his daily life. Leisure time, a prime requirement for advancement, was pitifully small. The opportunity to dream dreams and to plan for the future was seldom present. Until he achieved this boon, his development would be more or less completely impossible.

It is difficult to understand how he broke away from this status at all.

Our knowledge of this period is severely limited. It would be helpful if we knew how he did begin to gain control over his environment so that it would make possible a greater fulfillment. How did he tame the forces of nature so that they would contribute more effectively and fully to his needs? One thing appears evident. However it happened, this stage, whereby a transition was made from a food gathering to a food producing system, was a momentous one. It may have been the most revolutionary transition which man has made in his entire history. It began to transfer him from a position of dependence to one of independence. He could control the creative powers in the world and mold them to his requirements. The subsequent advances have been developments of this initial thrust. Further efforts to take control of the powers in the universe were made. Our forebears should be honored because they did somehow turn man into an entirely new direction.[1]

B. PASTORAL STAGE

The initial breakthrough was achieved by the domestication of animals. Some evidence points to the dog as the first creature to be brought into subjection. The value of this accomplishment can be appreciated. This animal offered a variety of assets for his master. It would provide protection against other natural enemies; it would assist in obtaining food; it would guard any surplus which was at hand. Another less tangible value would be possessed in that the dog would provide companionship to offset the loneliness which would be adverse to his well-being. It would serve to help man to move to a more social mode of existence. The relationship which was established may have aided in the development of his mind through an interacting of activites by the two. It could also be used for warmth in times of severe weather.

Of greater importance would be the domestication of other animals like sheep, goats, and cows. They would serve in a middleman capacity. They would do the gathering, collecting, storing, and making food available to people. Therefore, the human responsibility became radically transformed. Man must seek out the places where the raw materials, pasturage and water, were available; he has the duty to protect the animals from predatory enemies; then he could take from the flocks and herds whatever met his needs. Milk and milk by-products became major parts of his diet. Animal skins provided materials for clothing and shelter. The result was a substantial enlargement of his resources.

Human life was still terribly precarious. Man was still a wanderer in search of suitable grazing land. He had to assume responsibility not only for his own safety but also for his possessions. This latter factor often made him even more subject to physical harm at the hands of the varied enemies which surrounded him.

He had, however, earned some leisure time and was capable of taking advantage of this gain by participating in other activities. Most important, he had the opportunity to direct his mind to things other than sheer existence. One can certainly appreciate the possibility that he began to ask questions about himself and his universe. These queries were elementary in nature, but they served to establish the foundation for a continuing quest for understanding.

Some advances in socialization could occur. He could associate himself with others to carry forth the common search for the needs of existence. Tribal organizations became evident at this time. Ethical, political, and religious patterns of behavior assumed greater importance. Laws, organized groups, and religious patterns became more highly developed. There was even the beginning of literature through the preservation and transmission of tribal traditions through oral communications.

C. AGRICULTURAL STAGE

Even as man had previously gained control over animal life, eventually he did the same for plant life. He discovered that when seeds were planted, they grew into maturity. Rather than depend on the ordinary forces of nature to carry out this process, he found it advantageous when he performed the act himself. Through it he gained control over the productive operation. Not only did he receive rewards from the standpoint of economics - important though this element was - but also there

was a sense of creativity and control over the forces of nature.
He was beginning to assert himself. The psychological values
would be advantageous notwithstanding the danger of arrogance
when this exhiliration became excessive. It would give him a
greater confidence and a sense of selfhood not heretofore present.

As his abilities developed and greater success was achieved,
he had the opportunity to settle down. He ceased his wanderings
and established his own homestead. Of course, it could be said
that he became a slave to his environment since he no longer
enjoyed the freedom to move about and to seek new adventures.
The demands made on the farmer are always tremendous. There is
scarcely the opportunity for substantial leisure. The actual
farming operation may have been assigned to the woman since
the male members spent considerable time in searching for food.
The society may have been organized along matriarchal lines.
Only with continued improvement in agriculture was it possible
for the homesstead to be taken over by the husband and father.

That which ultimately proved to be the greatest asset which
this mode of living afforded was a new and enlarged form of
sociality. Various types of cooperative activities were seen
to be desirable. For example, the demand for protection required association. Through extending the experiences derived from the older tribal order, it would be possible to
erect a walled village where the members could establish resi-
dence. This group arrangment necessitated a new type of political system.

Slowly, the society experienced an increase in the surplus.
From this factor greater leisure time was made possible. Expanded activities could be engaged in. Man set aside some
time for improving himself by enlarging his interests and
knowledge of the world. He learned to read and write; he
could paint and create other forms of artistic expression.
He could even invent tools by utilizing his enlarged knowledge coupled with the motivation stemming from his greater
needs. In other words, he gradually achieved a life-style
which offered more than a minimum. He could do more than
eke out an existence. In comparison with the experiences of
his forebears this life was exceedingly rich. More significantly, it opened the door to greater things yet to come.

D. INDUSTRIALIZATION

Throughout his early existence man had utilized tools. From the time that he had used the tree limb as a club, he had recognized that the capacity of his bare hands would be greatly enhanced if there were instruments which he could employ. Subsequently, improvements began to be made. The stone age produced some substantially more adequate implements. The progress was slow, but advancements were made.

The tool age would come into its own when he discovered various types of metals which could be forged into more effective instruments. They were more malleable and, therefore, capable of being fashioned more according to human desires. The whole range of activities would be greatly improved as a result of the creation of different types of implements.

Perhaps the most important factor at this stage was the growing recognition that some division of labor was not only appropriate but would make a major advance in the social order. Individuals could develop their talents so that they could increase their contributions to the other members of the group. Not only could they provide for the needs of their associates, but they could gradually improve upon them and even discover new types of instruments.

This same type of specialization was employed in yet another way. Certain individuals were entrusted with functions whereby life could be made more complete. Those who were selected were given the necessary food, clothing, and shelter from the surplus of the group so that they would be freed to engage in the special affairs and make their contributions. Through this approach, painters, record keepers, religious leaders, politicians, and teachers fulfilled specialized functions by utilizing their unique talents. Their efforts provided other members of the society with substantial benefits. Obviously, these developments came slowly and painfully. But through persistent dedication human progress was achieved. Gains appeared to be inevitable notwithstanding those occasions when these organized patterns of life entered into a stage of decline. Even with the deterioration and fall of advanced groups, other people entered in-

189

to their labors and built on the foundations which they had laid. The disintegration of a society will open the way for the eventual beginning of a renewal, and the next step in human endeavor will have been taken. The tools of the past will have been improved upon, and additional discoveries will be accomplished.

E. INDUSTRIAL REVOLUTION

The culmination of this industrialization was the Industrial revolution. Just as the domestication of animals in an earlier period had made it possible for man to have his tasks performed for him - at least the muscle for the work would be supplied by the beasts of burden - now he would discover forms of energies in other parts of nature which could be harnessed and put at man's disposal.

The newfound leisure which this development provided opened the door to freedom to move more extensively in many different and original directions. The enlarged productivity, which resulted from the fact that one person could now do the work previously performed by many individuals, meant that opportunities were greatly enhanced to live life more fully. The basic requirements could be more easily supplied; there could be provided comforts which removed many hardships; but, most importantly, man could employ his ingenuity so as to become more creative in relationship with the universe. Unfortunately, he has too often lost this opportunity. He has become so absorbed in catering to his physical desires that he has deprived himself of enrichment in the distinctively human sphere - aesthetic, moral, and spiritual. Even these areas, however, were not totally neglected as a consequence of the employment of the energies in the universe.

When this new period opened, developments were made quite rapidly. Greater specialization contributed to this expansion and the capacity to utilize the discoveries more effectively. The complexities of the universe became more evident; therefore, it required that one person had to devote his time and energy in mastering a particular segment of the process. He would have to become an expert in a special realm which would be his prerogative. This division of labor set in motion a phenomenal increase in knowledge. Moreover, it accelerated

190

at a pace far greater than man could possibly have anticipated. As a matter of fact, it may be argued that the human predicament was made worse rather than resolved by this factor. The socio-economic problems grew in complexity as a result of the rapid diversification, specialization, and expansion of the system so that the human position in the universe deteriorated rather than improved. Gradually the machine which man had created began to dominate and control his life to the degree that its liabilities outweighed its assets. Human values were subsumed under economic values. Man became a tool of the industrial order rather than the one who directed its destiny so that it would serve mankind. On the one hand, it is accepted that the industrial revolution has enriched life. But the cost of this enhancement may have become much higher than was considered likely in an earlier period. While few individuals desire to turn back the clock, we should be willing to recognize the difficulties and to seek solutions to them.

E. ATOMIC AGE

Before we have resolved very adequately the excruciatingly severe problems of the industrial revoltuion, we have entered another age which proposes new promises in economic development and achievement. The two areas in which the period impinges upon us may be considered simply extensions of the preceding era. But the tremendous possibilities for both good and evil suggests that it should be examined as a new order.

On the one hand, there is the new type of machine, the computer. What this device will be able to accomplish has scarcely been recognized. Its productivity to date is startling enough to cause us to pause and ask ourselves if our abilities to utilize this tool are sufficiently mature. Its ability to perform tasks heretofore done by people is most impressive. With greater sophistication, it is not beyond the realm of imagination to believe that it can be programmed to achieve anything that man can do. Further, it can accomplish the result more efficiently and produce a superior product. The disturbing question meets us, Where does man go to fulfill his role in life? Theoretically, he will be free to participate in many activities and interests which he has not been able to do heretofore. But is he prepared for these experiences? For example, it would appear that he would now

191

be free to use his mind for expanding his knowledge and understanding. But the efforts to educate man so that he can do
so in a much more significant way seems to have been almost
totally disappointing. As a matter of fact, our education facilities devote few resources toward this end. The primary
thrust is to develop man as a part of the economic system
when the latter is rapidly eliminating him as a participating
factor. It has been predicted that within a decade ten percent of the population can produce all the material goods
which people require. It has even been hinted that complex
mechanisms are now available, or could be made, which would
vastly increase production with a corresponding diminution of
manpower. But the captains of industry have been concerned
about the social dislocations which would result that they have
been reluctant to put them into use. While this point of view
is questionable, it is understandable.

On the other hand, there are potentially new forms of energy
which will contribute extensively to economic development.
Nuclear energy is already been produced and utilized in many
areas of human affairs. More rapid expansion will occur as
soon as problems relating to the environment are resolved.
A far-reaching program in this area known as the Project
Plowshares has been organized in the United States. It is
planned to employ nuclear devices to excavate canals and
harbors, to move mountains, and to extract oil, shale, and
minerals. A few years ago the United Nations Atoms for Peace
Conference was held at Geneva to explore this program. It
appeared at that time that the Soviet Union might become a
joint participant in this venture.

Altogether this new age offers potentialities which could
totally revolutionize the economic order. A century or two
of experimentations could easily result in meeting the basic
economic requirements for all people. But the social problems
and dehumanization of personality could be disastrous. This
two-fold result is a distinct possibility. We shall almost
certainly pursue the explorations in these areas, and the results can be fantastic. Unfortunately, man is prone to ignore
the personal and social issues which accompany the achievements.
There is too much of an inclination to consider human needs
only in physical terms. Whatever may confront man in other
dimensions of life will somehow solve themselves. Consequent-

192

ly, efforts in other than the technological and related aspects of the atomic age will no doubt be ignored. Everything else takes precedence over personal fulfillment and human relationships. In other words, the religious needs of man are essentially denied even in western societies which assert very high evaluations of man as being superior to all other creatures. In previous periods of change, the transformations developed slowly. Even then there was an intolerable amount of suffering. There was, however, time for a sense of gradualism so that the social changes could be effected. It appears most unlikely that similar accomodations will be present for the current age.

Consequently, we are entering an era of abundant promises but one with grave premonitions. The ultimate result will be determined by the presence or absence of an adequate, dynamic religion.

CHAPTER XIV

PAST RELATIONSHIPS OF RELIGION AND ECONOMICS

A. DIRECT INVOLVEMENT

In introducing this section, which will trace out the course
of the interactions between religion and economics, a prelimi-
nary statement should be made that is currently a factor in
the total picture. American churches and synagogues are direct participants in the economic order. They constitute institutions which are associated with other forms of organized
life in this country. This relationship is carried out in essentially the same manner and utilizes the same techniques as
do other groups. Business operations follow the same motifs.
Services are rendered, and some forms of compensation are received. Since the days of pew rents have passed, the amount
of revenue is uncertain. Some groups attempt to preserve a
steady income by urging their constituents to contribute the
tithe, ten percent of their income, to charitable purposes
with all or most of it being channeled through the churches.
In the smaller churches there are indications that members
follow this practice more regularly than do those who are
affiliated with the larger ones. Many of the latter, however, secure some knowledge about the financial status of its
communicants and exert some pressure to make contributions
accordingly.

In the utilization of these funds, the churches follow, in
a general way, the same procedures which operate in other areas
of the economic life. Personnel are hired on an agreed basis
of financial arrangements. There are even some forms of labor
organizations beginning to take shape. For the most part, the
physical requirements for the church plant and its operations
are secured in the market place. Budgets are drawn up and
adopted on an annual basis. The amount of funds is modest,
but not insignificant, in relationship to the total economy.[1]
For example, in the year 1972 contributions totaled $14,061,
400,000. In addition, there was building activity to the extent of $844,000,000.

Another phase of the financial picture exists in investments and direct participation in business. Since religious organizations are not required to make financial disclosures, information in this area is imprecise. Nevertheless, both investments and profits are believed to be considerable. Several factors have contributed to an increasing concern about this feature of these groups which has been expressed by those who are within, and others who are outside, these institutions. First, the income of these organizations is tax exempt, a factor which can give them a substantial competitive advantage. For example, it has been estimated that an investment can be recouped in a maximum of twenty years because of this tax status. It has even been suggested that were the religious institutions in the United States to utilize fully all of their resources, they could secure control over the entire economic order in this country in approximately ten years.[1]

Second, questions have been raised relative to the nature of the investments. On the one hand, financial ties with certain types of businesses have appeared to be inappropriate.[2] On a more positive note, churches have been urged to express their social concerns by directing their investments to projects whose prospects for large profits are limited and, even more, the loss potential is high. Some denominations have adopted a forthright program which states that a substantial part of the investments are to be made in these businesses. Finally, a greater interest has been expressed in the utilization of voting rights through stock ownership in an effort to create an improved social attitude on the part of corporations.

Third, in an effort to improve their financial condition, religions have entered directly into the business world. Often, in these instances, they operate as competitors to secular companies. The most obvious example is the publishing activity which is quite substantial in most groups. Then there are schools, hospitals, nursing homes, homes for the elderly, and similar activities where there is some measure of competition.

Fourth, it is interesting to observe how many communistic communities have been developed by religious societies. In America there have been many including the Oneida Community

196

in New York, the Ephrata Society in Pennsylvania, the Amana Commune in Iowa, the followers of George Rapp in Indiana, and others. While, undoubtedly, the initial motivation which led to the establishment of these groups and provided the basis for their continued existence was religion, in practice it may be questioned whether they were not just as concerned about the development of the economic interests. The Brooks Farm experiment in New England gives some support to this assessment. The religio-philosophical foundations were present, but there was not an equal involvement in the financial efforts by the members. Consequently, it did not prove to be a very successful undertaking. A serious fire brought about its demise.

While religious societies can scarcely avoid financial operations and, thereby, run the risk of losing their integrity by imitating common business practices, they do as a rule attempt to keep this dimension of their affairs in a secondary position. Their major energy is poured into the spiritual realm. Both historically and currently, direct involvement in this operational phase has been kept in perspective with every effort being made not to allow it to be an intruder in the primary interests.

B. RELIGION AND THE ECONOMIC ORDER

In contrast to the above, however, the extent to which religion has been indirectly related to economic activities has been considerable. It is doubtful that one could find a period when it has not been substantial. An examination of those forms of participation which have contributed most fully to the developments in this part of human experiences will be useful.

1. Primitive groups. The most thorough dependence on supernatural powers to aid in the securing the necessities of life can be observed in primitive societies. The sheer magnitude of the difficulties and the impotence of man in the face of the tremendous forces which confronted him made it imperative that he seek whatever assistance could supplement his own actions. The later theological term would be the grace of God. Without the support of these powers even meager success would be denied. It was, therefore, of the utmost impor-

197

tance to have these powers favorably disposed so that the necessary aid was forthcoming.

In this type of society, the inducing of the supernatural power to provide aid was accomplished by magic. It required a three-fold operation. First, persons must be direct participants in working toward the desired results. One could not rely simply on assistance by the spirits to perform the tasks. Second, those powers who were being depended upon must be enticed to contribute their part. The procedure whereby it would be done was a performance of a symbolic act which was designed to initiate action. Should the normal modes of seeking response be unsuccessful, then other efforts must be put forth. One might cajole or heap abuse on the power. Should there still be failure, the spirit might even be abandoned. Third, the supernatural being acted. Primitive man did not construe his successes as having been accomplished solely through his own work. Religion was decidedly a contributor to the economic order.

2. Calvinism. At a considerably later time, a similar, yet distinctive, idea prevailed. It has long been recognized that there was a close association between the rise of Protestantism and the development of Capitalism. The major voice which contributed to this course of events was John Calvin. His legacy in the realm of economics would be produced from two vantage points, theological and moral. The doctrine of divine election proved to provide a great impetus for financial success. The conviction which was bred in followers of this movement that they were God's elect served to do more than simply to give them an assurance of a blessed life hereafter. It was, also, a powerful force in their economic destiny. God had not only chosen them for heaven; they would go far toward making that heaven upon earth. It is difficult to estimate the impact which this assurance has had on western economics. One of its most impressive expressions occurred in New England. The Puritans came to the bleak shores of the new world with full certainty that they were the chosen ones; and, therefore, they could not fail. The confidence which it created was so great that even major disasters did not deter them from their proejcted goal to set up a theocratic regime. Further, the same theology provided sufficient justification for enslaving the benighted heathen, both Indians and Negroes.

In the subsequent history of western capitalism, there has been a perpetuation of the same impetus toward economic success. The very presence of the latter would be taken as evidence of divine election. More often this ideas has worked subtly in that it has been so woven into the social environment that there was no overt recognition of it as the motivation for the endeavor to succeed. Moreover, it has, indirectly prompted the general disregard of human values and the substitution of material worth as having greater significance since it was a measuring device whereby the status of man could be determined. That is, one who failed to make economic progress might be considered a lazy, unambitious person. On the other hand, his lack of success could be a sign that he was one of the damned. Therefore, any exploitation of his services could be appropriately justified.

The moral aspect of Calvinism toward making its contribution to capitalism can be observed in the encouragement of those qualities of character which assisted in obtaining economic success. It placed particular emphasis on industry, thrift, and sobriety as virtues which were God ordained. The elect could demonstrate their status as the chosen by manifesting these characteristics. Or it might be said that they were the result of God's grace since He had chosen them to receive these attributes. Whatever the explanation might be, the consequences for capitalism were tremendous. It would not be proper to minimize the role of science in creating new forms of energy and technology in forging the new economy. At the same time, the phenomenal success of capitalism owes not a little to the religious fervor which assisted in the rapid expansion of this economic system.

There were other religious groups which were infused with spiritual fervor that served to aid them in the new economic society. The utter simplicity and singleness of purpose which characterized the German Pietists and the English Quakers had signal importance in their success. The attitude which enriched their religious life was no small factor in adding to material riches. They operated from the point of view of a carefully articulated work style which would make it possible for them to produce goods and services of exceptionally high quality and sometimes less costly. Further, the commitment to honesty established a reputation which was an important asset.

3. Religion assists in maintaining the status quo. One basic problem which has confronted man throughout his history arises from the fact that he is a social animal. His personal fulfillment depends heavily on his ability to relate himself to other individuals. Consequently, he has made persistent efforts to socialize. Many and varied organizations have been created in order to reach this objective. Unfortunately, he relies so extensively on these institutions as instruments to make his dreams become realities that, once they have been established, he cannot possibly allow them to be disestablished or even to be changed. Very rapidly they become hallowed with age, nostalgia, and, even, sacredness. The social entities have attributed to them intrinsic value. The original basis for their existence may become obscured.

This social development may continue until the society reaches the point that it is essentially a comprehensive order composed of the several institutions through which the people operate and engage in their several activities. This constitues what is called the "establishment." It is worthy of note that there must be a considerable degree of rapport among these several bodies in order for this arrangement to be solidified. It does afford great strength to the society in that it provides orderly means through which individuals can pursue their interests by interacting with their fellowmen.

Usually, however, this arrangment does not provide opportunity for change. The latter will most likely be discouraged because, among other things, there is a fear that any modification will affect adversely and weaken an efficiently operating mechanism. Human existence is so fraught with difficulties that there is a fear of tampering with the existing arrangements. The latter have proven themselves whereas novelties are untested.

There are several weaknesses in this situation. First, the directing of affairs in society are inevitably placed in the hands of certain individuals. As these persons become entrenched in their positions, they place a high value on them. There is power, prestige, and monetary rewards. Consequently, any meaningful modifications could remove them from their offices or, perhaps, destroy the organizations themselves. New forms of social orders would reflect new types of goals and purposes or new methods for engaging in old activities. Almost certainly new personnel would be required to direct these operations. Members of the old power structure, understandably, are reluctant to surrender their positions. Moreover, they will be thoroughly convinced that the established order is the only one which can operate adequately in meeting the needs of the society. Since they will be closely related with other individuals and groups which are equally well established in the social order, they will be concerned lest their friends and associates, also, be disfranchized. A coalition to resist change will inevitably develop.

Second, in the continuing operation of the society, there will be a persistent trend toward social division among members of the society. One segment will advance to a higher position while the other will reach a lower status in the social, economic, and political areas. Slowly the original basis of the fraternization will be lost or pushed into the background. It will be forgotten that the only grounds for society is to further the common interests of all members of the group. The outcome will be an intensification of the polarization among the constituents. Were there not the substantial values to be received by sustaining the cohesiveness, the appropriate solution would be for each of the several segments to go its separate way in order to form an independent association.

The formation of new societies has occurred repeatedly. Since the earth's habitable surface has become fully occupied, this approach is almost impossible. Furthermore, the several groups have become so extensively interdependent in fulfilling their lives that it is very difficult to effect this procedure. We have seen some of the problems which have resulted from the division of Ireland in 1923, the establishment of two Germanys after World War II, the subsequent split in Korea, and other similar operations. In 1968 a group of black nationalists met in Detroit to form a separate Negro nation to be composed of five southern states. It was stated, however, that, although they would renounce their United States citizenship, they would retain the "prerogatives of American citizens. . . ."

A third problem is the difficulty for an organization, after it has been established, has become operative, and has gained years of experience, to engage in any meaningful self-examina-

tion and to propose and engage in changes which will serve to
meet the needs of people more constructively. Even in our
democratic structure, which necessitates this review, it happens only to a limited degree. We go through the motions of
this process at intervals, but the perspective from which the
examination is made is the establishment itself. The result
is too often simply a reshuffling of the same old furniture.
We have discovered by experience that the only way to make
any meaningful change is to have such severe upheavals that
some adjustments must be undertaken in order to preserve the
society. It has been suggested that the only way that laws
can be changed is for the old ones to be broken. Even after
these radical disturbances and the modifications have been
effected, there is often great difficulty in finding any
noticeable restructuring. It is the same system with new
labels.

Fourth, there is the problem which arises from changing
conditions of various types. New ingredients are brought
into the picture, and new modes of personal living result.
We have seen this situation developing very rapidly when
education has been provided for on a wide scale. As new
discoveries are made, they have severe difficulty in securing
the appropriate institutional means for their social expression. That is, new forms of organization have to be established in order to provide for the socializing process to
occur. But these forms of social order have to be made a
part of the whole society. Oftentimes it is not easy to
accomplish. How can a land economy make provisions for an
industrial order? The aristocracy of the former are predisposed to take a cavalier position to the nouveaux riches
of the latter. When the latter has gained its position,
it will very effectively push the former into oblivion in
the new society.

Attention has been directed to these factors in order
to emphasize that religious affairs do not escape. In order
to effect a socializing of religious concerns, some type of
organization is needed. Those who become affiliated with
it are human beings with some understanding of other organizations. Consequently, the religious societies are no different, essentially, than other groups except that there is
a source for a considerable amount of additional power which

202

can be called upon to sustain them. These organizations receive a label of sanctity which is attached to them not only
from their antiquity and established pattern of operations
but also by the acceptance of their divine credentials. The
latter give them a status not enjoyed by ordinary human orders.
In a more general way, however, they are very closely associated
with, and partake of, the nature of ordinary groups. They consider themselves, and are recognized by others, to be part of
the established system. Sometimes it is difficult to determine
whether religious societies really consider their own divine
credentials to be exclusively their own or whether there is
some sense in which they see the whole order of the society
as being so closely intertwined that it is in its entirety a
sacred phenomenon. At any rate, the result is inescapable.
The divinely established order operates from the stance of
this divinity to give strength to resist the efforts directed
against the other social institutions. The maintenance of the
status quo is a divine imperative.

The economic order benefits immensely from this support.
The institutionalized religion can bolster the economic forces
with its power structure. Several factors contribute to this
arrangement. First, the structure of the religion developed
concurrently with the economic order. There is, therefore,
a parallel development wherein leaders in one of the structures will achieve high positions in the other. The administrative direction in economics and religion will come from
the same personnel. There will be a coalescence in the aims
and the implementing actions carried out by both orders.

Second, with this close affiliation of personnel, the individuals in the economic sector will claim that they are the
mainstay in providing for the financial requirements required
by the religious institutions. The success of the latter
necessitates that their supporters be affluent. The logical
conclusion is drawn. If the religious establishment is to
flourish, the economic segment of society must prosper. A
careful examination of this description may raise doubts concerning its accuracy. In modern day church life there is
little evidence that the religious organizations do receive
their major support from the wealthy members. The per capita
giving in less affluent churches far surpasses contributions
in the more prestigious ones. It suggests that the commonly

held belief that members with considerable financial resources constitute the main support of churches may be a myth.

A third factor is the extent to which the churches become direct participants in the economic order with their own investments. Therefore, if business does not prosper, their revenue will be reduced. That is, there is a genuinely vested interest in the financial establishment. There is a conflict of interest. One of the functions of religion is to keep alive and active the prophetic judgment in matters pertaining to the social order. But it is very difficult for human beings, either individually or collectively, to engage in criticism of themselves or of their institutions. Since the financial expectations are substantially tied in with the goals of the economic order, the sacred organization will be loath to direct unfavorable assessments against the secular societies. The more closely these two sectors are tied together, the less likelihood that negative evaluations will be made.

The ultimate outcome of this course of events is that the concept of elitism will develop. As the benefits of this order of things accrue to the few, the opportunities for the rank and file will be correspondingly diminished. Their role will be to assume a status in the social order as supporters of those who govern society. It proves to be difficult for them to object to this state of affairs since it has the divine stamp of approval. To rebel against the system would be tantamount to rebellion against God. As long as the general theology of the society can be inculcated to support this interpretation, it is all but impossible to effect any genuine change. The power structure which is created is all but impregnable. The two forces together can resist transformation for an exceedingly long period of time. As long as the economy is vigorous and dynamic, there is little hope for any other course of action. Modifications occur in most institutions only when the establishment becomes weakened by indolence and lassitude.

The religious organizations have traditionally assisted in retaining an acceptance of the established system through several other ways. First, for its constituency, there are offered the values received in a common fellowship with others who are suffering similar economic deprivation. Of course,

this service is not restricted to this concern. Life provides
vicissitudes of many kinds. Hence, religion fulfills a major
service when it helps to cope with the exigencies of human experience. It provides what has been called a "fellowship of
suffering." Through it, the losses of life, whenever and wherever they arise, are shared by those who are bound together by
a common faith. Each member helps the other in bearing the
burdens in all their manifestations. The economic problems
are no exception. The economically dispossessed not only discover that there are many others who have this difficulty, but
there is a sense of mutual support in enduring the agonizing
experiences. In dire circumstances, the institutions may give
some practical assistance. Individuals at this level of deprivation do not very often attach an excessive significance to
material worth. There is a generosity of spirit which can be
of exceptional importance. The religious organization provides
not only a psychological union, but it establishes a financial
interdependence. It may eventually become a communistic society where there is a common sharing in the possessions which
are available. Even if the community does not operate according to this system, the activity will approach this form. If
one or more members of the institution suffers a reduction in
his financial status, the other persons will contribute to his
needs.

In this type of society, a considerable value is derived
from the condemnation which is heaped upon those who are the
elite members of the larger group. Since these individuals
constitute the source of the suffering, either real or imagi-
nary, which are born by the subordinate class, the latter
takes delight in the judgment which is meted out against the
wealthy sector. Moreover, they are quite certain that eventually, either in this life or the next, they will be adequately punished. There is oftentimes a real delight derived from
the visions of the pangs which people of affluence will have
to endure. They have been so vividly drawn that they would
almost deter one from attempting to amass a considerable amount
of possessions.

Religion may contribute toward the maintenance of the status
quo by providing to the dispossessed members of the order some
theological explanation for their suffering. All religions
project this part of their teachings with evident sharpness.

The conclusion which emerges from this examination of the problem is a degree of fatalism. That man must suffer in various ways, including economics, is written in the structure of the universe. Further, as a general rule, there is no provision for effecting any change in the matter. At least it is true for the present life. One must submit to the inevitable. The Marxists express a partial truth when they say that religion is the opiate of the people. Lenin portrayed it in these words: "Religion is a kind of spiritual gin in which the slaves of capital drown their human shape and their claim to any decent life."

More important in sustaining the status quo is the offering of future rewards which is held out by most religions. If one accepts his lot in this life and conforms to the order which has been determined, he will be in an infinitely superior position in the future. Those religions which teach reincarnation promise that on the occasion of the next rebirth one may arrive on a higher level. Other faiths describe another type of existence after death. If one is successful in achieving this blessed state, he will enjoy the greatest delights which can be imagined. In the traditional terminology, there will be "pie in the sky by and by." If one can focus his attention on the glowing picture of the future, he may not be particularly discontented with the present order of things or overly concerned for greater economic justice. He is willing to allow the present system to continue without interference because his religion is essentially other-worldly. Present realities over which he acknowledge he has no control are minimized in favor of directing intense attention on the future. In Christianity, the doctrine of substitutionary atonement is paralleled with a concept of substitutionary rewards.

4. Totalitarian systems. There is evidence that we have arrived at another critical crossroad in the course of man's religious aspirations. Throughout the world there exists considerable turmoil and upheaval in every area of human experience. Questions are being raised concerning all the established orders through which man has sought to pursue the human enterprise. Many persons have expressed a complete loss of confidence in the traditional institutions of society. Rebellion is the order of the day. There are individuals and groups who are aware of the inadequacies and are trying

to make the necessary changes. But the most popular trend appears to be escapism, seeking to get away from the situation.

Given this general unrest, it is not surprising to find that religion, too, is on trial. It is especially observable in the western world. There are those who would burn the churches down; others are endeavoring to work within the establishment, Oftentimes against tremendous opposition; then there are those who are seeking to discover new modes of meaning and purpose by creating new patterns of spirituality. A not inconsiderable part of the difficulty in the field of religion is the fact that its institutions are considered to be a part of the total economic order, and the latter is no longer acceptable. Consequently, the only way to alleviate economic ills is to change or eradicate the religious societies. Where new perspectives concerning the social order have come into existence, some type of reaction to these institutions has been inevitable.

Economically speaking, the most distinctive form of change has been introduced by the establishment of Communism. From the time of its inception is Russia, church and state have been at war with each other. The latter has obtained greater success. The situation in Russia depicts in an extreme way what this new ideology says is wrong with the traditional religion. In that country the church had become so closely related to the Czarist regime that it would probably have been impossible to change the political and economic institutions without altering the religion. The church had become so wrapped up in itself that it had lost its power. Its major goal was to sustain and perpetuate itself so that it was ignoring its responsibilities to serve mankind. Religion had become decadent and moribund.

Under these circumstances the leaders of the new movement stated forthrightly that the religious establishment had to be eradicated along with the remainder of the social order. It was considered as much an enemy as the rest of the establishment. Lenin put it in these words: "We must combat religions - this is the ABC of all materialism, and consequently, Marxism." Lunarcharsky, the Russian Commissioner of Education stated: "We hate Christians and Christianity. Even the best of them must be considered our worst enemies. Christian love ia an obstacle to the development of the revolution. Down with love of one's neighbor! What we want is hate. . . . Only then can we conquer the universe." Following upon the successful establishment of Communism in Russia, the church was put under severe restrictions. Positive efforts were made to eliminate it. Many of the church buildings were confiscated and put into service as museums. Anyone who sought to continue his faith would quickly discover that his advancements in all areas of life were substantially limited. Special attention was given to the youth. Religious education and youth organizations were proscribed. In the educational system there was a distinct antireligious indoctrination.

There was a positive side to this program which made these dictators (the same can be said concerning the other new form of social organization which has been created in the current period, National Socialism) unlike some autocrats of the past. They were trying to establish their power with the techniques and fervor of religion. In the genuine sense of the word, the effort was put forth to make the system a faith. There is, for example, the dogma of economic determinism which is central to their philosophy. It asserts that the order of the universe is implemented in terms of this program. Commitment to it is the only way the individual can obtain salvation. If he does not accept and conform, he will be crushed. In other terms, for example, excommunication, other religions have proclaimed this threat. Authoritarian religion asserts that there is a divine power who is the creator and ruler. Conformity to his will, which is woven into the very fabric of the universe, is the only way one can relate successfully with him and achieve personal fulfillment. To resist is to ally oneself with the forces of evil, and the inevitable result will be destruction by the powers of the universe.

In other parts of the world, this form of economics is not necessarily being accepted. Nonetheless, there is a genuine revolt against the established capitalism, and closely tied with the economic reaction is a rejection of the religion which is considered its handmaiden. A young theological student expressed herself quite forthrightly after attending the Eighth General Assembly of the National Council of Churches of Christ. "The Detroit assembly may mean . . . that the NCC is dead. The wake was an effort to see if there was any hope of reviving the corpse. Their conclusion, I'm afraid, was negative.

"The NCC General Assembly is meaningless to the student community. It is not a real part of the world in which we live. Eight hundred persons gathering in plush hotels to pass a long agenda of resolutions is a familiar White 'liberal' game. Words alone no longer have meaning or strength when they come from an ecclesiastical body structured so that it can easily sidestep the most pressing issues of the day."[3]

All of these movements, unfortunately, are following an approach to the issues of the day which will ultimate fail to arrive at appropriate solutions. What is being done is perpetuating the old dualism and asserting that there are two realms. The difference between the present and the past is the question of priority. Historically the religious order has created its institutions for the expressed purpose of responding to the human desire for spiritual well-being. The distinctive trend today is to achieve material success. Hence, there is either an implication or an overt assertion that the economic fulfillment is the only basis for living. Everything which relates to the spirit must go. We must put our hands to the wheels of industry to produce that which will satisfy physical needs.

One can understand and appreciate this perception of the universe. There are many parts of the world - the overwhelming majority, in fact - where people do not have the necessities which will provide for their existence, to say nothing of their general well-being. When half the world goes to bed hungry each night, it is futile to be concerned with other interests until this need is met. But it is not going to be solved until that part of the world which has made phenomenal progress in satisfying physical needs and providing for human comforts rearranges its priorities. It will not do this as long as the basic philosophy is that of materialism, whether it is supported by capitalism or communism. The recent history of the United States demonstrates this position. The greater the affluence which has been achieved, the less has been the effort to work toward the elimination of poverty in the world. On the contrary, the order of the day for Americans is to achieve more creature comforts. The amount of stark hunger

even in this country is appalling. Whenever efforts are made
to establish a welfare system which will provide a minimum of
decency, the cry is always made about the ones who are taking
advantage of it unworthily. But every study which has been
made shows that, with the exception of a very small group,
the recipients are people who would not be capable of supporting themselves under any conditions.

Is a religion of the whole person capable of meeting the
issues when the old dualism has failed? Many individuals believe that it can amd must do so. Failing in this task, it is
doubtful that mankind will continue to exist. A devastating
war or plague or some other equally horrible calamity will destroy him.[4]   But this form of religion must assert itself.
The problems are immense. Discouragement is all but impossible
to resist. It must accept the words of Jesus, "Man does not
live by bread alone,"[5] as its basic guide. It must direct its
attention to persons so as to seek out solutions which will
result in fulfilling all of life. While keeping this vision
alive, it must move immediately and vigorously to solve the
problems of economics. The approach of the Salvation Army
which is operated on an individual basis might serve to guide
the world-wide effort. Physical needs must be met while, at
the same time, keeping alive the possibilities of a life with
total meaning.

CHAPTER XV

COORDINATION OF RELIGION AND ECONOMICS

A. THE PROBLEM

It has been shown in the preceding sections that human concerns in the economic dimension have always occupied a major place among his several interests. From the beginning, when he could expect no more than a bare survival, to the present, when, for some people, luxuries of great variety and quantity have become available and even expected as a normal part of life, man has directed the major part of his energies in this area. It is not surprising, therefore, that religion has always maintained a vital interest in, and made substantial contributions to, human living in this sector. It would have been impossible for this state of affairs not to have existed. In other words, to have religion and economics occupying separate and independent fields has never been feasible. It is not a case of whether there is to be a relationship between the two; rather, the problem is to find the most meaningful and constructive basis for association. The unfortunate feature which has characterized too much of past history is the fact that religion has generally been used to support a particular economic system. This coziness has served to aid in the exploitation of the great majority of people for the benefit of a small segment of humanity. Religion has been used as a tool to sanction the limited goals of the economic establishment.

It is time that religion take a larger view of its role. It must respond to human needs in the area of material values in a way that will make the process of securing one's "daily bread" contribute to the total fulfillment of human living. There will have to be a close association with the whole process so as to understand the needs in this area, the tools and processes whereby they are met, and the manner in which human personality is involved in the production and distribution of goods and services. Religion cannot contribute its most significant services whenever it sets itself on some exalted pedestal. At the same time that it is deeply involved in the actual operations of the economic order, it must keep its per-

211

spective in terms of the requirements for the "whole person."
They will include material values, but the needs of man are
much greater. This is the short-sightedness of the Marxist
system. Its anthropology is deficient. The ideal would be
to weave a tapestry wherein economic goals would be realized
in conjunction with the many other possibilities.

The proposed program is especially difficult to achieve
since the modern economic order not only is organized almost
exclusively to meet physical needs but also the latter are
described in terms of the individual. Consequently, each participant observes the nature of his involvement in the system
only as it contributes to his own personal rewards. Not only
the mechanism but the persons involved are seen only as means
for reaching his own distinctive satisfactions. As a result,
we see human beings developing a ruthless disregard of everything which does not contribute toward his own goals. We become individuals who are so relentlessly directing our efforts
toward these fulfillments that we build outselves a private
shell wherein we dwell except as necessity requires us to be
involved with others. Our eyes focus on other persons as
tools which we can manipulate.

Moreover, we evaluate people from the standpoint of their
success or failure in the economic realm. This concept, in
turn, must inevitably lead to the position that the only
goal is to secure those values which will elicit a high rating.
There is no interest in the method which is employed. If one
can suceed by working within the system and conforming to its
stipulations, he will work enthusiastically in this manner.
On the other hand, if his efforts do not bring success, he will
adopt those processes which are frowned upon by the society.
The important rule for the latter is to avoid detection. There
is a premium on skillfulness in not getting caught. Additionally, society itself contributes to this approach. The patterns
of deceit which are used by those in the lower economic order
will be severely condemned, but more sophisticated methods of
others will be censured only modestly, if at all.[1]

B. NEW ECONOMICS

From the preceding description, it would appear that some
new direction needs to be taken in this area of human experience.

212

While the satisfaction of physical needs has advanced at an accelerated rate and the success in this area has been stupendous, the price of these achievements has been exorbitant. Moreover, the possibility that we are heading toward some destructive end cannot be dismissed as improbable. In biblical terms, there is ground for thinking that we have sold our life for a dish of pottage.[2] Or, in New Testament terminology, we have gained the whole world but have forfeited our lives.[3] It is mind boggling what man will do in order to attain financial success. Our present situation would appear to be not unlike that which prevailed during the period of the Roman Empire. At that time, the physical well-being of the upper class was most attractive. But the support for it came from a slave economy. When we return to examine it and the ultimate result, the question must be faced, Was it worthwhile? One of the dominant characteristics of that society was the presence of fear. The slave was kept in line by repression. But the masters were deeply concerned lest the slaves rise up in rebellion.

In our current western civilization, a similar situation exists except that there is not a clear-cut line of distinction between the masters and the slaves. Every member of society can be identified in each of these categories depending on the particular relationship which is operative at any given time. A person will be subjected to some power force in one area, but he will be the dominating individual in another. Throughout,the same psychological attitude prevails - we are afraid that the other person will take advantage of us. Given this perspective, there will be the inevitable response of hate. Consequently, we are divided up into myriads of small units. Each of them is concerned to take advantage of others. At the same time, each elicits hatred in this relationship. The only thing which prevents the situation from degenerating into complete destruction is the personal element. That is, the attitudes described are developed against the impersonal economic order, both in the form of the system itself and the separate parts of it. It will, however, be kept in check when one is relating with a particular individual unless the latter gives some reason to make the person more clearly identified with the structure. In these instances, the built-in attitude will surface very quickly and express itself. It indicates that there is only a thin veneer of appreciation for persons.

To effect a transformation in the state of things will require a tremendous effort and dedication over an extended period of time. A major task will be an educational one. It will be necessary to convince people that the present mode of economic procedures is rapidly reaching its zenith, if it has not already arrived. We have sown the wind and shall reap the whirlwind.[4] A continuation in the present direction can only lead to the point where the entire system will collapse. For example, how long can the present form of confrontational relationship between capital and labor remain operational? Is it possible to maintain a financial structure wherein the top one-fifth of the participants obtain forty-five percent of the income while the bottom one-fifth is forced to be satified with only four percent? We can take a defeatest attitude and believe that nothing can be done about it since it is just the nature of the system. If this attitude is widely prevalent, the evolutionary process must surrender to the revolution.

But it may be that another way is open if we are willing to pay the price for it. It is the proposal which prophetic religion has proclaimed throughout past ages. It has never been expressed better than by Jesus himself: "Neither be called masters, for you have one master, the Christ. He who is greatest among you shall be your servant; whoever exalts himself will be humbled, and whoever humbles himself shall be exalted."[5] What is primarily expressed in this new perspective is an altered direction for life and its values to be guided. Instead of perceiving those who are below us as subject to our power and control and requiring obedience, it will mean that we shall look for ways and means whereby the economic order can be most constructively created for the benefit of all segments in the society.

C. COMPOSITION OF THE NEW ORDER

1. Process. The first change which must be undertaken is to move away from the idea of a rigidly structured system. We become so committed to one economic pattern that we are incapable of making an objective examination of others to see if they may have some features which could be useful. We get ourselves into a tightly bound system so that we are afraid that any alteration in it will be disastrous to the whole. As a result, we steadfastly refuse to modify the order unless an

irresistible force compels a further examination. The system comes to have so much sanctity attached to it that it is considered irreligious to alter it. Consequently, changes are often attempted only after the economic difficulties have become so overwhelming that the effort is largely defeated. One would not deny that some alterations have occurred notwithstanding the obstreperousness. We have witnessed these changes in both the capitalistic and communistic programs. For example, in the latter there have gradually been introduced some elements from the western society whereby greater freedom has been given to the management, incentives have been offered for achievements, and consumer demand has been used to guide production. Suppose there had been greater flexibility in the early days so that these methods could have been introduced at that time. It is conceivable that Russia would have been able to advance much further in meeting the economic problems of the nation.

It was interesting to observe the changes which the administration of former President Nixon made some years ago in its economic policies. At first it vigorously opposed all suggestions that controls should be introduced into the national order. Later they were accepted. It was unfortunate,however, that, in adopting these new procedures for guiding the economy, it was categorically asserted that they were temporary and that a return to the free market would be made very quickly. There was no recognition given that the totally free market was no longer a workable basis for these activities. Strictly speaking, this type of economy has not existed for many years, probably never. Can it exist today with the control of the financial affairs being rapidly assumed by a very small group of capitalists?

The principal need is to recognize that a particular system is not necessarily the answer to all requirements. The important demand is to continue an examination of the latter so that techniques can be devised to fulfill them. There is nothing sacrosanct about a particular mode of production and distribution of goods and services. It has its worth only to the degree that human living can be enriched by it when observed from the standpoint of the total meaning and purpose of life in its entirety. The process of assessing the system and keeping experimentation alive is essential in a society.

215

2. Freedom. The preceding factor is not feasible unless there is provided a setting wherein freedom exists. This quality does not mean simply that no interference is permitted. In a more comprehensive connotation it refers to the opportunity to engage in making the examinations, trying the untried, and developing new instruments for economic operations. Support will be given to those who are innovative. Huge sums of money are expended to create more efficient machines. Very few grants are available to seek out more adequate economic organizations.

3. Cooperation. The key to the type of order which is being proposed is one in which all segments of the economy will recognize an interdependence and realize that expansion and development of the economy will be widely beneficial and not restricted to a select group. For example, if a labor saving device is introduced into a business, our present system has no mechanism whereby the laborers who are displaced by it will benefit. Their reward is to be deprived of their means for earning a living. The fact that the general good will be greatly advanced is not particularly appealing if one will incur adversity from it. If our system were to accept a responsibility so that the people who lose their jobs would not suffer financial loss, there would be less fear about the changes. We have limited programs, but they are far from satisfactory. The long drawn out struggle between management and labor in the railroad industry illustrates this problem. Some of the work rules needed to be modified because they were archaic. But as long as the owners accepted no responsibility for those who were to be eliminated by the new methods of operation, then labor could scarcely be receptive to the proposals.

The whole purpose of economics is to secure the satisfaction of human needs. To the degree that one individual is deprived, to that extent the system is imperfect. While it is not expected that we can ever attain the absolute ideal in this area, it should be our goal. Consequently, the first step is to accept the objective, keep it constantly before us, and examine the operations with the idea that we are genuinely concerned that all members of the society will be served by it. We should expect and work toward securing greater provisions for everyone. The primary change must be in motivation. Our pres-

ent egoistic drives should be subsumed under the larger guiding
motif of the general good.

D. RELIGION IN THE NEW ECONOMIC ORDER

1. Religion must sets its own house in order. The new economic system which has been projected cannot get off the drawing board if left to the varied sectors of the business world.
The established patterns in this mode of social organization
are simply too intransigent to make the necessary adustments
in and of themselves. Further, the institutional arrangements
have been so carefully drawn and have become so deeply in-
trenched that it is most unlikely that they can be revised by
the several groups cooperating together. The basic presuppositions would inhibit the radical revisions required to create
a more equitable society. The general theory is that individual
enterprise is the most successful form of economic endeavor.
Therefore, it is incumbent upon each person to strive toward
his financial success regardless of the cost to others.

If progress is to take place, it is inescapable that religion must provide leadership and motivation. This source must
be particularly active in the initial phase. After the new
direction has been set and indications indicate that the economy will not collapse on account of the changes, the new order
may be able to continue largely on its own initiative.

Before religion can assume its responsibility, there is a
problem which inhibits it. The organizational structure of this
sector makes it ill-equipped to respond to the situation.
There is the same competitive spirit wherein the emphasis is
to achieve success notwithstanding the price. The source of
this attitude is the concept of exclusiveness which has been
imprinted deeply throughout the history of the faiths. It
is asserted that a particular religion offers the only true
hope for everyone. Traditionally, it has been expressed in
the words, Nullus ex ecclesia servabitur? While these words
come from the Roman Catholic tradition, it has been accepted
in fact by Protestantism. While the most destructive forms
of this sentiment are being toned down and a more ecumenical
spirit is being born,[7] there are still major hurdles confronting the churches in achieving a genuine sense of unity and cooperation.

217

Consequently, the voice of the church, as it may seek to achieve greater cooperation in business affairs, is hampered by disunity. The great challenge to religion is to achieve a common base from which it can speak to the human condition with conviction. This ideal does not necessarily mean one organized body, but it does require that there will be a unity of spirit as it faces the monumental problems of modern man. The strength which will be required to confront the economic establishment can be provided only by a common approach.

2. Having achieved an underlying oneness, the religion will be able to create an environment wherein the spirit of cooperation will be given life. When people within the religious groups are discovering avenues through which harmonious relationships can be made operative, the process can scarcely fail to have an impact on the larger society. Many of those who have positions of leadership and responsibility in the secular world are identified with the several faiths. In fact most of the major positions in the latter are filled with individuals who have previously demonstrated their ability in other areas.

Moreover, an example will have been presented to the world. As presently operative, with all the antagonisms among the organized religious groups, these societies would sound very strange if they urged a new form of economic order wherein the several sectors would enter into partnership arrangements. But a living faith, permeated with the dynamic spirit of brotherhood, must inevitably spill over into the whole order of mankind.

3. At this point the religious societies would be able to move more concretely to generate the actual process required for the new order. Historically, religions have produced some of the most creative minds that the world has ever known. It is not unreasonable to expect that it would occur in this new area. Actually, many able men and women have explored this issue and have provided some substantial contributions. But they have been hampered in that their words have not carried much weight since the religious institutions, which they represent, are so ill-prepared to give spiritual guidance in this situation. If the institutional foundation were more firmly laid, these distinguished and competent individuals could speak

218

effectively and with great understanding concerning the actual process whereby the goals of the new economy could be fulfilled.

4. Substantial assistance to the new form of social order could be given through religion's recognition of accomplishments in this area. Through the many publications at its disposal, the individuals and groups who not only catch the cooperative spirit of the new age but make a signal contribution toward its realization can be identified and an appreciation for their achievements expressed. This service would have an additional value in that it would encourage other individuals and groups to participate in similar creative experimentations and stimulate new thinking along these lines.

5. There may be instances where agencies of religion might enter more directly into the economic order to lead the way by concrete expressions. Most obviously, many opportunities could be found in their own institutions. While, comparatively speaking, they are small operations,and do not contribute signifcantly to the economy, they could serve as pilot experiments. The programs could be established with greater ease since these organizations are not caught up in the ruthless competitive struggle which prevails in the ordinary business exterprises. Nevertheless, their examples could be encouraging.

Another type of direct participation in this area would be to become involved in ordinary business enterprises. Special problem issues could be probed and responses made. There have been limited efforts of this nature. Religion has worked with various union enterprises, movements seeking greater racial equality, various types of boycott, and similar activities. The industrial chaplaincy has been established in some factories. Roman Catholic priests have secured employment in order to become more directly related to the workers.

There is grave danger in this approach. The individuals who participate in these affairs run the risk of becoming so deeply involved in one segment of the economic order that they lose their perspective and become adversaries to the other parties to the issue. The very purpose which they might serve can be lost. Their own objectivity will have been compromised. When this occurs, they become special pleaders and lessen their influence. The prophetic voice must be heard in the marketplace, but its authority must come from an external source.

6. One of the major contributions of religion to the economic order will be to bring to all persons a new sense of the sacredness of their economic activities. As long as we operate the present system, it will be difficult for a person to have any sense of a religious significance. It is merely a means whereby he is satisfying his own monetary requirements. The job is a task to be performed so that the financial compensation will be received. With a reconstructed outlook, tasks should become means for the most concrete expression of faith. Work becomes the basis whereby contributions are made toward the satisfaction of human needs. Instead of drudgery, they would become acts of creative love. Even the most menial and monotonous work would take on a meaning which would serve to provide fulfillment to the worker's own life.

7. In all this experimentation to create a new economic order, one thing must always be kept alive. It is the prophetic spirit. The "man of God," as seen of old, was ever alert to the insidious dangers of human debasement in the world wherein people were earning their daily bread. He was always sensitive to the injustices wherever they were found. When these were observed, he did not hesitate to cry aloud: "Thus saith the Lord, You are your brother's keeper." It is the permanent and ever recurring role of religion to maintain this high calling. All other activities will be carried out from the perspective of this spirit. Consequently, it must be careful not to become so deeply involved in the manifold duties that it is lost.

E. CAPITALISM

The proposed new order might be more concretely illustrated by portraying a development of capitalism wherein it could be implemented. The usage of this label may be questioned since, as stated previously, it would be impossible to have a finalized and firm structure. The latter presupposes fairly definite patterns, procedures, and operations. But the ideal, which has been previously described, must be a dynamic process

220

It must be allowed to pursue its own fulfillment however much it may deviate from some structured order. Moreover, it must be encouraged to experiment without interference from the established society.Given these characteristics, there may be an objection to calling it capitalism. The term is retained, however, on the grounds that the past history of this economic theory actually has not been too severely limited in the achieving economic goals. From a historical viewpoint, it may be argued that to conceive of capitalism as a precise system is contrary to its real nature. Therefore, what is being proposed is simply the full realization of the ideology.

1. Laissez faire capitalism. As the feudalistic order began to break down and merchantilism was emerging, the primary emphasis exhibited by the leaders of the new idea was negative. There was expressed a dissatisfaction with the inadequacies in the traditional organizations. The continued operation of the latter not only resulted in an increasing amount of distress, but also it provided roadblocks in the creation of new modes for meeting human needs. The resistance came from the feudal estates, the church, and the state. This powerful combine made change all but impossible.

Centuries later, a similar unfolding of events took place in the United States. In the beginning of its history, agriculture was king, and the other institutions were designed to support this activity. Since the best land and the most suitable climate were in the South, the latter exercised substantial control over the entire nation. Economics, politics, and religion were so inextricably intertwined that to effect any modification required a heroic effort, even a war. Many students observe that the Civil War was only incidentally related to the issue of slavery. The real cause was the struggle for power. The South had dominated the whole country; now it saw its control eroding. The North was gaining industrially, and even the monopoly in agriculture was being broken as settlements opened in the West. It is not surprising that southern churchmen became substantially involved in the controversy. They were too deeply related with the social order in the South to fail to join in the endeavor. They provided ammunition from the Bible to support slavery as a legitimate and sacred institution. When war erupted, they encouraged the

221

southern soldier by saying, in effect, that he was engaged in
a fight on behalf of God and the Bible. Of course, his fellow
clergyman in the North, who was probably an abolitionist, performed a similar service for the Union Army.

At this stage, therefore, the thrust of the new order has been
to weaken the power structure by developing the point of view
that man should be free to follow his own interests in economic
matters. He did not wish to be restricted by the inhibitions
which had evolved over the centuries. This concept, labeled
as "rugged individualism," has often been asserted to be the
genuine nature of capitalism. But in a pure form it has probably never been operative. As a general pattern it is unwork-
able. It is simply too chaotic in that no guidelines are inherent in this approach. If everyone does as he pleases, as he
conceives his own economic interests, there will inevitably be
so much conflict that the possibility for some success will be
extremely limited. Lack of order in any society inhibits the
efforts to provide for human needs. It is not as serious in
agriculture. The farmer, for example, can arrange to engage
in military activities in his "off season." But the merchant
and the manufacturer have no period of this nature. Consequently, it was early recognized that some type of ordered
direction in the society had to be established. The issue
waw expressed quite well by Adam Smith who is generally considered as the spokesman for the early form of capitalism.
He stated that every man should direct his own economic interest "as long as he does not violate the laws of justice."
It is in the latter words that the problem exists. What
is the just order which the entrepreneur is not to violate?
Some provisions are required to provide a standard for judging
actions.

2. Controlled capitalism. Gradually, the shape of an economic system began to be formed in which regulations were enacted whereby the members no were engaged in this type of
activity could be guided in their procedures. Ideally, it
would mean that the several segments of the economy would
formulate those policies which would be accepted and implemented. Unfortunately, this mode of operating did not prove
to be very effective. The individual is almost always predisposed to interpret rules according to his own personal in-

222

terests. There was the obvious necessity to secure the services of a disinterested party. It was at this point that government began to be involved by assisting in meeting the needs of the group. But the older form of the state was not equipped to perform these functions. Consequently, we see a gradual diminution of the feudal system in the governmental sector. The Holy Roman Empire was to be succeeded by the rise of the nations. In the beginning, the power of the state was in the hands of one individual, the king. He served initially as a very useful instrument since he was a powerful personality eliciting the loyalty and support of inhabitants of an area against outside interference. The same authority which had been vested in the old order was transferred to him. He ruled by "divine fiat." As long as the new forms of enterprises needed to be safeguarded against outside depredation, the monarchy was an appropriate form of government. It would have been difficult for any other type to work. The strong arm of the king, undergirded by his subjects, gave a solidifying basis for the social order. After it had become firmly established, however, the tradesmen and artisans began to realize that the king could be as destructive to their operations as the preceding power. He could operate as capriciously as anyone. Even if the laws had been codified, they were subject to the king's personal interpretation. As a result, another long struggle ensued in which efforts were directed by the middle class society to gain control of the governmental machinery. The power of the king had to be weakened, and a new tyep of organization had to be created wherein the control would be placed in the hands of the governed. The representative assemly was the eventual outcome.

The significance of this transformation in government was to provide a basis whereby the economic order could be guided in its operations. Controls were promulgated which would be designed to limit the freedom of the participants to act in those areas which would interfere with the actions of others. Since laws are essentially negative in nature, the enactments were primarily prohibitions. They were designed to prevent certain occurrences. Some positive aspects would come as provisions were made whereby some guidance was set forth for some activities. For example, rules could be proclaimed so that two individuals might form a partnership and, thereby,

enlarge their business. It would be necessary to establish
the rights and responsibilities of those who engage in this
form of activity.

This process of designing new procedures for business has
continued, and the government has assumed an ever enlarging
role. The increasing complexity of economic organizations
has required this involvement. One often hears some deroga-
tory remark from the business section about governmental
controls. It finds them onerous If they were removed
and it could act freely, conditions for everyone would dramatically improve. If this expressed dissatisfaction were
examined, however, it would be discovered that in most instances the source of the objection is some recently enacted
regulation to which the community has not adjusted. The
managers had had to make some changes in their mode of operation and found this requirement to be distasteful. Were they
asked to survey the whole history of governmental control in
economic activity from the beginning of the capitalistic system, they would probably conclude that it would be unthinkable
to eliminate most of the procedures which had become permanently ingrained in the system. In each instance, after a period
of adaptation to some new stipulation has been made, it would
be impossible to return to the old order.

3. Corporate capitalism. It is against this background
that it is proposed that there is a need for capitalism to
move toward a new stage of maturity. It will occur through
the full realization of the corporate structure. It may be
argued that this system has been accepted. It is true that
a beginning has been made, but only a beginning. The failure
to enlarge the scope of it is the source of the difficulty.
The full nature of the corporate enterprise has not been
discovered and implemented. There is too much of a tendency
to operate according to more limited forms of organization as
they have existed in the past. The system is still "pretending
to be individual enterprise" and has not recognized "its essential elements in their corporate character."[8]

Gradually, economic necessity is compelling a recognition
of a need to develop fully its potential. The several parts
of the enterprise have their discrete interests so inescapably

224

tied together that failure in any one part will have serious repercussions throughout the system. A new sense of responsibility must be created so that all sectors of the economy will be given appropriate consideration in the fiscal activities. The real challenge will be to recognize the disparity within the present order and to discover means to cope with it. For example, it is estimated that ninety percent of the wealth in the United States is controlled by ten percent of the people. This severe imbalance in the economy, if it is not corrected, must lead to growing tensions among the people.

Therefore, a full blown corporate system must be created or, better, completed. We have made a beginning. Basically, it will involve the incorporating of the four major elements, which go into the composition of the system, into the one structure with an appropriate distribution of power to each part.

First, there is the investor. He has made a capital outlay in some activity with the expectation that a profit will be made by it, and he will be rewarded accordingly. Under the older order, he was the key to the entire operation. Everything was performed with his rewards in view. It is now being recognized that his interests will be jeopardized if the actions are performed solely with this objective in view.

Second, there is management. In some instances, there may be overlaping with the first segment. But, increasingly, it is separate and distinct or only indirectly related with the capitalist. This sector is brought in on the basis of an expertise to guide the operations of the organization so that it can achieve its goal In the past, the emphasis has been almost totally on profit. It is no longer true. The problems of management have come to include many other matters. Managers have profit in mind only as a vague, uncertain expectation. The proposed new order would simply accentuate this enlargement of the managerial concerns. Profit must be included only as a part of the whole outlook. In the day by day operations, attention must be directed to efficiency of the plant, maintaining an orderly flow of materials into the business and of finished goods out of the plant, successful sales, consumer satisfaction, and labor contentment. Each of these items will have to be considered on its own position in the structure apart from the ultimate profit. Decisions by management will be made in terms of the effective operation of the institution as a contributing agency in society.

Third, there is labor. Under the old economy, this section had only one objective, the periodic wage or salary received. The employee was interested in other matters only to the degree that they affected it. It is not surprising, therefore, that a failure by this part of the order to accept any meaningful responsibility is growing. Their concern is simply to perform whatever tasks are inescapable and to do them with the least effort feasible. Were the laborers recognized as integral parts of the whole system, given an appropriate role in determining the operations, became participants in the success or failure of the organization, and shared in the rewards, a totally new attitude could be created. There has been a distinct reluctance on the part of management to accomodate itself to this type of order presumably because it fears a loss of power. It has been encouraged to take this stance by labor organizations since they see that their positions are threatened by this arrangement. Nonetheless, some serious restudy in this area is long overdue.[9]

Fourth, there is the consumer. This element is the ultimate recipient of the enterprise. If there is one segment of the economy which must become more deeply involved in its activities, it is the user of the products and services. It has already been accepted that this group must be introduced significantly into the system. Sometimes there appears to be a danger that the pendulum will swing to the other extreme. But there is a definite need that they will be provided a place in the structure of business affairs. Primarily it would be to see that the goods and services meet the needs of the user. But this sector will have to be involved in a related matter, that of ecology. Business operations, with its modern technology, can have severe impact on people. Responsible considerations will have to be directed to this side of the activity. To some extent, too, this concern must take into the picture future generations. There must be an insistence that the consumer be given a voice in the determination of the economy.

CHAPTER XVI

THE NATURE OF POLITICS

A. ORIGIN

At an early period in history, man found it necessary to develop a type of organization which would serve to exercise control over his activities. He discovered that when two or more
individuals began to associate together, some bases for guiding this relationship were required. Out of this need came
that form of social direction called government.

States have emerged as a result of the conflicts between
two feature of human nature which have had to be reconciled.
On the one hand, man is the most sociable of animals. He does
not desire to live alone. Existence itself cannot be sustained
by human beings separate and apart one from the other. The
attainment of human values at a signifcant level requires sociality. These interests and concerns are realized only as
cooperative enterprises have been projected and implemented.
Moreover, to meet the dangers which surround him requires the
associated efforts of two or more persons. Additionally, when
projects are conceived, it is found that the combined energies
of a group will assure the accomplishment with greater ease.
A considerable part of human history has demonstrated the
enrichment of life in this manner. As one surveys the past,
he is amazed at the continually enlarging scope of activities
which have been attempted and successfully concluded through
cooperative effort. History is basically the story of endeavors to form these associations.

On the other hand, man is characterized by individualism.
His very approach to the achievement of sociality has been
marked by a deeper search for personal values. Too frequently, he has seen things only in the light of their meaning to
himself. He may have some awareness that the accomplishments
have not been entirely his own doing; nevertheless, he wants
to take credit for them. This attitude is understandable since
he has, in fact, been vitally concerned with the undertakings

227

and has participated whole-heartedly in their realization. It is difficult to give credit to others for those things which seem to be the result of one's own labor. The effort to survive and to move toward a more adequate life has involved the sweat of his brow, the facing of untold dangers, and the ever present possibility of failure in the enterprise. The struggle upward has been an exceedingly difficult one. The fight has been directed against every conceivable type of enemy. At many points man has appeared on the verse of losing out in the struggle. Very often the anticipated success has not been forthcoming. The line of demarcation between fulfillment and falling short of the objective is a tenuous one. When the former has been realized, it is understandable that the individual wishes to claim credit for it. He can rightly insist that it was the result of his own perseverence. This emphasis on his own role has contributed to the continuation of the efforts to move ahead. Whatever anyone else has supplied is perceived as minor by comparison. The individual develops an exalted sense of his own importance.

Social arrangements have often been established to face the exigency of some particular phase of a project. As soon as the peril has been overcome, it has been difficult to acknowledge the efforts of anyone other than himself in achieving a successful conclusion. The inclination has been to revert back to an assertion of individualism. He proclaims himself as the sole participant in the action. Should anyone attempt to claim some of the rewards, he turns against that person or group and resists the efforts to obtain recognition of some involvement.

Two results of this affair can be observed. Most immediately, there is the conflict which erupts. However small a person's contribution to a project, he is unwilling to forego his payment. As a matter of fact, he will probably be predisposed to take the same attitude as the other individual - the compensation for the enterprise should belong to him alone. Tension is created between the two parties. Moreover, this factor can be a serious hindrance for their future associations. It becomes necessary to devote considerable time, energy, and ingenuity to the resolution of the enmity so that participation in cooperative tasks can be assured. If this problem did not

exist, many more projects could be brought to successful conclusions. Sometimes, too, individuals and groups who had no
part in the endeavors attempt to seize whatever has been achieved.
Human beings have expended a stupendous amount of himself over
the centuries in conflicts with his fellowmen.

In the early period of human existence, progress moved very
slowly as a consequence of conflict and the inability to find
ways to establish cooperation. Advancements were made at an
almost imperceptible pace. When social organizations were
formed to cope with the matter, they were often incapable of
keeping up with the increasing complexity of the issues. Hence,
from time to time there has been a reverting to conflicts as
a means to solve the difficulties. Then the institutional
machinery would come abreast of those situations. Everything
would remain peaceful until something arose for which provision
had not been made.

Out of these described conditions, it gradually occurred to
man that society was needed and provisions had to be made to
preserve it intact. Notwithstanding his inclination to resist
efforts to restrict his individualism, he did accept the inevitable requirement to submerge himself in order to acquire
the values of relationship with his fellow creatures. This
meant that there was a need for a control factor. Some one,
or a group, would be accepted as the basis for determining the
relatedness in the society. Thereby, it can be said that
government arose as a major institution which would provide
for and guarantee the maintenace of human sociality. It
would have to accomplish this task without destroying the
initiative and activities of the person.

B.   THE FUNCTIONS OF GOVERNMENT

What is government? It is that social entity which represents the best interest of each individual and of all the individuals together. It can be said to have a two-fold function. On the one hand, it must restrict absolute individualism.
Should no restraints be imposed, man would simply return to the
jungle. Progress would become impossible, and past achievements
would be destroyed. Any government has a fundamental responsibility to enter a situation in which one person, or a group of

229

persons, becomes capable of operating in a manner which will prove to be detrimental to others. All societies have made provisions for extensive police powers and established substantial rules which proscribe anti-social behavior. The essence of a state is often limited to this described function.

The other side of governmental operations has been accepted with greater reluctance. Even yet, there is a widespread denial of this role as a proper prerogative of the state. One political theory contends that if the individual is provided with an environment wherein he can carry on his own personal interests without the danger of external interference, he will be able to live successfully and engage in substantial accomplishments and advancements. Some evidence is available to support this point of view. Governments have generally limited their operations, and major achievements have been made. Unfortunately, however, the beneficiaries of these accomplishments have been limited to an exclusive group. They have profited by the exploitation of other elements in the society.

Consequently, it has become necessary for governments to enlarge their function and become involved in most activities of individuals and of groups. For example, in the purchase of a house for himself and his family, the state has assumed a substantial role. On the one hand, this institution protects the purchaser's investment in that the limits of his property are clearly established. It prohibits others from intruding across his boundary line. But it insists that the owner must respects equally the rights of others. This is the police power, and it has been recognized for a long period of time. As long as government restricted its power to this area, however, the number of home owners remained relatively small. The control of the economic machinery was so tightly maintained by a small sector that it virtually prohibited ownership by many individuals. Through the enlargement of governmental involvement in the economic enterprise, greater flexibility has been provided with the result that home ownership is now feasible for a greatly enlarged number of citizens. Furthermore, considerable protection of the investment can be secured by those persons who would other-

wise have difficulty in providing it for themselves. Several
governmental agencies supply these services.

It should be stressed that even with this enlarged function
of the state, it is the individual, in the final analysis, who
is the performer. The political order must do its work by
providing the setting for personal accomplishments. The differences in the two-fold functions performed by the government
are matters of extent and character. Should it be restricted
to police powers, the contributions are primarily negative.
It enters onto the scene only to prevent distruption of individual enterprise. If the focus is on the positive operations,
authority is extended creatively in assisting human ingenuity.
In the former instance, the work of the state usually is performed after an event has taken place. In the latter procedure, governmental efforts precede those of the individual.

C. THE OPERATIONS OF THE STATE

From this larger view of government, several areas of its
operations can be suggested. First, the political order must
establish its basis for governing. Many political philosophies
have been developed. From them one must be chosen to give
the primary guidance. The nature and extent of its power
must be determined; the supportive basis for its control must
be asserted and accepted; the division of responsibilities
need to be worked out. One of the principal decisions will
be to choose among the two alternatives which have been de-
lineated. Should it choose to have individuals take the initiative in the affairs of the society, then its participation
will take place only at that moment where there is conflict.
The primary emphasis will be to assure the adequacy of the
police efforts. On the other hand, the affirmative approach
will subordinate these efforts. The presence of the state
will be observed at all stages of human activity. It will
be a main factor in unifying the citizens to assure the highest degree of cooperation. The people will do the actual work
which is undertaken. But the government will be the steadying
hand and support the endeavors toward a successful conclusion.

The second duty of the state is to formulate and initiate
common goals and purposes. The determination of these aims

231

will be based largely on the type of government. In a Communistic order, the deciding factor will be in, theory, that element called the proletariat. The owners of the tools of production will be forced to give up the control so that the laborers will be the recipients of the values which are created. In a Fascist society, there will be an increased enlargement of the industrial sector so that the most successful production will be achieved by these instrumentalities. The industrial and banking elements become very closely associated with the government so as to determine the goals. In a Democratic community, it is anticipated that the electorate will be the key to the social order. By electing their representatives, the goals and purposes will be decided and implemented.

Up to the present time, the economic demands of mankind have been so pressing that provision for the satisfaction of material values has occupied the greatest involvement by all three types of government. Increasingly, it is being recognized that other interests require attention. For the most part, however, even these have been examined primarily from an economic perspective. For example, a national forest can be excluded so as to contribute to the conservation of national resources. At the same time, certain areas can be utilized for recreational purposes. It is becoming accepted that even bolder programs must be developed in order to promote the common good. By their very nature Communist and Fascist states can and have operated more extensively in this regard. Democratic societies necessarily move more haltingly since these programs must emanate from the people themselves. Once these objectives have been undertaken, they will receive wider support and provide desirable results for a larger segment of the population.

It is at this point that states following the more comprehensive procedure will introduce the police powers as a third dimension of its role. But the control can be implemented more easily since the operations underway will be those which are congenial to the people as a whole. They will have accepted the objectives. In order for the political institution to be successful, the police power must make certain that the programs are, in fact, being carried out for all members of the state. Force will be required essentially

232

to restrain a minority who will always be found opposed to any enterprise. Should extensive force be required, it may be indicative that the project was ill-conceived in the first place and that it needs to be reconsidered.

It is in this area that there is substantial difference between Democratic societies and those which follow authoritarian principles. The latter governments make decisions based on the guidance from a limited part of the people. Consequently, the proposed goals may elicit an unenthusiastic response and even substantial opposition. The democratic process performs somewhat more effectively although the mechanism appears to operate much more slowly. Too often, however, vested interests which represent small segments of the people succeed in manipulating the governmental process so that it works to their own advantage. It has contributed to increasing unrest and alienation among the citizens.

But the tradition in democratic countries has been to utilize police power reluctantly. Ingredients like search warrants, trial by jury, and diversification of powers attest to this procedure. The opportunity is given for a minority point of view to be expressed within limits. Ultimately, it may affect the course of events in the state. Occasionally, there have been instances of rigid enforcement; but they have been exceptions and usually to meet extenuating circumstances. To many people, who do not fully understand the nature of this form of government, certain groups or individuals have appeared to operate in defiance of the law. Unless their activities become unduly destructive or disruptive to the ordinary course of life, they may not feel the heavy hand of authority. Very often a confrontation is forced by some one or a few individuals who press their freedom too far.

A fourth operation of the state is an extension of the police powers. It sometimes appears to be more in evidence. These are the military forces which are deployed against outside groups which appear to have aggressive intent. While there has never been a time in human history when this part of the state was not in evidence,   certain current conditions have increased its role and its call upon the resources of the state. Previously, to a very considerable extent,

it has been possible for each political order to achieve its
fulfillment within its own boundaries with very little in the
way of dependence on other states. When it did become necessary to look beyond its own land for resources, the military
power was sufficient to establish colonies which were incorporated in a limited manner within the state. More recently,
however, this state of affairs has undergone considerable
change. Industrialization has demonstrated a substantial
amount of interdependence. The interactions among nations
have been facilitated to the extent that modifications in any
one part of the world have considerable repercussions on everyone. Developments in heretofore subservient societies have
brought them to the point that they anticipate some participation in the accomplishments of mankind. They have become
less willing to see their own resources exploited with little
to show in return.

These several factors has served to develop a concern to
effect some form of socialization that will be applicable to
all mankind. The need is evident for that same type of organization which has been effective in the individual states to
be created for the entire body of people. Nationalistic interests have thus far been effective in limiting the scope
of multilateral relationships. Instead, there has been a
proliferation of military organizations to sustain the aims
of the separate sectors.

The failure of this reliance on military power is evident
to everyone. The hawkish members of the societies simply
are convinced that there is no alternative. But the increasing awareness of the dangers in these unilateral operations means that the need for another approach to the
problem cannot go unfulfilled.   It is to be expected,
therefore, that this type of police power will gradually be
taken from the individual states and placed at the disposal
of some larger organized body. The latter will have the
responsibility to provide that service for the states which
local police units have done for individuals. It will intrude when there is the danger of conflict between two or
more societies. A major hindrance is the failure to achieve
a fully developed system of common interests and the legisla-
tive machinery which will be able to express them by enacting

laws suitable for the new realities. The whole process can be accelerated by a constantly enlarging communication among the peoples of the world.

The fifth dimension of government is education. It is one of the most promising instruments for the creation of an adequate political organization. Today it stands as one of the highest priorities in the modern states. Dictatorial governments establish and operate these programs for the expressed purpose of leading their people to an acceptance of themselves and their plans for the nations. The success attendant upon these indoctrinations has been remarkable. In the long run, however, a major flaw in its operation will become increasingly evident. As the quest for knowledge proceeds, it can scarcely avoid bringing in materials which will be different than, or even antithetical to, their own systems. However extensive and thoroughgoing the instilling of their own ideas, the variant points of view may raise questions about the correctness of the traditional positions. If the Soviet scientist finds that his American counterpart has made some remarkable discoveries, the former may begin to question the anti-American propaganda. In a rather interesting, indirect way, it may be seen in the manner in which claims have been made for Russian discoveries when, in fact, they had been achieved by people elsewhere long before the present system of government came into existence.

In the democratic nations, too, there has been excessive exploitation of education for nationalistic purposes. The demand that greater attention be given to American history in the schools reflects this effort. It is anticipated that the glories of the United states will be so apparent that students will develop an unquenchable loyalty to this country. Traditionally, the theory of American education has been to further the development of the democratic system which says that the government is "of the people, for the people, and by the people." In other words, it is social education. The individual is to be prepared to take his position in society. He is to be education to become a creative citizen of the nation.

The wide range of the curriculum underscores this tremen-

235

dous goal. First, there is the field of economics. Each one
must select and be trained in an area of employment where he
will be capable of contributing to his well-being. But, in a
larger sense, this achievement will be an important part of the
sucess which is attained by the nation. His economic productivity will be valuable in satisfying the employee's own needs;
but, in the work which he does, he will be creating social goods.

Second, he must be educated to become a participating individual in the social institutions which have been created and
others which he himself will contribute toward their formation.
One of the major functions in this process is the establishment
of an attitude. The person must be brought to an awareness and
appreciation of social accomplishment. He lives in a society
and partakes of the benefits which accrue from this arrangement.
He must, also, realize that the continuation of this mode of living
depends upon him. When changing needs arise in the course of
personal interactions, the challenge will be faced to create
that form of institution which will meet effectively the situation.

Third, that special form of social institutions known as
politics, must occupy his attention. The continued operation
of government as the solidification of the varied interests of
the people will depend upon his awareness of the processes
of political life, the achievements of the past, and the requirement for alertness in his duties as a citizen.

Fourth, the realm of aesthetics must be supported and encouraged. The enlarged value of human living through the
production and employment of the arts will be an asset for
a more complete personality. An educational system which will
provide the foundations for acquiring an understanding of,
and appreciation for, these forms of human expression will
have contributed to a signal accomplishment. Should it
extend to the development of personal expression in this
realm, its value will increase significantly.

Fifth, the place and function of religion in the life of
the individual and of the nation will be an inescapable part of
the educational process. The most demanding factor in this
field will be an extensive acquaintance of the individuals

236

with the wide-ranging operations in this dimension of human endeavor. More limited programs will be destructive since there will emerge from them a narrowly construed perception of faith. It will result in the encouragement of conflicts among the several societies as they advocate their own particular points of view.

The sixth area of governmental operations is taxation. It is required to support the several activities to which the state is dedicating its efforts. This part of political life has, undoubtedly, incurred the greatest opposition on the part of the citizenry. A failure to appreciate the nature and importance of the state and, even more, the disinclination to take an active role in its affairs have contributed to this attitude. It is especially evident in our modern states because of the complexities of their functions and the difficulties experienced in conveying an understanding of fiscal policies. Therefore, one of the most demanding requirements for all branches of government is to continue the search to find more successful means for making explicable the total procedures - both the levying of taxes and the disbursement of revenue.

Moreover, the financial affairs should be subject to constant examination and experiment. States must realize that their operations constitute only one element of social life. Hence, tax policies should impose as little limitation on the citizen in his total commitment to social goals as is necessary. To secure a proper perspective is difficult to accomplish. Pressures brought to bear by special individuals and groups increase the misunderstandings and becloud the issues. In our modern form of government, the voices of the experts, especially economists, have to be given emphasis. But, here, too, the voice of the people utters the final word. The specialist has fulfilled his duty when he has successfully presented his recommendations so that they receive the full support of the majority of citizens. Moreover, retaining his status depends on the results when they have been implemented.

D. THE CHARACTERISTICS OF THE STATE

To conclude this section, a portrayal of the state will be

237

presented in terms of its being a functional entity in society.
First, it has limited power. Its control is rather rigidly
defined as being operative for a particular segment of the human race. Historically, its boundaries have been determined
on the basis of land area. It was a fairly simple device since
the delineation could be accomplished with a high degree of
accuracy. Problems arose, however, when two or more political
organizations claimed authority over the same territory. To
solve this problem, a second form of regulation had to be used.
Powers began to be assigned along lines of function. Each unit
of government had its own area of duties and responsibilities.

This problem has grown increasingly troublesome. The complexities of modern life have added immeasurably to the roles
of political organizations. To decide which one is to adminis-
ster a particular office requires a very acute analysis. An
additional part of the difficulty is the high mobility of the
population and the activities engaged in by both individuals
and groups. Consequently, governmental operations determined
by land division are often not suitable to the situations. In
the United States, for example, there is the question of dif-
ferentiating the powers which can be allocated to the federal
officials as distinguished from the responsibilities claimed
by the individual states. There may be substantial
overlapping of functions and duplication of activities. Even
at the local level the division of duties can become acute.
With the growth of large metropolitcan areas, inherited forms
of government may no longer be meaningful. Cities and coun-
ties may coincide as far as land area is concerned. But the
most pressing need is to find solutions to political relationships among the several nations of the world. With the
modern methods of transportation and communication, national
boundaries can no longer be impervious to the demands for new
forms of international agencies.

Second, when the extent of the authority of the state has
been settled, its powers extend to everyone who falls within
its province. In the usual meaning of this concept, it involves the inhabitants of a certain geographical region whether
on a permanent or temporary basis. On certain occasions, the
exercise of the authority may be forfeited on the basis of cer-

238

tain agreements or procedures of protocol. Even under these agreements, however, the sovereign government of that realm does retain determination. While a representative of a nation with which a country has relationships may not be subject directly to the laws of the land, he may be declared persona non grata and his recall be demanded.

From the foregoing, it is recognized that anyone who resides in an area permanently or temporarily must acknowledge that he is subject to what stipulations may be established by the legal government of the state. Should one not be satisfied with the enactments, he has certain alternatives. First, he may seek to effect a modification in the regulations which have been legislated. This effort may be carried out peacefully or by violent means including the fomenting a rebellion. Failing success by this approach, he may defy the authorities. This act may be done in order to achieve a personal goal which the law prohibits. The civil disobedience may be performed openly in order to attract attention to what the person holds to be injustice. Thereby, he anticipates that pressure will be brought to bear so that change can be achieved. Finally, he may leave the country either permanently or temporarily and seek asylum elsewhere. In this instance, he has simply substituted one form of government for another. He has not, it should be emphasized, escaped government itself.

A third characteristic of the state, which has been implied in the preceding, is its prerogative to compel obedience. Since it is working to attain the common good, certain procedures must be stated. Common goals are accepted, and the individual members of the state must perform in keeping with them. Or, to put it more accurately in a negative form which is often the methodology followed, the individual cannot be permitted to interfere with the aims. Should he act contrary to the regulations, the political society must assert its will so that the accepted procedures of the state affairs may proceed uninhibited. A government, therefore, is scarcely viable if it does not possess the instrumentalities powerful enough to enforce the policies.

The representative of the government is provided with a a variety of forms whereby power can be exercised as the oc-

239

casion may demand. They fall, generally speaking,into two
categories. In some instances, physical force must be used.
So long as individuals or groups attempt to countermand the
political policies by overt defiance, this tool is av .lable
and must be utilized. The other form of authority is expressed
in the person of the political representative. While he is
supported by the recognized power of direct restraint, his
achievements are effected in the normal procedures by his
presence and the symbolic prerogatives of the land which
he manifests in his person. The degree of civilization
which a political order demonstrates is indicated by the extent
of state functions which can be accomplished through these
procedures. These processes have been widely and successfully
implemented at the level of local and national life. We are
still, however, essentially in a primitive condition in the
dimension of international relationships.

In the fourth place, a state acts according to law. Rights
and duties, crimes and punishments have been rather carefully
stated. One of the major factors contributing to the stability
of a society is formation of   carefully conceived pronouncements whereby citizens can be directed. A member of any well-
governed state has a fairly good idea concerning what is required of him and those actions which are proscribed. Even in
countries with authoritarian forms of government, a large
body of law will be fully established to provide guidance
in ordinary affairs. It will probably make more extensive
use of the rather anomalous principle of the general welfare
whereby the political body can proceed without "due process
of law." In extreme cases, even democratic countries may
employ this technique. In this instance, however, the actions
are subject to confirmation or condemnation by a court of law.
Basically, a state cannot be too arbitrary in its operations -
certainly not indefinitely.

Finally, membership in one or more jurisdictions is all
but inescapable. Theoretically, one might search far enough,
even on this earth, and find a place which was not subject to
the control of any political order. In a more practical sense,
there are territories where government in any real sense of
the term is non-existent. It would, however, be a most unusual individual, one with a considerable spirit of adventure

in his blood, who would care to attempt this way of life. The day of the frontiersman, which prevailed a relatively short time ago, has disappeared. Hence, it is imperative that we recognize the inevitableness of government as a starting point. We may then become sufficiently concerned to recognize the need for it, the possible programs which may be fulfilled, and the techniques which may prove to be succesful in achieving these ends. A more responsive citizenship could be created. Individuals would seek to identify themselves more realistically with governments as they engage in their tasks. They would rejoice in the gains as reflecting their own involvements and would accept the failures as the products of their own inepitude.

241

CHAPTER XVII

PAST RELATIONSHIPS OF RELIGION AND POLITICS

In examining the subject concerning the past relationships
between religion and politics, the most concrete approach is
to explore the institutional associations and interactions.
It is recognized that this methodology will not give a totally
complete portrayal of the subject. In any society there are
relationships which are carried out on a more personal and individual level. We shall introduce some proposals of this
type in the following chapter.

A. CLOSELY INTERRELATED

When the issues of life are excruciatingly demanding for
the persons and the social order, tensions among the individuals
and groups may become submerged. The opportunity for closer
connections and increased cooperation will exist. This situation is most commonly experienced when a society is engaging
in war. There are, however, other equally demanding conditions,
if they are severe enough, which elicit the same response.

It is not surprising, therefore, that historically the
period which provides the clearest examples of political and
religious coordination are to be found among primitive groups.
Our ancient forebears lived under exceptionally perplexing and
uncertain conditions. Consequently, there was that pressure
which would force all segments of the people to bring to bear
upon every issue of life all possible sources of assistance.
They simply could not afford the luxury of too much internal
conflict or division. As a result, politics and religion were
partners in a cooperative effort to meet the exigencies of
tribal life. The chieftain and the shaman might be one and the
same person. Even if the offices were separate, they coordinated their efforts in the respective sectors so as to cope
with the manifold difficulties involved in survival. The position of tribal chieftain imposed very heavy responsibilities.
This person would want to avail himself of every resource, including religion, which could be utilized. His every act must

243

be undertaken with the assurance that it had been given approval
and support by the supernatural powers. In return for this aid,
the religious order was fully backed by the state.

The cooperative association of these two powers resulted in
a tremendous accumulation of authority for controlling the lives
of the people. Man's destiny was totally determined for him.
While this type of collaboration was necessary in order to
meet the needs at this time, there was the inevitable danger
that the power could be abused. It would especially mean
that members of the society would be liable to harsh punishment, meted out by the political representative but sanctioned
by the religious leader. Additionally, it would be used to
maintain the status quo. It would be extremely difficult for
anyone to take exception to, or to resist, the entrenched
order. Most individuals would be deterred not only by the
potential punishment which might be inflicted but also the
possible loss of divine favor.

While primitive society has manifested this position most
fully, it has prevailed widely throughout human history and
in every part of the earth. In the narratives of ancient
Hebrew history, one observes this phenomenon. The king was
the "Lord's anointed;" that is, God selected the person who
occupied this office. Consequently, he was established in
this political position with almost unlimited control over
his subjects. His rights were divine rights. With this
status, the ruler assumed responsibility for the religious
institution. When David organized his court, he brought in
a priest; his son and successor, Solomon, had two. After the
division of the kingdom, the state assumed even wider domination. One of the constant complaints of the prophets was
the assertion that prince and priest engaged in infamous
activities which undermined the condition of the people. In
rebuking the work of Amos, the priest Amaziah cried out that
Bethel was the king's sanctuary. Centuries later, when the
Jews had been incorporated into the political regimes of other
nations, substantial social control was entrusted to Jewish
leaders who were apparently parts of the religious institution. In one of the most stirring episodes in Jewish history,
the Maccabean Rebellion, the leadership was in the hands of
a priest and his sons. As they achieved success, religious

244

self-determination was first received. Later, political power was regained. The ideal order wherein a priest-king ruled had been accomplished. Unfortunately, the latter part of this era demonstrated the apparently inescapable evil of this coalition. Political and religious corruption became pervasive. Nevertheless, a popular idea in Jewish eschatology was the predicted arrival of one who had this dual prerogative.

B. SEPARATE: RELIGION SUPREME

Another form of relationship between religion and politics arose where each was identified as a discrete activity with religion claiming the higher position. The foundation for this arrangement was built from a theological plan which was essentially otherworldly. The sojourn of people on earth was seen as temporary and, essentially, preparatory for the next life. While there was no denial of needs in the terrestrial existence, the significance was decidedly secondary. How could one compare a life of extremely limited duration with one which would extend throughout all eternity? It was obvious that faith was the prime factor in guiding man to his destiny. Insofar as the political sphere observed its subservient status and did not intrude into the domain of the spiritual, it would be given appropriate recognition.

This idea was developed and articulated very clearly by St. Augustine. God is the omnipotent Being; hence, He cannot be divorced from politics. His omniscience makes him alone capable of comprehending the requirements for the secular life. In an ideal situation, therefore, man would follow God in creating a successful political order. Through his faculty of reason he would apprehend God and the latter would reveal the requisite understanding for the society. The difficulty, however, is that from his birth man's nature has been beset with sin. It has beclouded his vision and interferred with his clearly perceiving God's will. When man has attempted to determine his own destiny, the result has been disaster.

This condition has been most obvious in politics. Instead of ruling in terms of the true religious spirit and governing by service, the politician ordinarily has sought power to satisfy his personal desires. Since, by nature, all men are equal

245

each possesses the faculty of reason. Therefore, it is illegitimate for one person to control and oppress another. Man is permitted to exercise this prerogative only over the subhuman. This divine idea does not deter the ruling powers. They destroy morality in order to achieve their own goals. Since the real goal is to be moral, this means that politics cannot succeed. Further, it should warn the person who aspires to the higher level that he should eschew political ambitions.

Augustine does not deny that politics may be inevitable on earth. It performs a useful function in that it can use its power to secure social order. This task is performed by arranging the parts of the state in their appropriate places. In this way the lives of citizens become fairly predictable. But this activity relates only with that which is superficial. The state does not, indeed it cannot, serve man in striving toward his real goal which is to arrive at the heavenly city where God rules. It is the church which consummates this greater mission. Its authority comes from God Himself. Eventually, Augustine was convinced, as man, following the teachings of the church, moved toward the sublimely richer life, the function of the political state would diminish.

Since the state's responsibility is a very limited one and is precisely stated, it should not overstep the boundaries. It simply maintains the order as it now stands whose condition has been brought about by sin. Specifically, it is not the function of government to attempt any reforms in society. It does not have the prerogative, and it would fail were it to try. Instead of stability, there would be instability. Those who suffer deprivation in the present situation will have to recognize that their lot would be made worse by any attempted modification. At least, there is presently an orderliness and continuity which they can enjoy. Even slaves must accept their position and acknowledge that slavery is the result of sin. Moreover, they should realize that their masters are caught up in the maelstrom created by this system. Suffering, accordingly, is their fate; and it will eventuate in their destruction. Consequently, the slave should serve his master with love.

Throughout his reflections on politics, it is obvious that

Augustine is portraying an overwhelming pessimism and negativism. The only encouraging note that he can assert is scarcely comforting. This institution does prevent conditions from getting worse. The only genuine hope for humanity is provided by religion. It can guide toward the City of God wherein love rather than power will be preeminent. As this ideal is realized, the political society will vanish into oblivion.

A concrete historical expression of this relationship is observed in the establishment of the Holy Roman Empire. It emerged as the successor to the political order wherein Roman had been both the capital and the determiner of the social order. There had taken place some changes in the geography. The eastern sector was now ruled from Constantinople. Moreover, those who ruled in the West were of German lineage. But the new political entity had a source of strength which had not been present in its predecessors. Its establishment took place under the auspices of the church. It was Pope Leo III who had crowned Charlemagne on Christmas Day, 800. Thereby the seal of approval by the divine institution had been affixed, and its authority could be drawn upon to support the political establishment.

The centuries which followed demonstrated the failure of this mode of social order. Since there were two powerful structures, it was inevitable that conflict would arise. Arguments could be adduced to support the priority of each one. Since the temporal welfare of the citizens depended on the state, its operations had to be acceded to by all other social instruments including the church. As a matter of fact, if the personnel of the latter did not prove to be amenable, it would be justification for the political sector to substitute persons in positions of leadership who would be more cooperative. When the secular rulers had the requisite ability to sustain this posture, they did not hesitate to depose members of the religious hierarchy and to name their replacements. In order to create a permanent arrangement so as to assure the appointment of acceptable individuals, the investiture of church officials became a joint venture.

The church, however, was not lacking in ability to exert influence on the determination of the political system. When the prince or king or even emperor proved to be detrimental to the church, it was not impossible for the latter to take steps against him. On the one hand, there always would be persons standing on the sideline ready and willing to be chosen. Should the reigning individual prove to be weak, or should he incur strong reistance, the support of the church could provide the balance of power for the removal of the ruler. On the other hand, there were penalties which could be imposed under religious auspices. He might be excommunicated with the ensuing weakening of his control by virtue of being outside the church. It was possible for the church to go further and direct the subjects not to be submissive to the secular ruler.

Under these circumstances, it is not surprising that an almost interminable period of conflict resulted. Many factors gave great strength to the religious organization; nevertheless, the state was not devoid of substantial influence. At times it appeared that the papal authority, especially, was completely dominated by the emperor. The situation almost demanded that the pope be responsible to the latter if his status was to be sustained. The conflicts among the several political contenders for the imperial position served to make the pope excessively dependent on whoever could most effectively provide him with protection.

This consolidation of power made for an intractable system both religiously and politically. The common man could only submit to both structures. Furthermore, society was engaged in almost perpetual warfare as ambitious individuals sought to gain the vast power which was available. The church suffered because of the ensuing corruption which made the ancient institution an object of ridicule.[1] The religious establishment attempted to curb the aggressive struggles in the political sector and to lessen the military affairs. But its "Truce of God and "Peace of God" were simply not effective.

As long as the feudalistic society remained essentially unchanged in its general structure, the Holy Roman Empire and the Roman Catholic Church would remain intact and would continue their associated roles in guiding the destiny of the people. Each had sources of strength as well as areas of lassitude. Neverthless, there was a certain commonality

which made any appreciable change in their affairs virtually
impossible. This assessment is demonstrated by the recurring
efforts to reorder the two institutions. Individuals and groups,
feeling a disquietude in the failure of the church to fulfill
its mission in terms of the moral and spiritual values, sought
to effect reforms. But these endeavors were swallowed up by
the religious establishment. Similarly, strong political persons essayed to bring order among the contending governmental
factions, especially the nobility. Had there been a continuity in their programs, it is conceivable that greater success
could have resulted. Unfortunately, too often a competent
ruler was succeeded by one who was inept. Coupled with the
opposition from the church, the projects fell into disarray.

C. SEPARATE: STATE SUPREME

As a result of new forces at work, which would gradually
change the medieval posture, the social structure would be
altered. The expanded contact with non-Christians, especially growing out of the Crusades, broadened man's horizons. The
new intellectual climate, which restored an acquaintance with
Aristotle, deepened human understanding. A renewed consciousness of human values broke the exclusive emphasis on other-
wordliness. New forms of educational institutions, the Cathedral Schools and the Universities, provided the means for
a freer intellectual pursuit. But, most importantly, there
was the economic factor, the development of merchantilism.
It was a form of human activity which could not flourish under
the restrictions enacted by the old order. Both church and
state imposed too many handicaps for the successful pursuit
of goals in this field. Consequently, new organizational
techniques had to be created to meet the needs which were
arising in the new age. Religiously, it meant the rise of
the Protestant Reformation; politically, independent states
governed by kings would emerge.

In the beginning, there was a substantial inheritance from
the past. One could scarcley distinguish the two orders -
the religious and the political - from their respective
parentages. The state asserted its prerogatives on the traditional grounds of its being a divine entity; the king had received power from God. At the same time, the church had

249

its source of authority in God's revelation as recorded in the Bible. Therefore, there were still ample conditions for conflict. Initially, the more powerful order was the state. It was even supported by some of those who were leaders in the new religious movements.

Martin Luther was, in many respects, a medievalist. Further, he reflected the views of the church father whose name was born by the monastic order in which he served, the Order of St. Augustine. These factors were reflected in his political philosophy. He accepted the belief that there are two realms, the Kingdom of God and the Kingdom of the World. Those who belong to the former have no need for government and the secular law. They will do more than is required by political authorities since they are taught by the Spirit. If all persons were Christians, there would be no need for these institutions.

Moreover, Luther was careful to limit the power of the state. Its role must be confiend to secular affairs. It would be overstepping its bounds were it to enter into spiritual affairs and seek to exercise governance over them. Specifically, he says that only life and property are subject to the state's jurisdiction. The things of the souls are outside its competence. In his definitive theological position, each person must decide what he believes. He does set forth a standard for faith, the Bible. But conscience is to determine the ideas in religious issues. The state cannot compel belief any more than the church hierarchy. Were the police powers to be directed at man to compel religious conformity, it would simply lead man to lie. In accomplishing this end, the state would be held responsible.

His medieval heritage was also shown by an attitude which many in the modern world would consider to be cruel. For example, he argued that should a murderer die a natural death before his execution took place, then God's law would be broken.[2] Moreover, he asserted that a Christian must be willing to accept his political responsibilities as they may be demanded of him. Whenever he has the requisite qualifications, it is his duty to serve. He included bearing arms and even performing executions.

Although Luther set certain limits to the state, especially in the area of religious beliefs, his real contribution to political philosophy was to strengthen and expand the role of government. Therefore, he can be considered a representative of the school of thought which asserts that there are two discrete institutions. First, he legitimized the state by showing that it owes its existence to God. It is His will which has brought secular law and the sword into the world. The Bible provides evidence for this viewpoint. He expounded extensively on Romans 13 and I Peter 2 for support.

Second, he stated that the law is applicable to everyone, including Christians. His reasoning is that no one is by nature a member of this select group. Furthermore, secular law has a religious foundation in that it contributes to the identification of sin. Hence, in his obedience to the state, the person obtains knowledge of his sinful state, and it can point him to Christ. In addition, there are those who are only nominal Christians; they have been baptized, but their faith has not really been confirmed. Since they have not the Spirit which would be the guide for their lives, they must be restrained by the law.

Third, he perceives that the state performs a useful contribution for those who are Christians and, consequently, without need for the law. The unrighteous far outnumber those who are the redeemed and would bring great danger into the world. The police power can restrain the unrighteous persons from engaging in evil deeds. Thereby, peace can be maintained. Thus, from a practical point of view, Christians should recognize the Godgiven status of the political sector.

Fourth, since the state has this lofty status and provides some highly signficant services, it is incumbent even for the righteous to be obedient. To be sure, this type of person has no need for the government to direct his life. He will live on a much higher plane. Nonetheless, he must recognize the great benefits which it offers. In his being responsive to it, the Christian actually fulfills one of the divine laws, the love of neighbor. Luther argues that the latter, by which he means the unregenerate individual,does need the law. It would, therefore, be a disservice if the redeemed person did

251

not support that institution which the ordinary individual required for his own well-being.

While Luther did not attribute absolute power to the state,
his major influence was to confirm this institution as the dominant one in human affairs. There is a higher law, the law of
the Spirit; but only a few individuals are subject to it and
conform to its requirements. Even these persons are not Christian by nature. It is obvious that secular enactments are appropriate for everyone.

This emphasis on government grew out of a practical necessity,
the dependence of the individuals in the new religious movement on the state for protection. Otherwise, the all-powerful
church would have quickly brought into operation its tremendous
force so as to destroy the emerging faith. Luther himself responded with courage in proclaiming his religious beliefs when
they conflicted with those supported by the established church.
But it was Frederick of Saxony who gave him support against his
adversaries. The German reformer, therefore, readily recognized
and reciprocated the values received. In a manner reminiscent
of St. Paul, Luther perceived that the secular state did offer
many advantages. Hence, it could only be concluded that the
political instrument was ordained by God. Every citizen, both
Christian and non-Christian, was confronted with the duty to
be obedient.

Another important individual who contributed to this point
of view was John Calvin. He, too, divided power into two
separate parts, and each has its own responsibilities. First,
he portrayed the spiritual realm wherein piety and the service
of God constitute the responsibilities of man. Herein the interior part of man - his mind - is operative. It provides the
context for human freedom. Man's conscience is operative and
serves as a medium between him and God.

God has provided an institution, the church, which can supply the necessary guidance and discipline for a proper association with Him. To it the keys, i. e. the signs of authority, have been bequeathed. It has been entrusted with the duty
to discipline the people. Everyone is subject to this common
agency, even kings. Calvin insists that without this power,

the entire dissolution of the church would occur. Those who resist the doctrine of Christ can be controlled; the inactive can be stimulated; and those who have fallen can be chastized. Rulers ought to welcome the discipline of the church when it is meted out to them. They seldom hear other than flattery from their associates. Surely they will feel no dishonor in prostrating themselves before the King of kings.

In carrying out this discipline, even excommunication, the elders will execute the punishment. But the entire church should supervise the affair to see that a few persons do not perform from an improper motive. Neverthless, the church body does not direct the proceedings; they can only express their approval.

The other area is the political realm wherein duties of humanity and civility are to be encouraged and safeguarded. But its area of operation is external conduct. In a sense, the two realms are to be considered separately; yet, in a more comprehensive consideration, this approach is impossible.

Those who do not recognize that God is lord over all the universe may exalt the state over against God. It would give to the political regime supreme power. On the other hand, one may deny to the secular ruler any control. Some professed Christians have followed the latter course and supported anarchy. The basis for this error has been the failure to maintain a distinction between church and state or religion and politics. The same liberty of conscience whis is appropriate for the soul3 is considered equally as a principle for the political sector. They insist that their submission is to Christ alone. But, says Calvin, "while we are aspiring toward our true country, we be pilgrims upon the earth. . . ." If the church of God could be perfected, it would suffice to supply the place for all law. But this ideal can never be found in any community of persons. Therefore, politics is both desirable and necessary. The state has a variety of functions including giving protection against offenses which, if committed, would adversely affect religion. The secular rulers will serve to protect the true religion "contained in the law of God." It is the duty of politicians

253

to defend the honor of Him whose vice-regents they are and by whose favor they govern. Actually, the Scriptures praise certain kings because they restored the worship of God.

Thereby, Calvin has declared that the very position of rulers was established by God. Hence, "the first duty of subjects toward their magistrates is to entertain the most honorable sentiments of their function, which they know to be a jurisdiction delegated to them from God." Obedience which is rendered to princes is given to God. This response should be made even though the person who holds the office is a reprobate. Two factors are involved. First, the office itself is worthy of honor and reverence. Second, if the individual occupying it fails in the designated duties, it means that God has sent that person to punish the iniquity of the people. Both the just and the unjust rulers have been invested with the legitimate authority of the office. Even a conqueror must be obeyed since he, too, has received the power from God.

Is there, then, no relief from tyranny? Calvin answers succinctly that it cannot come through our own efforts. We can only pray to God to send a deliverer. Sometimes God will heed our petition. If it occurs, it will be a magistrate chosen by the heavenly lord. A private individual can do nothing on his own accord.

There is one exception to this submission to the magistrate. One cannot accede to him if it means disobeying God. If the ruler commands what the latter has proscribed, it means that the limits of his office have been exceeded. In this instance, then, one is not really failing in his duties of citizenship.[4]

It is against the background of this theological politics that one can observe the course of history in Europe. The Peace of Augsburg (1555) enacted the principle that the ruler of the country will determine the religion of its citizens.[5] If one did not agree, he was free to emigrate. But it meant that Germany would be denied the development of toleration as occurred elsewhere on the continent. Frederick the Great referred to himself as the "pope of the Lutherans," and until 1918 this preeminence continued. The rulers of the Protestant states in Germany were simultaneously the supreme bishops of their state churches.

Calvinistic influence became more widespread. As we have seen, the French reformer provided for resistance to tyranny only under some magisterial direction. In practice, it was stretched to encourage more active resistance. In Holland it became allied with the growing nationalism with its opposition to Spanish rule. Eventually, the effort triumphed; and this form of Protestantism became generally accepted. However, it seldom rejected minorities. As a consequence, the persecuted from many lands sought refuge there.

Protestantism made great headway in France since there had already developed a strong anti-Roman spirit. In the country's conflict with the Hapsburg, however, a strong national unity was required. Since Calvinism advocated local autonomy, it was considered as opposed to national unity. For many Frenchmen it was unacceptable. The eventual outcome was the Thirty Years War between Catholics and Protestants. The latter invited German and English troops to support their cause. This move further alienated the nationalists. The climax came with the Massacre of St. Bartholomew on August 24, 1572 in which thirty thousand Huguenots died. Rome celebrated this event with a public procession and solemn mass which was attended by thirty cardinals.

In England, too, the beginning of Protestantism was closely interrelated with the growing nationalism and merchantilism. The kings had emerged as the solidifying force in the struggle. Henry VIII utilized his popularity and the anti-church sentiment to impose restrictions on the Catholic power. He capped it with naming himself as "head of the church." At first, the concept of the divine rights of kings gave power to the monarchy. But it could not withstand a growing demand for representative government. Concessions would be painfully won. Nevertheless, the idea of a state church was solidly established with the ensuing persecution of dissidents. A different basis of government than that of divine rights of kings was required before a concept of separation between church and state could be accepted.

255

D. SEPARATION OF CHURCH AND STATE

To a very substantial degree, the establishment of Protestantism in European countries resulted in another form of authoritarian control in religion. It assumed the form of a state
religion which was operated under the auspices of the political
rulers. To many, this solution was as displeasing as having to
submit to the papacy. There was an even stronger feeling on
the part of some adherents to this faith that the Reformation
had not proceeded far enough, especially with the strong emphasis placed on institutional affairs. In Germany there
arose a movement known as Pietism which rejected the Lutheran
insistence on adherence to dogmas and participation in the
sacraments. There was a need for an inner religion of feeling.
While many supporters of this expression of faith remained
within the Lutheran Church, they did provide the source for
a considerable migration to America.

In England the dissent was expressed in the rise of Puri-
tanism. Theologically, they were disposed to follow the teachings of Calvin. But they were disturbed by the retention in
the Anglican Church of many elements from Roman Catholicism.
They advocated that the church be purified by removing the undesirable features. As expected under these conditions, they
did not agree on a common program. Some would introduce as
many Puritan principles as possible into the church and wait
patiently for further reforms. In modern terms, they would
work within the establishment. They were identified as non-
Separatists. Others, however, insisted that it was sinful
not to follow the teachings of the Bible and to separate from
the nonelect. The true church was composed of those whom
God had chosen. They formed themselves into a body of believers bound together by a covenant with Christ and with one
another. Herein is to be found the beginnings of Congrega-
tionalism. The ensuing persecution led many of them to seek
refuge in the hospitable climate of Holland.

Some of the immigrants came into contact with the Anabap-
tists who had been forced to flee from Switzerland. They were
convinced that infant baptism did not conform to bilical teachings. Consequently, they introduced another divisive element

into the Puritan movement and established the Baptist church in England.

As a consequence of these religious persuasions, coupled with economic and political factors, there was set in motion a continuous migration to America from the several European countries. While Englishmen provided the majority of the settlers, the other countries were not without substantial representations.

While the motivation for these undertakings came largely from the persecutions at home, the colonies in the new world were scarcely more inclined to provide a hospitable environment for dissent. The general procedure was to establish a government which would supervise the religious order. Nonconformists were not welcomed and suffered disabilities, especially in the area of politics. The situation would have undoubtedly been far worse had there not existed the great need for settlers in order to make the enterprises economically profitable.

Two major factors which contributed to the rise of religious freedom in America were economics and a political theory concerning the separation of church and state. The first existed to some extent in all the colonies. It has often been noted that the Puritans who sailed to this country on the Mayflower had with them a not inconsiderable number of other individuals, including the renown John Alden and Myles Standish. But the most distinctive expression of this motif was found in the Quaker colonies. When William Penn received his grant in the New World, he sent advertisements throughout Europe urging settlers to migrate to Pennsylvania. Individuals who held very diverse religious beliefs accepted his invitation. It is not surprising, therefore, that toleration was generally practised. One of the first political documents enunciating this point of view was produced in New Jersey.[6]

The most distinctive exponent of this philosophy was Roger Williams. From the moment he set foot in Massachusetts, he was in conflict with the authorities. Eventually he was banished. He secured land from the Indians and formed his own colony which he called Providence Plantation, now known as Rhode Island. In 1664 he traveled to England to secure a charter. While he was there, he was confronted with opposition from Cotton Mather, one of the great Puritan divines. His reply was presented in a document known as the "Bloudy Tenent of Persecution for Cause of Conscience." In this writing he refuted the idea that the political state was divine in origin. On the contrary, he held that it arose out of human need. People associated together and required some basis for sustaining this relationship. Government was created by man, and its area of competence was restricted to civil affairs. By the same token, the church had its jurisdiction in spiritual affairs. The two, therefore, should maintain separation from each other. In his own colony, Williams did not require church membership as a prerequisite for suffrage. An inhabitant only had to possess property therein.

In this same period, political theorists in England were formulating an explanation of the state in a similar vein. Thomas Hobbes portrayed man as living in a state of nature. His natural proclivities to seek for personal ends brought each person into conflict with every other person. Hence, in this state there was war or an inclination thereto. In order to eliminate this evil and to provide an opportunity for man to receive the fruits of peace, power was conferred upon one individual or a group of persons. It would be the responsibility of this governing body to reduce all other wills to theirs.

Luther had propunded the idea that religion was to be found in the individual's relationship with God; now, approximately a century later, the idea is presented that the political order grows out of individuals. A society is simply an aggregate brought about for purposes of achieving certain goals for the individual. Religion and politics have arrived at a very similar perspective.

Subsequently, John Locke gave impetus to the significance of the individual to an even greater extent. For Hobbes, the formation of the state meant that the individual had surrendered his rights permanently and had made himself completely subject to the political order. The only basis for rebellion would be the failure of the state to fulfill its responsibilities; that is, it did not maintain peace and tranquility.

258

Locke, however, not only starts but ends his political theory with the individual at the center. The state is always the
servant of the person, and its powers must be kept under control. It has authority only to the extent that the individuals
have bequeathed to it. It is a limited institution and cannot
transgress the established boundaries. Moreover, he observes,
man enters into other social arrangements. The political order
has no jurisdiction over them. Among these other organzied
bodies are the religious. He would deny any control of government over the church.[7]

The culmination of this process was reached when the First
Amendment to the Constitution of the United States was adopted.
It affirms that "Congress shall make no laws respecting the establishment of religion or the free exercise thereof." The
principle setting forth the separation of church and state had
been formulated into a basic constitutional precept.

Since all asserted ideals have their real value in the implementation, the First Amendment provides no exception. Its
meaning has varied over the course of its two hundred years
history and will continue to do so. The American form of
government requires that government must operate on the basis
of the wishes expressed by the people.

But, more importantly, it needs to be recognized that there
are still many difficult areas wherein this particular Bill of
Rights is inoperative. First, the state does interfere with
religion. It is demonstrated by the fact that financial support is granted to the churches through the policy of tax ex-
emption. The church receives services from the government
but does not compensate for them. Consequently, all citizens
pay the costs in the same manner as in countries where the
religion is state supported. This policy can create a critical situation. In 1950 California passed a law which required
all officials of tax exempt institutions to take an oath of
loyalty. Clergymen were included. Some churches accepted the
obligation; others refused on the basis of separation of church
and state. Finally, in 1967, the entire law was declared to
be unconstitutional.

Indirect assistance has been given to institutions which

are controlled by religious groups. One of the most significant has been the funds granted hospitals under the Hill-Bur-
ton Act. Baptists in Alabama and North Carolina have refused
these funds on the principle that they violate the doctrine
of separation between church and state.

Particular religious groups have suffered adversely at the
hands of the state. The Jehovah Witnesses assert that their
male members are ministers and, appropriately, should be granted draft deferment. The government has generally disagreed.
Consequently, some of them have been sentenced to prison. When
this same group has refused blood transfusion for their children, the courts have interferred, taken control of the latter, and compelled the medical practice.

Religion can exercise an influence on government. In
Arkansas, Mississippi, Texas, and South Carolina, office
holders must not deny the being of Almighty God. In North
Carolina and Tennessee, there is a further requirement that
these officials must believe in a future state of rewards
and punishments. Moreover, there are various blasphemy and
Sunday laws in many states. Until recently, the teaching
of the theory of evolution was proscribed by some codes of
law. Almost every religious society has representatives in
Washington to keep abreast of legislation which affect its
interests.

E. CHURCH AND STATE IN TOTALITARIAN SOCIETIES

A modern form of government which has become increasingly
widespread throughout the world is that of totalitarianism.
In the countries where it has arisen, many problems concerning the relationship of religion and politics have become evident. In general it can be said that this type of
political philosophy does not permit opposition from any source.
Therefore, religious groups are automatically in a difficult
position. They represent potential or actual sources of divided loyalty. If the state is sufficiently strong, it will
be successful in suppressing the movements. Since the strength
of these powers usually resides in the military, any meaningful opposition is simply out of the question. Sometimes the
two institutions will arrive at a compromise whereby provi-

will be created so that each can fulfill its own functions with no obstruction by the other.

There have been instances where the dictatorship and the religious authorities share common interests. If the authoritarian regime arises as a means to oppose another form of political and economic order, the religion may accept the political group as an ally since it, too, opposes the other form of social organization. Apparently it occurred in Spain when Franco rose to power. The alternative would have been a Communist regime which the church in Spain would have found more unacceptable.

Some types of dictatorships in recent years have organized in a unique way. The traditional position is asserted by this type of political organization that the government is supreme. It will permit no opposition. Consequently, since there is the potential conflict between it and the religious society, the latter has been suppressed. But the state has not stopped at that point. Rather, it has proceeded to utilize certain features similar to those to be found in religion. The state will become the object of reverence. That spirit of religious devotion which had been given to God will now be transferred to the political sector. First, there are the sacred writings of the leaders; second, organizations will be created to guide and encourage the adulation which is given to the system; and, finally, it reaches its height in the elevation of a personality to the position that he becomes virtually an object of worship.

The Nazi system in Germany presented many of these ingredients. The foundation of the order was set forth in Hitler's Mein Kampf; organizations were formed, especially among the youth; some expressions of faith were formulated; and Hitler became idolized by the populace. For example, in February, 1937, the Hitler youth society adopted the following statement: "We believe in this earth solely in Adolf Hitler. . . . We believe that God has sent us Adolf Hitler so that Germany may receive a foundation for its existence through all eternity."

Communism has initiated the most extensive operations in this regard. On the one hand, it has quite successfully associated the church with the old regime and declared, there-

261

fore, that it must be destroyed. But, in turn, it has attempted to develop a religious structure based on the philosophy of dialectical materialism with a sense of eschatological expectations. Moreover, it has elevated its major leaders to positions where they receive homage from the people. It is possible that one of the most damaging acts of Khruschev was his program of deStalinization. If one idol can be broken, it endangers the confidence in the others who are enshrined.

Through history there has existed the widest range of relationships pertaining to religion and politics. Since both sectors have a profound interest in the manifold concerns of people, it is impossible to maintain a policy of complete and permanent separation. A more positive approach is required. It would appear profitable to see how the two institutions can relate together successfully without establishing a power structure which would prove to be exceedingly damaging to human fulfillment.

CHAPTER XVIII

COORDINATION OF RELIGION AND POLITICS

A. SEPARATION OF CHURCH AND STATE

"Congress shall make no laws respecting the establishment of religion or the free exercise thereof." This mandate is found in that part of the Constitution of the United States which is considered one of the most valuable collections of political ideals existing anywhere in the annals of government, the Bill of Rights.[1] It grew out of a long history both in Europe and America wherein it had been found impossible to effect a satisfactory relationship between church and state. One or the other gained so much power that it dominated the entire life of the people. The possibility of man's expression of his own way of life was thereby limited. With this accumulated experience, the founding fathers early gave expression to the idea that these two forms of social order were to be separate one from the other.

Subsequently, the wisdom of this proposal has been increasingly recognized as an eminently desirable approach to the problem. In the United States the continuing enlargement of the pluralistic nature of the population would make a reversal of this principle inconceivable, at least in the foreseeable future. Ideally, one might project a rapprochement of all religions which exist in this nation so that a state church would be feasible. The possibility that this development will occur is most remote. Therefore, the principle must be sustained that, as organizations, church and state must remain independent. Any infringement of the right to seek for religious values wherever and however one may wish is considered to be impermissible.

But it should be noted that the constitutional provision, like most laws, is a negation. Congress is denied the right to enact any regulation which either establishes a religion or prevents its existence. While this amendment has been

subject to continuing litigation, the courts have endeavored
to draw a narrow line while recognizing that these two institutional arrangements cannot be totally separated. The
state is composed of people who are seeking to achieve certain goals and values in life. In a similar manner, religious
organizations are engaged in a quest for the bases in human
living. Given these functions, it is inevitable that there
will be many instances where they overlap.

It would appear appropriate to recognize two different sides
to this issue. On the one hand, the constitution will prohibit
the government from doing anything which supports a particular
religion or religion itself. Nor will it be allowed to take
any steps which would curb the operation of a religion. On
the other hand, there is the inescapble necessity for both
forms of human experience to recognize that they share many
common areas. The major problem is to seek out the processes whereby religion and politics can respond to human
needs without any dictation on the part of either sector.

B.   THE FUNCTIONS OF THE STATE

1. State will support religion. In an earlier section, it
was urged that the major role of the state should not be negative, a denial of certain forms of action. This function,
while it continues to be a necessary though vexing part of
government, should be incidental or auxiliary to the fulfillment of its principal purposes. It should devote itself to the
providing of primary guidance in the enrichment of human personality with the establishment of common goals and values.
It is in this context that the state can make an important
contribution by supporting religion. It is the latter which
serves to integrate the varied interests and concerns of the
people whereby they will be able to live meaningfully and pur-
posefully. Therefore, government must perceive its own tasks
from the understanding which is furnished by the religious
dimension of society. It is inescapable that it will be
vitally concerned that every effort has been made to contribute
toward the developing, strengthening, and advancement of religion among the people in its society.

In affirming that the state should support religion, it

is not meant to say that the Bill of Rights will be violated by having Congress make laws "respecting the establishment of religion." Certainly, it is not intended that the assistance be construed in financial terms. This aid would be especially detrimental since it would almost inevitably eventuate in the exercising of control over whatever faith was supported. Thereby, the very purpose of religion would be circumvented since it would then become an arm of the state to formulate its position from the vantage point of the political organization rather than its own independent perspective.

What is being proposed is that the state will seek to provide a proper environment wherein the religious quest can function in an independent and untrammeled fashion. It is in this respect that dictatorial governments fail to serve their societies. They take the position that the state can establish the requisite goals and purposes which become the ends toward which the people will strive. This action is accomplished without any outside contributions.

There is a similar problem in democratic societies. The determination of human values tend to be formulated in economic terms; and, therefore, the business community assumes the prerogatives which do not rightfully belong to it.

What the state must do is to see that religion is given a free hand to pursue its activity and to project the aspirations which will serve to direct all aspects of human living. When it creates this milieu, the state cannot be accused of establishing a religion or supporting faith itself. It simply states that neither the state nor the economic society is equipped to explore the whole dimension of life in order to formulate the bases for its fulfillment. After the latter have been constituted, then all the other sectors of the society will work toward implementing them in their respective dimensions. As these activities are accomplished, religion will be free to evaluate the results and the means by which they were reached.

With the great diversities existing among people, it is to be expected that in this setting that many different religious groups will emerge. Moreover, there will be indivi-

duals who will maintain an aloofness from all organized faiths
so as to project their own independent views. The state will
assure all people and groups the right to proceed and will not
be unresponsive to any position which will be developed and
presented. From this perspective, there is no question of religion as over against antireligion. The two positions are
simply different forms of religious expression. For example,
a so-called atheist is clearly acceptable and recognized as an
appropriate medium through whom certain ideas and interpretations are presented. His insights into the meaning and purpose
of human existence will be recognized as simply another form of
religious understanding.

What is being urged is that the state will give the religious
efforts the necessary undergirding which will make their mission
feasible. Since there will be many diverse points of view, one
of the most important functions of the government in fulfilling
its duties will be to make certain that the varied groups and
individuals do not interfere with one another. While holy wars
appear, for the most part, to be episodes of the past, there
can still be confrontation in many other ways. Since the disputes are carried out in a more subtle fashion, the work of
government is made very complicated. The attacks are not as
easily detected. Oftentimes, it would be difficult to present
adequate proof that untoward actions had occurred. Since members of religious groups have favorable standing in the community, there may even be a disinclination to interfere in
these affairs. Furthermore, the political sector has a natural
desire to escape involvement in quarrels except in case of
necessity. Lastly, it is not easy to know how to resolve
this type of problem.

For example, in a region where members of a particular faith
constitute a substantial majority of the population, other
groups may be discriminated against on religious grounds.
Thereby, they may suffer economic, political, and social dis-
advantages. In order to fulfill its defined function, it
would be required of the state that it prohibit this type of
conduct. Obviously, there are many barriers which handicap
it in accomplishing its duty. In that immediate area, the
governmental officials will almost certainly be affiliated
with the dominant faith and will owe their continuation in

their offices to the majority. Consequently, there will be a
disinclination to do anything which would potentially disturb
the religious societies.

One may examine the difficulty as it would appear in another
context. Some religious groups are so thoroughly assured concerning the rightness of the beliefs that they will engage in
a very vigorous missionary operation in a community in order
to make converts. This form of propagandizing may elicit a
negative response from the established religions. The latter
may insist that the new group is disturbing the tranquility
of the community and insist that they be restrained. There
may erupt conflict with members of the new group so that an
unfortunate turmoil will prevail. In either instance, the
state will be confronted with an all but insoluble situation
if it is committed to uphold the principle of religious freedom.[2]

2. A second contribution of the state will be to encourage
religion. From the standpoint of organizational structures,
this function will be performed by extending a welcome to all
religious groups to be participants in the community's quest
for moral and spiritual values. It will indicate to the many
societies that every effort will be made to enable them to
pursue their faith without interference. Further, it will
express a readiness to receive advice and counsel in matters
related to the affairs of government. In this respect, religions outside the Judaeo-Christian tradition could make
an increasing contribution to the paramount issue in our
modern world, the necessity that nationalities understand
one another so that a more peaceful order can be created. As
the several religious groups fostered association with one
another, opportunities would be substantially increased
for people to reach an appreciative understanding concerning
the diverse elements of humanity. The basic determination
of life in any society is to be found in the group's faith.
To establish a constructive relationship among people can
never be accomplished unless there is, at a minimum, a tolerance for varied beliefs and practices. Ultimately, it
would be hoped that a spirit of profound appreciation could
be engendered. In America the conflicts among the different
religious groups have been substantially lessened as the

communicants have had opportunity to associate together in
social situations. Internationally, the same process could
be accomplished.

It will be of even greater value for the state to encourage
individuals to be religious. It would mean, in terms of our
idea of separation of church and state, that each citizen
would be challenged to seek for a personal understanding of
himself and his role in the universe, the meaning of human
existence, the purposes and goals which should guide each
one in his own life and his contributions to society, and
a basic commitment to the moral values which he would find
contributing most effectively to a social order. Again,
there is a fine line that must be recognized and maintained
intact. The state should not extend its duty to include the
position that a person should affiliate with, and support,
organized religious societies even if no particular group
received special attention. Its function would be restricted
to expressing a recognition that the community supports persons in their commitments.

3. This assessment leads to a third significant function
of the state in relationship to religion. People need a society which is fulfilling its duty so that both individual
and social values can be obtained. If government is to
fill this responsibility, it must be able to make decisions
and to act upon them. These tasks are not performed by some
impersonal entity but by officials who have been selected for
this purpose. These men and women, however, do not operate
in a vacuum. Decisions are made and carried out on the basis
of many influences which impinge upon them. Ideally, each
citizen would inform the governmental bodies concerning his
expectations. Then each one would speak to the issues on
the basis of his total experiences, including religious.

Unfortunately, this mode of influencing decisions is not
feasible. From the standpoint of political realism, people
find it necessary to unite into organized bodies in order to
receive meaningful hearings. It has been proven how effective this type of methodology can be, and politically oriented
groups have been formed widely. They represent diverse objectives and exert pressure on officials to support them.

Religious groups cannot be immune from political issues. Many of them, in fact, represent concerns which have emerged out of the spiritual background. It would be inconceivable for these organizations not to be desirous of expressing their points of view to the state. Since the latter is attentive to some associations with their interests, it should perform in like manner for the religious societies. Ideally, they could contribute more fully to the analysis of the issues and proffered solutions since they speak from a perspective which is developed out of the whole structure of life. Their observations and advice should be more comprehensive than organizations which reflect narrow interests. It is unfortunately true that the ideal is severely tainted by extremely circumscribed and parochial views. Consequently, they do not always fulfill their appropriate tasks.

The state, therefore, must be receptive to the contributions presented by religious societies at least to the same extent that it is responsive to the spokesmen of other groups. Neither the sacred nor the secular groups should be the determiner of state policies and actions. The government alone must bear these responsibilities. Consequently, it must, in the final analysis, rise above all the voices which have been heard and arrive at the decisions and determine their implementation. Political representatives simply should not ignore the insights which proceed from individuals and groups which make their contributions from the standpoint of their faiths.

C.   THE FUNCTIONS OF RELIGION

1. Concern for politics. Historically, the dominance of institutionalized religion in governmental affairs has proven to be detrimental to society. As a result of these unfortunate experiences, efforts have been made in many countries to maintain the separation of these two sectors. There has sometimes been the insistence that religious societies should refrain entirely from any and all involvement in political affairs. Furthermore, some religious groups have rejected the idea that they should have any participation in these matters. A small number even insist that the policy of noninvolvement should apply to individual members of their groups. The justification

for these latter positions has been that the function of religion relates to concerns other than political. Religion should maintain an aloofness so that it can devote its resources to "spiritual" affairs.

It is unfortunate that this general attitude has been accepted. Immediately, it denies that religion can respond to governmental issues notwithstanding the fact that the very nature of the state and its citizens will be substantially determined by the governmental acts. Therefore, these religious groups almost abdicate their ability to influence the lives of their people. The latter cannot very easily insulate themselves from the social order. If the state proceeds to guide its citizens, the latter will have extreme difficulty in being responsive to the teachings of religion. For example, if there were no minimum wage law, it would be virtually impossible for a business man who, from the religious standpoint of justice, wished to provide a more adequate income for his employees to be capable of doing so. Were the religious bodies to coalesce in order to seek for the enactment of regulations governing wages, they would probably contribute heavily to the achievement of them.

Equally unfortunate is the fact that the failure of religious groups to become active participants in politics can result in their constituents having only limited interests in this dimension of life.

The inescapable conclusion would seem to be that all organized religions have a responsible duty to relate themselves to the formation and enforcement of state policies. Their leaders can provide considerable input from the resources of faith whereby the resolution of public issues can be affected. In a pluralistic society the diversity of groups can greatly enlarge the bases for decisions.

Another service which can be rendered to the political process by religious groups is to provide information on the issues. Most organizations of this type have extensive literature which can serve as channels of communication. One can be certain that other institutions are attempting to influence opinions. The religious societies should not be restrictive or parochial in

270

their presentations. With a sufficiently inclusive editorial policy even partisan politics could be given opportunity for expression.

It is, therefore, of vital importance that individuals and groups address political issues from the background of faith. This interest could exercise a wholesome influence on government both directly and by enlarging the knowledge and understanding concerning the political process.

2. Second, the religious organizations should stimulate their constituents to be political involved. By keeping before them the issues which are current in governmental affairs, they can indicate the relevance of their faith to the problems of society.

There are two disturbing situations today. First, it is apparent that there is an ever widening gulf between the religious leaders and the lay members of our churches in the area of social issues. Three factors contribute to this state of affairs. On the one hand, the old struggle in the area of theology is less evident. As is usual in hostile encounters, there seems to have taken place a general mellowing following upon an extended period of conflict. Many people have lost the traditional fears about the dangers besetting doctrinal teachings. For example, the theory of evolution does not necessarily raise the spectre of lessening the dignity of man by sharing a common ancestor with the ape. At the same time, the traditional liberal is less likely to cut large blocks of materials from the Bible on the grounds that they lack historicity. The liberalism of the past has become somewhat the orthodoxy of the present. Even the "death of God" theory scarcely causes a ripple; most laymen have no conception of Bultmann's "demythologizing."

Consequently, the controversy now focuses upon social issues and the involvement of the religions. Some studies have suggested that expressions by church leaders, especially those at the top level of denominations, even when supported by the institutional machinery, result in a disenchantment and withdrawal of support by many lay persons. Attempts to explain recent declines in membership and contributions employ this

271

explanation. The laity, it is said, are not prepared to understand religion in this dimension.

On the other hand, those who are now attaining positions of
leadership in the churches have received considerable exposure
to the problems of mankind as set forth in classes of social
ethics. Curricula in seminaries have undergone extensive reworking in the past several decades. But the comprehension
of religion in this areas has not only been gained in the classroom but, concurrently, the students have become participants
in the social struggle. Therefore, when they assume positions
in the institutions, they bring with them a deep commitment to
the ideal of justice in its manifold exemplifications. Another
contributing factor has been the close working relationships
which they have achieved with the youth. Oftentimes, these
several features add up to a generation gap in the churches.
Since the institutions rely heavily on the elder constituency
for financial support, the cleavage between laymen and clergy
has been more sharply drawn.

It is obvious that the solution to this problem will require
a greater tolerance on the part of each for the other. It is
difficult to see that the clergy will surrender their ideals.
But they will need to develop a high degree of patience in
relating themselves to their parishioners. Moreover, they
will have to bridge the gap with an extensive program of
education so that the persons in the pews will grasp something of their own vision. This effort will have to be accomplished carefully, painstakingly, and continuously. It
should prove to be eminently worthwhile since it should result in the church assuming a much more comprehensive role
in human affairs.

3. Third, religious institutions can serve the state in
a very creative fashion by encouraging its members to exercise their rights of citizenship. It is especially needed
in America. One of the great disappointments in this country
is the failure of a substantial part of the electorate to
participate in the political process. Undoubtedly, some
of them fail to become involved for religious reasons. In
a small number of instances the faith positively discourages
or even forbids involvement. In an even greater number of

situations, the unintentional teachings of society more subtly undermines the concept of responsible citizenship. But from the standpoint of institutional religion, it is a matter of omission. The group fails to assume any obligations to make contributions in this area.

Were efforts exerted to encourage people to join in the political arena, the immediate result would probably be a renewed interest in the affairs of state and a greater involvement in them. In a longer period of time, those who were affiliated with organized religion might respond from the standpoint of their faith. The ideals of the latter could become a more dynamic instrument in determining governmental practices.

This function of religion could be directed at all levels of political activity - working in the political organizations, seeking office, taking part in voter registration, serving at the poling places, and assisting persons to vote by providing transportation or baby-sitting requirements. It is difficult to see how a greater responsibility being assumed could fail to improve the political climate.

Obviously, there is always the danger that this involvement will result in the institution becoming too partisan and losing its objectivity in political matters. But it is a risk which must be taken in order to attempt to contribute toward making a more viable political process. If the religious ideals are kept in the limelight, the potentiality can be effectively diminished.

4. At all times, it is the function of religion to keep the prophetical voice alive. It is the only human instrument which represents the whole person and all people. Consequently, its perspective is broad enough to examine political issues from a comprehensive overview. It sees the human personality from the vantage point of its having a lofty status with great potentiality. Therefore, all facets of life, both individual and social, are kept under continual surveillance and evaluation to determine whether they are contributing toward the enhancement of humanity. Not the least of the social instruments to be examined is government. It has so much

273

influence in determing the course of human existence that it
cannot be ignored. Religion would be derelict in its duty
were it not to exercise diligence in appraising all governmental bodies from the lowliest precinct organ to the highest office in the nation and, on the emerging scene, international instrumentalities.

To fulfill this requirement is extremely demanding. The extent of governmental activities make it difficult for anyone
to make an appraisal. It has been stated by newspaper colum-
nists that the Washington establishment has become so elaborate that there is simply no way for any administration to
influence the many departments and bureaus. This assessment
is understandable. Social problems which arise out of modern
life are so complex that they must of necessity become obligations of governments. Unfortunately, however, as the latter
assume responsibilities in these areas, there is the temptation
to aggrandize power. Then it tends to feed on itself. Many
complaints have been uttered concerning big government. But
a considered assessment of modern man and the intricacies of
his personal and social experiences apparently reveals   no
acceptable alternative. It is certainly not feasible for
human affairs to be committed to any other organization, not
even religious societies.

The most serious handicap which interferes with oversight
in government whether made by religion or any other organization is secrecy. In recent months it has been brought to
light that a very large number of Washington bureaucrats have
the right to classify documents as being more or less un-
accessible to the public. Even in our American society, the
citizens are deprived of information whereby they could make
appropriate decisions. Then, too, elected officials employ
all kinds of devices to keep themselves out of public scrutiny. On the local level, the most frequently employed mechanism is that of holding executive sessions. In order to
lessen criticism, these meetings are held first and the
course of actions determined. Then a carefully structured
open meeting will follow where some limited disclosures will
be made.

Notwithstanding the extraordinary severity of the tasks, re-

ligion cannot escape its obligation to maintain careful oversight in the political sector and to speak out courageously
on issues. Several things may assist it in its work. First,
religious leaders must achieve greater political expertise in
order to understand the process, to develop capability in ascertaining relevant information, and to achieve facility in
performing its functions most effectively. Second, it must
improve the cooperative association on the part of the leaders
in this area in order to achieve the most efficient use of its
limited resources. The different divisions of governmental
activities should be assigned to specific persons so that each
one can concentrate his efforts on the particular operations.
Third, the political leadership must be apprised of the fact
that its actions will be examined and evaluated from the standpoint of religion. Moreover, it must not be an idle gesture.
Too often, groups initiate programs of this nature with great
enthusiasm. But the difficulties which are met, the time consumed, and the energies expended cause the interest to wane
very quickly. Finally, religious leaders should seek to enter into a working relationship with other groups and individuals who are involved in these areas. It should prove to be
particularly useful to develop a cooperative arrangement with
journalists. Members of the legal profession will frequently
prove to be useful sources of information and professional
guidance. Students of political science can contribute a
tremendous range of assistance especially in understanding the
governmental process. Of course, great care needs to be exercised since, unfortunately, these varied groups and individuals
will sometimes endeavor to exploit religious leaders on the
basis of the latter's inexperience.

Some effort should be made to provide regular interaction
among the religious leadership. These people are finite individuals with the limitations which this concept implies.
Consequently, there is the danger that the truly prophetical
voice will be blurred by a restricted perspective. There is,
in particular, the possibility that, as religious institutions
are organized, a leader will be governed in his approach to
issues by the interests of his own constituency and/or his
superiors. It may even occur that pressure will be brought to
bear so that he will uphold one position rather than another.
But assistance can be provided by the frequent sharing with

his fellow clergy his ideas in the political sector. For example, a minister from a wealthy church may view the political spectrum from one perspective while one who is serving in a less affluent community may have a quite different outlook. Through their associations and interactions, these partial viewpoints can be somewhat broadened. Moreover, in highly controversial issues a collective jusdgment can not only carry more weight,but also it will lessen the criticism emanating from particular religious societies.

5. Finally, it is the function of religion to provide for the cultural unity in the state. This task will be its most unique and important contribution in the political realm. As shown in the early part of this study, social culture finds the source of its most distinctive expression in the religion of the group. The defining identification of a people, therefore, will come from their faith. Again, it should be reaffirmed that a qualification enters into this assessment. There may be a considerable gulf between the expressed religion and the faith which is actually determinative of culture. This situation occurs when the former becomes little more than an appendage to the social order. It will take place when the institutionalized religion fails to achieve a viable interaction with the people of an area and their social expressions. In the present case, it would happen when the political entities failed to elicit a concern for, and participation in, their activities.

On the other hand, when religion is committed to achieve a genuine dedication on the part of its constituency to goals and purposes which will be determinative of their lives, it will do so on the basis of the broad relationship with every aspect of the personal and social life in the political division. The formative pattern of human living will have been created in the dynamic process provided by this interaction. In other words, it will not be a contrived devotion but one woven out in the very process of the group experiences. The objectives will not be established formally, but they will emerge in the active living of life itself.

This role of religion is particularly appropriate in pluralistic societies. The United States provides a good ex-

ample. There are many organized religions. Each has its own
distinctive heritage and its own conceptualization, values,
and institutions. Instead, however, of this multiplicity
being a liability, it provides a distinct advantage since
there is a wealth of religious resources to draw from. Further, the day is no longer present when each of these several
groups asserts its own position as the possessor of the true
faith and seeks to impose its views upon all people in the
nation. To the contrary, there are wide areas of associations,
interactions, and cooperation. As a result, the religious
groups themselves are enlarging their outlook and setting an
example for the establishment of a faith which will be comprehensive enough in scope to provide for the most diverse needs
of a complex civilization. That is, religion in the United
States slowly moves to a point where it can properly serve
the citizens of this country by forming a culture in terms of
the national requirements. Out of this development a cultural
unity becomes a distinct possibility.

The most direct consequence of this process is that the old
idea of the state having to remain completely neutral in religion has become of less importance. The relationships of religion with government need no longer be seen as a desire to
gain sectarian advantage. There is now the basis for faith
in its several dimensions to work toward a common culture
formed in the dynamic process of its concern for the total
needs of Americans. It should not be concluded from this
assessment that there is unity in this field. Obviously,
there are wide divergencies. But there has been a distinct
diminishing of the power struggle in influencing national
policy. The various bodies can interact with the political
issues along the lines of the same give and take, successes
and failures which characterize the whole democratic concept.

CHAPTER XIX

THE NATURE OF SCIENCE

Our present age is often called the scientific age or the age of science. We have become so accustomed to the preeminence of this discipline that we accept it as the determiner of all truths and values. Unfortunately, however, when this word is used today, the meaning given to it is a very restricted one. Consequently, we have had the misfortunate of seeing the perspective about the universe and man very severely narrowed. The cause of this occurrence is that we have either limited the term to the physical properties or we have reduced all phenomena to physical dimensions. We have come to think almost exclusively in terms of objects which can be empirically verified and mathematically measured. Space and time have been accepted as the only criteria for the determination of knowledge.

A careful examination of the historical quest for enlightenment should make one hesitant to circumscribe inquiry. Modern science does not stand alone. It has built upon the discoveries of the past. Furthermore, it depends on other human faculties to assist its operations. For example, imagination, which expresses itself in setting up hypotheses, must precede the actual scientific investigation. This factor is a peculiarly restrictive one since its projections are finite and limited at any given moment. As new hypotheses are imagined, the scientific inquiry must reexamine the evidence. Growing out of this procedure is the incompleteness and temporalness of scientific results. In many fields of study special attention has to be paid to exceptions uncovered subsequent to the formulation of the general principle. There is considerable questioning concerning the present trend in education where the thrust is on vocational training. How can it be accomplished? In the short run, it is possible to prepare a person for a job. Even in this context, however, the peculiarities of an employing firm will necessitate an apprenticeship so that the employee can be prepared specifically for the firm itself. But scarcely has he been made ready for employment when changes may

eliminate the job or alter it drastically. A high school began
sometime ago to prepare students to be service station employees.
Conceivably, with the energy crisis upon us, many gas stations
will close. Where does the graduate of this program turn to
find a job? Or it may be that some new form of energy will be
used to replace gasoline. Is the trained attendant prepared
for this employment?[1]

The initial concern should be to understand the nature of
science itself. A beginning can be secured by recognizing that
the word "science" does not convey the limitations which modern
man attributes to it. The term is a transliteration of the
Latin word scientia which simply means "knowledge." Whatever
serves as a basis for understandng the universe is scientific.
It was stated in the section on philosophy that every person
must be classified in this category. Similarly, everyone is
a scientist. From the moment of birth each individual sets
out on the unending quest for knowledge, that of understanding
his environment and his relationship with it. In the course
of this journey through life, many inaccurate assessments will
be made. But, at the time they are accepted, they must be accorded the status of knowledge; and the conclusions were arrived at scientifically. That is, they provided an appropriate
basis whereby the person understood his universe and made it
acceptable as far as he was concerned. Should he reject the
knowledge at a later time, it will have lost its previous
identification.

Learning consists in comparing different methodologies and
the raw materials which are used in the various investigations.
Hopefully, those persons whose education has been limited can
be brought to an expanded perspective. At the same time, one
who looks at the universe from the standpoint of modern science
will not be so superior that he will demean those individuals
from other learning traditions or be unwilling to recognize
the possibilities that may exist in ancient methods of knowing. Education means literally "to lead out of." Too often,
in the modern period, it has meant "to lead away from." That
is, ideally, education should be a broadening experience. In
point of fact, it has become a substitution of one form of narrowness for another. Given the parochialism which is beginning
to dominate the system, one can scarcely not fear for the future.

In the basic meaning of the term, the first scientist was primitive man. He was confronted with the same predicament which every succeeding member of this species has met. He found himself in the universe which acted upon him and to which he had to react. He had to secure a knowledge of it so that he could respond in an appropriate fashion. Therefore, he made observations and reached certain conclusions. He became convinced that his environment was alive with spirits which could affect him for good or ill. But he discovered that actions on his part helped him to cope with them. The scientific approach which he utilized is called magic. It was performed in two major forms. One of them was productive and served to achieve certain objectives considered to be desirable. The other type was aversive magic whereby responses of the spirts which were undesirable could be warded off. In both instances, man performed acts which were designed to relate himself to the universe as he had discovered it. It was mankind's first efforts to acquire scientific understanding which he could utilize to enrich his life. Hence, to put it in perspective, it was primitive science. He had begun a process of inquiry which set mankind on the pathway which has led to the infinite discoveries made since that early dawn.

It may be, too that there was something in his experience which is valuable for his later successors to recall. There was an initiative which he took to understand and to control the universe. At the same time, however, he stood in awe or reverence in the presence of the forces with which he interacted. His science contributed to his religion.

Unfortunately, there is an almost universal trend in the modern world to perceive the universe as something to be used. It has value only as it contributes to man's well-being. In the current scene the universe is to be exploited. There is almost a total insensitivity to the natural order. The more wealthy man has become, the greater his haughtiness. The result has been a profligate waste. Finally, there is beginning to be an awareness that this approach cannot continue interminably. A spirit of responsibility must be created. It is not surprising that there is an extreme difficulty in coming to terms with this realization. Too many per-

sons have the unquenchable expectation that modern science
will be successful in solving whatever problems arise in the
natural world. There is only the vaguest awareness that our
very existence requires some balance among all parts of the
universe. Until we develop a new sense of humility and indebtedness, it will not be possible to respond very adequately
to this fact. Therefore, our primitive ancestor made two
correlative contributions. He initiated science. At the
same time, he provided an example of reverencing the creator
and the creation.

The day when science was begun has been followed by a continuing development of human understanding about the universe
and the responses which should be forthcoming. Corrections
have been made where errors were discovered. The perception
has been expanded. New and improved techniques for acquiring
knowledge have been formed while older ones were perfected.
Consequently, human knowledge has gained greater reliability
although the increasing complexity of the universe has enlarged
the area of uncertainty. Ignorance is more evident today than
in the earlier period. Primitive man was ignorant but scarcely was conscious of it; his modern offspring is ignorant and
knows it.

How has the quest for knowledge been accomplished? First,
there has been the procedure of trial and error. This methodology is universally employed. It consists of several ingredients. Observations are made of occurrences. Certain items
appear to fit together. Upon similar occasions the procedure
is duplicated. As long as it works - or works most of the time -
this knowledge is utilized.

A second technique is reason. The mind surveys certain possibilities and arrives at some conclusions. Initially, it is
a very unsystematic performance, and there is an all too ready
willingness to accept any results. From an early period man
has dreamed dreams and had visions. From these mental operations, he has perceived many things about himself and his
world. Some individuals have relied heavily upon these experiences. In some societies, they have achieved an acceptance
as experts or have been considered as divinely inspired. The
Old Testament says that in an earlier time, the prophet was

known as a "seer."[2] Apparently, there was a recognized association between the two but, also, a distinct assertion that
the prophet was a more eminent person than his predecessor.
Nonetheless,there was great value attached to the earlier profession.

In time a more systematic employment of reason came onto
the scene. Its earliest formulation was in mathematics whereby precise knowledge was based on numerical factors. Subsequently, another type of reasoning began to be carefully
developed. When fully developed, it would be called proposi-
tional reasoning.

From both perspectives reasoning was accepted as a dependable tool for learning. Numbering gave a reliability which
was attractive. When it was extended, it gave increased
prominence to all forms of rationality. The mind was able
to transcend the fluctuations of the present world to attain
insights of a more permanent order. The world of experience
was considered as having emerged from this ultimate realm
upon which it was dependent. Pythagoras proposed that the
essence of things is number. Subsequently, a more comprehensive portrayal of reality was disclosed in a transcendent
realm which could be apprehended by reason alone. Hence,
it was the mind or the soul which provided man with the most
dependable faculty whereby knowledge could be gained. Moreover, it was an exclusively human possession.

A. THE BEGINNNNGS OF EMPIRICAL SCIENCE

1. Aristotle. In the early development of the methodologies
for seeking knowledge, some limited use would be made of sense
observation. It could provide some basis for distinguishing
between truth and error. All too often, there was a disinclination to give it a major role. One gets the impression
that there was a predisposition to reject this type of knowledge unless it was overwhelming. Prevailing traditions were
given a higher priority and served to restrict disclosures
made by sense experience. A major handicap was the lack of
a precise method of discovery. The process had not been reduced
to   an orderly operation which had been recognized in the
society. Essentially, it was an unknown method exploring

283

the unknown. It would require considerable development before
it would be considered a major method for gaining knowledge.

One of the most important persons in the development of empirical science was the Greek philosopher, Aristotle. He had
been trained in the rational system espoused by his teacher,
Plato. But he was too attracted to the mundane level of physical
reality to be satisfied. His biological interests, as contrasted with Plato's concern for mathematics and related fields,
caused him to observe the earth and its creatures. His epistemology was developed from this perspective.

The first step to knowledge is sense experience. As they
are repeated, the individual stores them up in his memory.
His common sense provides the basis for association of
those elements which share common features. Thereby, practical
knowledge is gained which can produce the necessary ingredients
for meeting the everyday demands of life. While the ordinary
person may not advance beyond this stage, even the philosopher
simply moves past these preparatory stages in order to form
general principles whereby he can understand the world.

In adumbrating this systematic process, Aristotle opened the
door to the possibility for a substantial extension of human
understanding. Almost immediately, however, he closed it by
asserting that this type of research could not be very productive. Its usefulness was quite limited. Some mistakes might
be corrected. Particular items could be adduced. But it
would be basically a futile undertaking. For all practical
purposes, everything which empirical observation could teach
one had been disclosed. It was a closed book. Is it any wonder that progress in knowledge in the ensuing period was extremely restricted?

There followed a long period in human history wherein the
intellectual efforts were made in other directions. An exception has to be noted in the practical fields especially
in the Hellenistic Era. Man continued to engage in extensive
affairs as he pursued economic, political, military, and social interests. In some instances he achieved remarkable results. Some enrichment of life, at least for a few people,
came out of these studies.

The empirical methodology was especially useful to the men in applied sciences since it enabled them to explore the universe. Advancements were attained in mathematics, cartography, astronomy, and similar areas. Most of these endeavors were undertaken by way of reason, aided and abetted by some empirical observations. Three deficiencies in the intellectual quest imposed severe handicaps on the continuing search for knowledge. The first was the lack of tools which could increase the capability of the natural senses. A second was the limited world view. Intellectual curiosity did not extend too far. The view of a three -story universe was generally held. The overarching sky, a relatively short distinace from the earth, embraced the earth. Then there was the unfathomable abyss below. Human thinking was not stimulated by gazing beyond the observable horizon. Moreover, the same limitations existed with respect to his relationship with the earth itself. It is not surprising, therefore, that the stimuli which might prompt man to ask an unending series of questions were not present. Within the limited world view, reason was the primary agency for knowing. Only within very narrow bounds did search for additional raw material operate. Finally, and most unfortunately, there was a confidence in the results of the intellectual process. Infallibility rather than tentativeness was the prevailing point of view. If errors were made, they could be corrected quite easily by proceeding more carefully. But it scarcely occurred to the investigators that the entire problem, methodology, and solution might be erroneously and incorrectly described. Nor was there any serious scepticism about the underlying premises which supported their system of thought.

One of the most interesting occurrences took place in Hellenistic astronomy. Aristarchus of Samos (ca. 310-230 B. C. E.) had proposed the solar theory wherein the earth and the other planets revolved around the sun. But he indicated that the revolutions were in circles. The geometry did not support this description. As a result, the whole idea was discarded in favor of the geocentric theory proposed by Hipparchus of Nicaea and, later, popularized by Claudius Ptolemy. Had the concept of tentativeness been prevalent, it may have been possible for the problem to have been reexamined. It would be centuries later that Copernicus would discover the error. Undoubtedly many similar mistakes occurred.

285

B. A PERIOD OF DECLINE

During and following the Hellenistic Age, a radical change
in the perception of the universe eroded the pursuit of knowledge. The decline and fall of Greece caused increasing difficulties in life which created disillusionment and negativism.
Religiously it brought growing popularity for the mystery cults
which offered salvation beyond this life. The optimism of the
earlier Greeks, as shown in their creative genius in literature
and the arts, declined substantially. Attention turned to
philosophical and religious systems which provided the means
to escape the present existence and to focus attention upon
the nonmaterial, transcendent realm. In this existence one
could find permanence, stability, and solutions to difficulties experienced in the turmoil of earthly life.[3]

Gradually, Christianity achieved a foothold in this environment. When it passed from its Jewish setting into the Gentile
world, it quickly adapted its nature to the pervasive spirit
of the latter. It would have moved much further had it not
been restrained by the perspective which had been so thoroughly established in its formative years under the influence of
its parent faith. It should have become a full blown mystery
cult with its mystic initiation which would assure one of a
permanent being in life after death. Some adherents did, in
fact, follow a more speculative mysticism by denying goodness
to the material world and urging man to achieve knowledge only of the spiritual. Christian Gnosticism presented in its
interpretation of the faith a revelation of the eternal and
the pathway by which sinful man could achieve salvation. But
a more traditional form of the faith succeeded in rising to
a position of dominance. Nevertheless, the heretical sects left
lasting impressions which the religion has not been able
to escape to this day.

This ancient period became characterized by man devoting
his energies and abilities to the science of God rather than
to the science of man. The latter related to the world which
was passing away and, therefore,had no genuine value. Essentially, it was evil and man's attention to it only led to degradation for himself. The superior way was to devote himself
to the everlasting and to count everything for lost which did

not contribute to its attainment. Through this process, one would succeed in escaping the enticements of the evil one, even Satan himself, who exercised dominion in the present world.

Growing out of this emphasis, science became an exceedingly restricted operation, centered as it was only on what had value for salvation. Even the ordinary forms of education were demeaned as not worthy of the Christian. In the sixth century, Pope Gregory I wrote a letter to one of his bishops in which he expressed great disappointment because the churchman was teaching grammar. Consequently, science, in the general meaning of the term which states that it is a systematic search for knowledge, existed. But it covered a narrow spectrum of issues. The problems to be solved were religious matters expressed in the most limited meaning of this word. The source materials consisted only of those items which had been accepted by the church; the methodology employed was to seek to draw out probable applications of eternal truths which had been previously revealed; and the spirit with which one engaged in this exercise was that of deference to the authorities.

Under these conditions, there was scarcely room for a continuation of investigation in the earth sciences. The situation is probably no better demonstrated than by the fact that the works of Aristotle were literally lost to Western Europe. Fortunately, his philosophy would be preserved and utilized in the Muslim world whence it would eventually return to the Christian schools.

C. RENEWAL

After a period of time, the period of intellectual darkness began to recede from Europe. A variety of factors aided this course of events. One of the most important was an expanded contact with the Muslim world. From this source there was received not only the classical learning but also the results of the studies which they had carried on. One major contribution was the philosophy of Aristotle. When a reacquaintance with this ancient Greek thinker had been achieved, it was necessary to take his ideas into account. Some scholars accepted and utilized them   most enthusiastically. It offered many values.

287

For many persons who had been trained in the older modes
of thought, the value of Aristotle was initially seen from
a limited religious perspective. He could be used to assist
in the furtherance of the real goals in life, namely, to discover God and to secure salvation. It was in this context
that theology was identified as the "queen of the sciences."
Neverthless, even this pragmatic perspective of this Greek
philosophy opened the door to the more comprehensive examination and utilization whereby modern science was started
on its course.

This transitional development can be observed by comparing
two theologians who lived about two centuries apart. First,
there was St. Anselm (1033-1109), Archbishop of Canterbury.
He was appreciative of the human mind and urged man to seek
an understanding of his faith by the use of reason so long
as the latter did not lead one to be skeptical about the
teachings of the church. He was, in fact, convinced that after
one had accepted the latter, it was appropriate to seek grounds
for confirming it. There was a confidence, in fact, that all
the teachings of the Roman Catholic Church could be confirmed
rationally. In this context, he set forth his ontological
proof for the existence of God. Man has in his mind the idea
of an absolutely perfect being whom he calls God. This perception means that all qualities had to be possessed by this
being. Therefore, existence has to be included. Otherwise,
one would be able to conceive of a being greater than God,
namely, one which possessed existence as one of its qualities.
Consequently, if God did not exist outside the mind as well
as an idea in the mind, he would not be the perfect reality
which our mind conceptualizes.

This truth, of course, is based strictly on rational thought.
One does not require supportive evidence beyond the mind. The
rational argument itself is conclusive.

Then St. Thomas Aquinas (1225-1274) entered upon the intellectual scene. He was greatly enamoured with Aristotle and
relied heavily on his philosophy. When he sought to prove the
existence of God, he followed Aristotle and turned to the
empirical world. In effect, he said that one might begin without any belief that there is a God. Nevertheless, by employing

288

the human senses in observing the universe, the being of God could be proven. By utilizing this methodology, he produced five arguments to support this conclusion. For him the most important of the five was the first which asserted that ane observed motion or change in the world. As he examined this phenomenon, he would discover that every instance of movement required a moyer. But it was impossible to carry this back ad infinitum.[4] Somewhere a beginning point would be reached, and there one must posit a being who was the source of motion but was himself unmoved. This mover was the cause of all change. He identified Him as God. In a similar fashion, he set out four other arguments - cause and effect; possibility and necessity; gradation; design.

Aquinas is universally recognized as a theologian. His influence on the Roman Catholic Church as a major creator of its faith is undeniable. He should, also, be given credit for his contributions to the rise of modern science. His proofs for the existence of God required that man open his eyes to the world around him. This experience could only lead to a rapid expansion of the methodology in gaining knowledge. A return to the world of physical nature was inescapable. No longer could man deny himself and turn away from world as essentially evil. On the contrary, observations would lead to the conclusion that all things therein were created by God and, hence, everything was good. For some investigators, it led to the presupposition that evil is not a positive reality but only the absence of good.

Medieval man was standing on the threhold of modern science although he would hesitate a long time before he developed enough courage to enter. The tremendous values which he found in the traditional ways were so great that he hesitaged to do anything which might jeopardize them or raise some doubt. How could one compare the worth which knowledge about the present existence would bring with that of God's own truth which He had unveiled to guarantee one's future destiny. Nevertheless, some did dare to venture out and eat the forbidden fruit. Oftentimes, they paid a tremendous price for their audacity. For many of them, there must have been a frightful internal struggle in addition to whatever penalties might be imposed on them by the authorities.

D. MODERN SCIENCE

A transitional figure appeared at this time in the person
of Roger Bacon(1214-1292), a major forerunner in the rise of
modern science. While his work was severely circumscribed
by his environment and the period of his labors, he did make
some salient contributions in several areas. First, he emphasized the importance of Aristotle for inquiry. He was particularly disturbed that teachers in his day depended on very
poor translations of the Greek thinker and refused to learn
Greek in order to produce a superior text. Second, he attached
great importance to experiences as the most valuable method for
gaining knowledge. He considered it especially superior to
deductive logic which was so widely employed in his day with
dependence on premises accepted on the basis of authority.
For him, the empirical process was superior to reason. He
has been considered as an investigator not too far from a
modern scientist. Third, he was in advance of his times in
recognizing the importance of mathematics for the scientist.
He spoke of it as the "alphabet of philosophy." Scientific
facts, to be most useful, have to be subsumed under mathematical principles. In this respect, he was anticipating the work
of Isaac Newton. Fourth, there is some evidence that he personally engaged in experimental work. He may have had a telescope. Burning-glasses were definitely employed by him. They
were used in his laboratory at Oxford. It appears that he
knew the principle of their manufacture. Eventually, the
University had him destroy them because of the attention which
he drew from the students. They would, in the eyes of the administration, waste their studying time looking through his
telescope and lighting candles with the burning-glasses. Moreover, he gave a fairly accurate description of the eye. He
prepared some work in goegraphy which may have been used later
by Columbus.

Unfortunately, he was a man so far in advance of his age
that he had to pay the price. Popularly he was considered to
be a wizard and magician; his works were condemned two years
before his death. As is generally the case, however, one may
interfere with an individual; but his contributions persist
and lead to their continual unfolding. Through his imaginative
insights there had been accomplished major steps toward the

introduction of modern science. His attitude was one which would elicit similar responses.

Many other forces were at work in the succeeding centuries to set the stage for the new era. To a greater or lesser degree, all of them had one ingredient in common, an emphasis on human experience. The Renaissance renewed an interest in the classics with the recognition of man as a creature of the world. Civil law gained significance over against canon law. The study of medicine was accelerated. Cathedral schools supplemented the monasteries as places of learning. Eventually, these institutions evolved into the universities; many of them exist to this day. In the fourteenth and fifteenth centuries humanism swept over Italy; from there it spread to other European countires. Art and literature flourished.

In the sixteenth century the religious movement known as the Protestant Reformation became firmly established. Initially, it was medieval in spirit. But its affirmation that man could achieve salvation through his own personal relationship with God gave that independence which would serve as the motivation for far-ranging forms of religion. It contributed substantially in providing the environment wherein modern science could flourished.

The foundation of modern science, and that which preceded its emergence, was mathematics. This discipline was extremely old, and it had been widely employed in serving a variety of goals. But it had been essentially limited to the practical affairs with an occasional use for moralistic and mystical purposes as in Pythagoras and Plato. The dominant motive which had guided man in his understanding of the universe was the view that everything which occurred was striving toward some end or goal considered to be good. The end might be in this world - the philosophical viewpoint; or it might be in the next world - the religious conception. Teleology provided the central perspective.

In this new era mathematics gained a more comprehensive status. In part, it was enlarged as a consequence of increasingly practical problems. Man began to be attracted to various technologies and investigated them from the standpoint of their

291

constituent natures in addition to their purposes. Especially
was he intrigued by the occurrence of motion. To be able to
understand this phenomenon by an exact mathematical description
facilitated the control of it.

Of greater significance, however, was the need for a more
dependable base for understanding the nature of the universe
itself. The traditional authorities were no longer universally
accepted. Among the many contributions of Galileo was the
fact that he raised questions about Aristotle. The latter's
predominant query was, Why? Galileo emphasized that it should
be, How? In this status of turmoil, with no longer any place
of refuge where certainty could be found, it was only natural
for man to renew his faith in mathematics. It had never been
discredited nor even called into question. Hence, it stood
firm when all other disciplines were collapsing. Gradually,
there emerged the basic and universal premise that the key to
the interpretation of nature was mathematics. To make this
assertion, however, was a radical break with the older and
prevailing assumption that teleology provided the best explanation for the universe.

By assuming the mathematical point of view, Copernicus
(1473-1543) was able to take the observed knowledge about
the universe (he is said to have added very little to the
known facts) and to work out a theory which was both simpler
and was more in accord with the evidence. Consequently, his
heliocentric hypothesis replaced the Ptolemaic principle
which had held securely for many centuries. Subsequently,
Johannes Kepler (1571-1630), through more accurate mathematical
calculations, corrected Copernicus by showing that the earth's
orbit is an elipse rather than a circle. Notwithstanding
this correction, the geometric constitution of the universe
remained intact.

The results of these scientific investigations were many.
The basic one was to affirm the dependability of the cosmic
order because it had to conform to mathematical principles.
Kepler asserted that the world was created by God in conformity with previously existing concepts. Hence, occurrences
take place because of necessity. Otherwise, they violate
the mathematical rules. Consequently, it can be stated that

292

the real world has quantitative characteristics only. Sensory qualities are only signs of the mathematical qualities. In this context, space or extension and time became the central categories in the intellectual quest. Knowledge had to be stated in terms of that which was extended in space and movable in time.

Galileo (1564-1642) participated in an even more exciting development. In 1608, a Dutchman, Hans Lippershey, had invented the telescope; but it was Galileo who made it into a useful instrument and employed it in his own scientific work. He made studies which supported the new astronomy empirically. It could then be said that mathematics and sensory experience conjoined to prove these positions. It was this methodology which made Galileo a danger to the entrenched authorities. Up to this time, the new ideas were interesting hypotheses which were arrayed against the older ideas. The latter had enjoyed a superiority since they conformed to the unaided sensory observations of the ordinary person.[5] A principal work of Copernicus had been published in 1543, but it was not placed on the Roman Catholic Church's "Index of Prohibited Books" until 1616, seventy-three years later.

Galileo himself was brought before the Court of Inquisition and forced to issue a statement recanting his approval of views set forth by Copernicus. The fundamental achievement of Galileo, therefore, was the formulating of the principle that truth must be ascertained by sensory observations and be mathematically measurable.

Herein, too, we find certain assumptions which support modern science. First, nature is a simple, orderly system whose every proceeding is regular and necessary, governed by "immutable laws which she never transgresses," and this order "of nature is fundamentally mathematical in character." It had been asserted by the Scholastics that God was a logician; the scientists insisted that He was a mathematician. Second, Galileo assumed that controlled sense experiences were valid. Third, he accepted the atomic structure of matter which had been proposed by Democritus and others among the ancient Greeks. Many of the transformations of material substances could be accounted for by this presupposition. In summary, he drew

293

from a wide range of sources in the intellectual history of
man to create a synthesis which would open the door to the
modern world.

A Frenchman who was a contemporary of Galileo, Rene Des-
cartes (1596-1650) was so captivated by the new direction in
scientific activity that he proposed to construct a philosophy
which would be suitable for explaining the whole of reality.
He was convinced that man had the faculties which could formulate a picture of all existence without resorting to the authorities. His confidence in pursuing his ambition was greatly
enhanced by the development which he achieved in mathematics.
By combining geometrical analysis and algebra, he was able to
create analytical geometry, a simplified tool for mathematical
studies. If reason could accomplish this feat, would it not
be possible to utilize this same faculty to embody all existence in a comprehensive pattern? He initiated his project
by the assumption that nothing was true unless it could pass
the test of reason. Through the uee of this technique, he
arrived at a description of the universe which was totally
mechanical. Everything occurred as a result of mechanical
necessity. He boasted, "Give me extension and motion, and
I will construct the universe."

The intellectual system which had emerged was accepted,
in its main features, by the educated men. Modern science
had become a viable reality. But its main thrust thus far
was a mathematical discipline. Some of the main contributors,
however, had seen possibilities inherent in the sensory faculties. Initially, the latter's primary function was to give
support to the conclusions which had been achieved by way of
reason through providing evidence from observations. It was
a stupendous gain since there now existed a dual source for
truths. Moreover, each sustained the other. It was only
necessary to firm up the empirical approach and adopt it in
conjunction with mathematical methodology as a complete system.

One individual who contributed substantially to the further development of securing knowledge by sense observation
was Francis Bacon (1561-1626). He proposed a philosophy of
empirical science and a method to implement this point of view.

294

That is, he would take the work which had been done by the scientists of his day and set out the general principles which they had employed. While his understanding of these efforts was less than complete and, therefore, his philosophy and methodology were unduly narrow, he did contribute substantially to the evolution of science. There was, also, a reflection of an emphasis from a much later period of time. He appreciated the good things of life and saw in the new tools the means to achieve them. He was seeking "that knowledge whose dignity is maintained by works of utility and power." He proceeded with his efforts enthusiastically, convinced equally that virtually everything which had thus far passed for knowledge was erroneous. The medieval studies had relied almost exclusively on accepted premises especially as they had been provided by revelation and church authority Deductive logic served to provide explication for these presuppositions. For example, the Professor of Philosophy at Padua refused to look through Galileo's telescope to see the satellites of the planet Jupiter because he could already prove that these bodies did not exist. How did he know? The divine number which God had employed in forming the universe was seven. He could point to numerous instances which made it an acceptable assumption, especially the importance of this number in the Bible. Therefore, only seven planets could exist. Deductively it was a valid argument. The reason for mistakes like this, says Bacon, was that the mind had lost its pristine purity. Let it recover its original nature, and it could move successfully toward gaining true knowledge. It could accomplish this task by establishing propositions not by argumentation but by observation of particulars. An inductive logic was needed which utilized the "evidence of the senses." Bacon contributed several proposals for this purpose.

First, when one starts out to study a problem, he should ferret out as many instances wherein the occurrence takes place as possible. The medievalists made their fundamental failure at this point. They were content to find a sufficient number of instances for their purpose and stop at that point.

Second, one should then find those instances where the phenomenon does not occur. Then he could compare these two situations - the occurrence with the nonoccurrence.

Third, a comparison should be made regarding the different degrees of occurrence - in some, more; in others, less.

Fourth, then comes the climatic operation wherein one seeks for some factor which is always present when the occurrence takes takes place and always absent when it does not. Further, this same ingredient may be found in greater or lesser degree, even as the occurrence itself varies.

Fifth, one is now able to propose a hypothesis, really a guess. That is, the evidence collected will probably suggest a possible solution. Mode than likely, several of them will emerge.

Sixth, at this stage the most decisive process is undertaken. The hypothesis must be verified. It must be determined by the most painstaking assessment whether it can be accepted.

One of the great weaknesses in Bacon's system was its cumbersomeness. He proposed that evidence be collected first. Were this method followed, a considerable amount of wasted effort would ensue. Further, one would be likely to omit some instances which could be very important. Consequently, modern science recognizes the need to start with both a problem and a hypothesis. Normally, this procedure will be used. At least, the hypothesis should be formulated as quickly as possible.

It would be Sir Isaac Newton (1642-1727) who would make additional contributions to the methodology. Perhaps the greatest of his many scientific achievements was his synthesizing of rationalism and empiricism. His general principles would embrace both systems of inquiry.

He urged that the first step in acquiring knowledge is to make observations. The materials gathered by this means should be carefully studied and analyzed. Then one should formulate some fundamental principle by which the items could be understood. Thereby he would have his hypothesis, a tentative explanatory idea. To make it more workable, the hypothesis should be stated in a mathematical formula. It would now be possible to predict what ought to occur. But the real test of the hypothesis must be arrived at only by experimental or observational verification. Even then, the general law must be considered as true only to the degree that verification has been made. That is, future studies may require either a discarding or a modification of the law of nature. There is, therefore, the concept of tentativeness which has major importance in modern science. Newton had succeeded in uniting philosophy, mathematics, and empirical science.

In his own scientific work, the law of gravitation, or the universal attraction of matter, became central. Through it, he was able to provide a basic principle whereby astronomy and physics could be unified by a science of mechanics. His discovery (also independently accomplished by Leibnitz) of calculus provided the tool since it produced a method for measuring curves and, therefore, the processes of changes in the world.

As a result of his work whereby the description of the universe could be made, there emerged a vast and harmonious machine which was governed by the same laws everywhere - celestial and terrestrial. Not only was the whole physical order comprehensible under one fundamental system; but, also, the past, present, and future were seen as united in a continuum. Whatever happens today is the effect of mechanical causation from the past; and the future can be predicted on the basis of what is established about the universe today. In other words, the universe is dependable. It operates according to set laws. We have arrived at a scientific determinism. If the physical universe is mechanized and predictable, is it not conceivable that the nonphysical has its own laws by which it is governed? Even religion itself must be radically changed so that what is required is a natural faith rather than a revealed one.

Thus, in broad strokes,we have attempted to trace out the quest for knowledge from the primitive period when man haltingly and uncertainly attempted to identify elements in his environment until the modern period when he has set forth a methodology capable of giving him an assurance that he understands the nature of reality in terms of its physical properties which possess the qualities of space and time and are, therefore, measurable. The term used to embrace this reality

297

is "matter." Instead of ends, goals, and purposes, as had been the older emphasis, now the scientist speaks in terms of what is and its quantitative characteristics. The fantastic advances in the physical sciences have been built on this foundation.

But, as so often happens, man achieves success in one area and is inclined to devote himself exclusively toward it or to bend everything to fit that particular mold. Hence, there is the trend toward reducing all experiences to measurable terms. For example, the physicist tells us that we see the color red when two million ether waves per second are striking the retina of the eye. We rate persons according to their I. Q. But is this the whole story of the universe? Science's own insatiable curiosity inevitable interposes an uncertainty. Perhaps there are phenomena which are not explicable by empirical observation and numerical description. At the same time, the conclusions about them will not be contradictory to the perception of the universe by physical science.

CHAPTER XX

RELIGION AND SCIENCE: PAST RELATIONSHIP

Religion has been the matrix within which most of our cultural values have originated and been nurtured. Science has been no exception. From the most ancient times to the recent past, with some notable exceptions, the leadership provided by religion has served to bring to man whatever knowledge he has achieved.

When one observes primitive man, he becomes aware of people who observed various phenomena and sought to understand them in order to exercise control. But these things were experienced as being possessed by, and operated through, spiritual powers. Hence, the shaman was the one who possessed the ability to elicit a favorable response. In his magical performances, the medicine man was the first scientist. He began the slow process of organizing human understanding of the universe.

Eventually, in the river valleys of Asia and Africa, man began to settle down and to develop a more advanced life. His success in economic activity provided a surplus whereby he progressed more rapidly. Again, however, it was religion which developed the institutions wherein inquiry was promulgated. In ancient Babylon the priestly control over life was extensive. The temples were large buildings located in spacious compounds where varied activities took place. Among the duties of the priests was that of teaching. They knew about the universe and transmitted this knowledge to their students. The accumulation of the understanding had been accomplished through the performance of their religious duties. For example, they served as diviners who could determine a person's fortune. Among the several ways for ascertaining the future was by examining the livers of sheep. Careful examination of the structure and markings for this purpose would provide the beginning in the study of anatomy. Even more important were the observations made of the heavenly bodies. While their motivation was astrological, they accomplished their work so well that they were able to plot the celestial bodies with remarkable accuracy. Thereby, the groundwork for the science of astronomy was laid. In these undertakings, they made great contributions to mathematics. As early as 2300 B. C. E.they were using the multiplication tables.

Advancements in science under religious auspices in Egypt were even more dramatic. Egyptian theology gave a theoretical basis for it. Thoth was considered to be the divine source of knowledge from whom was revealed understanding about speech, writing, building, and calculation. Indeed, he was master of speech, lord of books, and inventor of writing. Consequently, it would be in temples that education and research would develop. Here were astronomical observatories where the heavenly bodies could be identified. During the Pyramid Age, some great building enterprises were undertaken for religious purposes. The mathematical skills needed for the pyramids, which would serve as the dwelling places of the departed pharoahs, would be extensive. Adjoining these burial places, magnificent temples would be build. The study of architecture would be required. The total impact of these building operations on the furtherance of engineering skills was substantial.

Of equal significance were the studies made regarding the human body. The signal importance attached to life after death gave rise to the embalming of the corpses. The internal organs were removed and the interior filled with pitch and other substances so that the human form was preserved. This process, however, had great value for medicine. It disclosed the nature of the human anatomy. This branch of science accelerated as a result. Some knowledge concerning the function of the organs was achieved although substantial errors were made. Surgery developed, and from carvings which were dated about 2500 B. C. E. the actual performance of an operation can be traced. At the priestly schools, physicians were trained, bone setters were instructed in handling fractures, and oculists were prepared to treat eye troubles which were common in Egypt.

These several contributions to science were transmitted to Greece and, therefore, provided substantially for the advancements which were made in the Hellenic and Hellenistic Periods.

300

Ancient Persia contributed to the development of science
under religious influence. Its theology was characterized by
a rigid dualism. There was the good God and his realm which
were opposed by the evil spirit and his forces. As a result,
the prime aim of religion was to direct man toward undermining
the forces of evil. Animal husbandry provided one area. By
the breeding and care of useful animals one contributed to
those powers which would weaken the adversary. One cooperated
with the good God to overcome the kingdom of impurity. Proper
farming would accomplish the same objective. A great amount
of attention was given to enriching the land by diversified
farming and the rotation of crops. Both were considered
religious duties.

While the intellectual quest proceeded dramatically in a
variety of ways among the Greeks, the relationship of this
activity with religion was minimal. Both reason and observation were employed, but neither reflected a deep religious
conviction. Even in the Pythagorean school, a mystic brotherhood, the operation of faith appeared to have had only limited
relationship to its scientific contributions. At Epidaurus
and elsewhere the work of healing was performed under the
divine power provided by Aesculapius, the god of health. It
is interesting that the temples which served as sanitaria were
located at places which provided physical environments which
were in and of themselves conducive to human well-being.
Neverthless, there does not seem to have been any overt
recognition of this factor in the healing process. It would
probably have been considered sacrilegious to have attributed
recovery from illness to environmental conditions.

A. RELIGION AND SCIENCE IN THE EARLY CHRISTIAN ERA

In the later years of the Hellenic Period, as well as that
era inaugurated by Alexander the Great known as the Hellenistic
Age, science continued to advance. Gradually, however, two
factors contributed to the decline of inquiry. One was the
increasing dominance of Platonic philosophy with its emphasis
on rationalism. The other was the growing other-worldiness
which caused man to turn to the mystery cults with their
initiations in order to be guaranteed a blessed life hereafter.

301

When the Romans gained control of the ancient world, they contributed very little to the advancement of science. Their interests were in other matters. Moreover, it was during this period that Christianity began to influence the course of events. This religion was not characterized by a concern for this type of intellectual activity. While many converts to the faith knew and appreciated the life of the mind, their conversion experiences usually altered somewhat their emphasis on these issues. They might be detrimental to their relationship with God. There was the special danger that one would be turned away from the more worthy life of faith and might even become so prideful of his achievements that he would lose his sense of humility and commitment to God for salvation.

When the Roman Empire fell in 476 at the hands of the Germanic forces, a very considerable part of what was left of ancient learning, except Christian teachings, disappeared. Only a few scholars tended the flames of classical civilization. The monasteries became centers of education, but they devoted themselves to copying the Bible and the theological works.

During this period, another religion arose and moved swiftly to extend its sway over a sizable part of the world. While Islamic theology was no more hospitable to science and intellectual inquiry than Christianity, yet, in many of its major centers, a considerable amount of valuable work was accomplished. Most importantly, they preserved portions of the classical heritage. In addition, they pursued their own independent investigations. A monastic order known as the Brothers of Sincerity produced scientific treatises of merit and otherwise stimulated investigation in the natural sciences. One important tool for research was the Arabic numerals which they had secured from the Hindus.

During the medieval period some medical studies continued at Salerno in southern Italy. Part of the vitality of this center was apparently due to its contacts with the Muslims of North Africa. In the succeeding centuries, relationships were enlarged and the Arabic studies in medicine, including those which had previously been received from the Greeks, notably the works of Hippocrates and Galen, were received.

During this period, one of the most important moments was the year 1000. The Muslims had captured Jerusalem in 637 C. E. Then about 700 C. E. pilgrimages began to be undertaken by Christians to this holy city. Since the New Testament contained a number of references to the millenium, many Christians reached the conclusion that the return of Christ would occur in the year 1000 C. E. As this year approached, their interests in pilgrimages greatly accelerated. As a rule, the Muslims had been quite tolerant of this religious act. However, this period of increasing journeys to the Holy Land was marked by the conquests by the Turks, and in 1071 C. E. they seized Jerusalem. Gradually, considerable opposition to Christians and their pilgrimages was expressed. In response to these actions, the European nations developed a plan to conquer the Turks and to rescue the Holy Land from the "infidels." Peter the Hermit rode through northern France, barefoot and with bare head, carrying a huge cross, preaching with fiery indignation about the desecration of Christian relics and the defiling of holy places. Finally, at the Council of Clermont, in 1095, Pope Urban II summoned the faithful. He proclaimed a Truce of God whereby peace would be established among the Christians. He, also, offered a plenary indulgence to all who enlisted. Then he called for the people to go forth under the sign of the cross (Latin, crux). It was the beginning of that monumental undertaking, the Crusades.

While the basic objectives of the Crusaders were largely unfulfilled, other results did follow. Overall, it meant an opening up of communication between the Muslim and Christian worlds. Given this setting, one of the major contributions to what is called the Renaissance was made. From the Muslim countries came the scientific knowledge which had hitherto been missing in Christian Europe. While Christianity had been partly responsible for the decline in learning, now it was the cause for its revival. The church served as a medium in laying the foundation for the beginning of modern science although it would be centuries before its appearance.

As it has been noted previously, one of the great recoveries for Western Europe during this time was the work of Aris- with the emphasis on observation as a basis for reason. Ini-

tially, the most profound influence was in theology since the
Aristotelian methodology could be used to support religious
beliefs. Nevertheless, there were those, even churchmen like
Roger Bacon, who recognized a much larger possibility. The
tool was at hand for making observations about the universe
itself so that previously held views would be questioned.
These radical conclusions were rightly seen as undermining
the very concepts which the empirical method had established.
For example, St. Thomas had produced his five proofs for the
existence of God. But a necessary premise asserted that one
could not continue to infinity. There had to be a Prime
Mover, a First Cause, who was God. But this presupposition
holds only so long as one has a closed universe – the earth
enclosed by the celestial bodies with God at the outermost
edge. The Copernican astronomy, especially as corrected by
Kepler, described the planets revolving around the sun.
This projection required space wherein to move. The door was
being pushed ajar for a much vaster cosmology than had
previously been construed. "Though the implications of
the new science were not worked out immediately, it began
even from the first to be suspected that, if the theories
advanced were true, man had lost his birthright as the creature for whose sake all else existed, and had been reduced
to the position of a puny and local spectator of infinite
forces unresponsive to his wishes and unmindful of his purposes. . . . With the possible exception of Darwinism, there
has never been such a blow to man's pride, nor one involving
such a complete subversion of all his most cherished prejudices.
The war between the old and the new beliefs was long and bitter."[1] The medieval church responded with the Inquisition
and the Index of Prohibited Books. As a result, the men of
learning were inclined to reject the church and to move in
the direction of secularization.

B. THE BEGINNINGS OF MODERN SCIENCE AND ITS
RESPONSES TO RELIGION

One of those who contributed substantially to the new direction was Benedict Spinoza. His parents were Portuguese Jews
who fled to Amsterdam in order to escape persecution. Benedict
was born there in 1632. Eventually, after his heretical views
became known, he was excommunicated from the synagogue.

The setting for Spinoza's thought is the very basic one in religion. Man is in need of salvation. This necessity is the result of human nature as it strives toward goals which it considers to be good. They are the various objects which we set our affections upon. For the most part, they fall into three general classes: riches, fame and sensual pleasures. The outcome of our activities, however, is disappointment. On the one hand, we direct our efforts toward the achieving of some good; but it continually eludes us. On the other hand, we may succeed in reaching the object of our desire. The results here, too, are disappointing. Therefore, either the anticipated satisfactions are not attained; or, given success in the quest, there may even be pain which outweighs the good.

It was obvious to Spinoza that were the tradtional religious views about the universe true, these experiences should have been the exceptions if they were present at all. If a good God had created the universe for human fulfillment, it would be expected that man's cravings should have been satisfied. Hence, the traditonal theological concepts were negated by the realities.

Spinoza was forced to the conclusion that it is not human good which provides the basis for the universe but the inherent necessity to conform to universal law. Just as mathematics operates from the point of view of an absoluteness, the same holds true for all things.

The human predicament has occurred because of the failure to accept the fact that there must be sufficient cause to produce an event. Man's welfare has nothing to do with it. His unhappiness, brought on by disappointed desire, is his failure to adjust his desires, emotions, and actions to the objective order. To be sure, he occasionally experiences some delight; but these occasions result from the accidental accomodation of outselves to the natural order.

Having recognized the universe operates in terms of a fateful necessity, we are prepared to turn our attention to that which can truly respond to human needs for a dependable object of our affection, that which never fails to bring "continuous, supreme, and unending happiness." In terms of what has been discovered, it becomes apparent that man's failure to achieve salvation has been due to his ignorance. Consequently, it is only through knowledge that salvation can be achieved. We must come to know the nature of the universe, the essence of our desires and emotions, and the relationship existing between the two. It should be noted that Spinoza was insisting on the dependability of human intelligence, a confidence which could be supported by the assembling of that rational system known as mathematics. There is no denying that the human mind is finite; he recognizes and accepts the fact. Nevertheless, he continues up to that point where truths fail to be established with clarity and certainty.

Where is that object which one can turn to with confidence in its dependability? Actually, it becomes increasingly evident that it is that knowledge whereby we are seeking this good which becomes itself the most satisfying reality. As the very nature of the universe becomes revealed to us, we come to see that it is the knowing which emerges intuitively to stand forth as the most firm and permanent reality. Therefore, as we engage in this operation, learning what man's predicament is, how he craves for that which fails to bring him happiness, we discover that which pointed man to the error of his ways has an attractiveness which cannot be denied. As we increasingly devote ourselves to it, joy and a sense of enhanced power in relation to our emotions and to the environing universe are received.

In the initial stages of this experience, we have difficulty in responding very enthusiastically. In our ordinary patterns of living, our emotions are often worked up to a white heat of desire. In contrast, knowledge may appear pale, cold, and weak. Consequently, there is a temptation, which we can scarcely resist, to turn back to the old ways. If our attachment fails, we simply try another. But the same end confronts us, disappointed desire. Yet, if we "come to ourselves" and recognize that knowledge is dependable, that it never fails, we must become more firmly attracted to it. Our emotions will be transformed. Further, they will be continually supported. Every experience enhances its worth and none undermines it. Former attachments correspondingly dissipate. Finally, love of truth becomes the all encompassing force. Salvation is ours.

The importance of Spinoza for religion can be summarized in several succinct statements. Instead of a teleological universe, he substituted a necessary order; instead of revelation or reason supplemented by revelation, he proposed intelligence; instead of man as the center of the universe, he made him a part of reality; instead of man being dependent on divine grace as administered through religious instrumentalities, he made him self-reliant. Nevertheless, Spinoza was so nurtured in the religious traditions that he could still retain the form, if not the substance, of the traditional order.

Therefore, it remained for the empiricists to create a more radical and, therefore, devastating system of thought. One of the basic factors in this school is its epistemology since its total metaphysics is determined by it. It has been noted and emphasized that Aristotle established the philosophy of empiricism. In order to gain knowledge, one begins with experiences. They are stored up in memory and associated together by "common sense." Only then does reason enter in to provide the basis for ascertaining the ideas or forms which determine the nature of reality. Having said all of this, however, Aristotle gave little place to the empirical process. He simply did not see that it could contribute substantially to human knowledge. Little, if any, additional data could be provided. Consequently, he, like Plato, emphasized the importance of reason as the distinctive human faculty which enabled man to organize the materials of the universe into a systematically organized whole. The unique nature of human reason was that it must be a substance which came from outside man, dwelt in the body as long as the latter survived, and returned to the source of its being. Hence, it came from God and returned to be reabsorbed into deity.

In Scholastic theology, this theory of Aristotle, perceived as agreeable to the biblical record, was taken over. Man was composed of body and soul. The former was constituted of matter and executed the vital functions which we call life. The latter, however, was of divine order and performed a dual role without itself being composite in nature. On the one hand, it was seen as creative intelligence which functioned to apprehend the Good. Since it operated without dependence on the body and focused attention upon that which was immaterial, it

307

was spiritual in character and not subject to dissolution.
Therefore, it was immortal. Seen from another perspective, it
was regarded as will. Having apprehended the Good, there was
set in motion that which was designed to realize the object
of its prior quest. Since the supreme Good was God, the
real function of the soul was to seek after God as the everlasting enjoyment. This factor, too, required immortality.

In Protestant theology, a somewhat similar point of view
was asserted. But, following St. Augustine, it was argued
that man had inherited the nature of Adam and dominated by
sin. Consequently, man was incapable of gaining a clear
perception of God. Without this vision, the will moved man
to persist in sin. The only solution was the grace of God.
If it was granted to the human soul, the latter could perform
its prescribed task, that of leading man to the blessed life
where he would be freed of the inhibiting nature.

It would be John Locke (1632-1704) who would set forth the
psychology for the modern empiricism. The traditional position stated that the mind contained ideas which were common
to all people. This view would be necessary if the concepts were universal. Under Aristotle's theory, for example,
a person may observe the phenomena. But he had the faculty
which enabled him to rise above the particular experiences
to the forms which served to explain them. Another person,
however, would proceed in the same way and arrive ultimately
at the same results. It could be concluded, therefore, that
the universal ideas were in all minds.

Locke denied that there were the general ideas present in
all minds. They simply did not exist. Rather, ideas differed
among various persons based on their own experiences. He concluded that the mind, at birth, was a blank writing tablet,
a tabula rasa. By virtue of empirical observations, there
were imprinted the ideas which the person possessed. These
experiences might be either sensations, that is based on external observations, or reflections, which are introspections
engaged in by the mind concerning its own content. Further,
there can be combinations of these empirical data. But the
content of the mind is derived entirely from the experiences
of the person rather than being composed of ideas from another

source. It was obvious that this theory had tremendous implications for religion.

For several centuries, there had been an increasing tendency
for man to be accepted as the determiner of truth. A compromise
was made by some scholars with the older preeminence of revelation. They asserted that there was a two-fold way to truth,
reason and revelation. Each pursued its own course in the discovery process. It was generally agreed that should there be
conflict, revelation took precedence over reason.

Another position, more generally accepted, held that reason
could be used up to a point. Then it had to be supplemented
by divine knowledge found in the Bible and in the teachings of
the church. Rather rapidly, however, reason was accorded an
even greater position of authority, especially as it was supported by mathematical achievements. With the reintroduction
of empirical observation as the ground of truth, it quickly
gained increased attention. The most radical theory, that
of John Locke, defined the soul itself as a tablet upon which
had been inscribed human experiences. With the trend toward
the domination of the intellectual scene by empiricism, there
would be raised the inevitable questions about religious ideas.

It was David Hume (1711-76) who explored the full implications of this methodology for religion. Starting with ordinary experiences, he identified the observation as an impression. It would be followed by an idea. But what is that
item? It is nothing more than a copy of the original impression presented by memory or imagination. Was the idea
true? To answer this question required a return to the original impression in order to compare the two. Obviously, this
action is impossible. The method which we usually follow is
to put the idea in juxtaposition with a present impression.
If they correspond, we say that the idea is true.

This theory was directed first against the mathematical
science of that day. It had contended that there is a necessity accorded to occurrences. Events happen because they must;
there is a necessary causality which assures that a particular
effect must follow. By utilizing the procedure, the general
laws of nature had been formulated. To be sure, Newton had

insisted that the laws were tentative. Additional knowledge might require a reformulation of the principles. Nevertheless, the corrections could be made without destroying the underlying assumption that every effect had to occur on account of a particular cause.

Hume denied this assumption of causality. If we observe the cause-effect relationship, all that we can find are two features. First, the two items are contiguous; second, the cause precedes the effect. But an examination of any event does not disclose necessity. The law of gravitation cannot assert that the apple must fall to the ground. Obviously, the idea of necessity was a reality. Not only was it held to be true in popular thought, but it was commonly accepted even in scientific circles. Therefore, there must have been something which gave rise to the idea, some experience which produced it. The idea, says Hume, grows out of a regularity observed in the cause-effect relationship. That is, every time the particular cause has been present, the effect has followed. Night has always followed day. From a series of these experiences, we have concluded that a particular effect must follow a particular cause. Then we reach a more fundamental principle that every cause <u>must</u> produce a certain effect. But the source of the necessity is in us, not in the cause-effect relationship. Next time, the apple might not fall.

A scientific law, therefore, does not describe a necessary and universal relationship to the objective world. It is, rather, a summary of certain regularities which we have observed up to the present time. We suppose, but we do not know, that they will hold in the future. Consequently, it should be kept in mind, modern science operates on a basic assumption. It is that given a cause-effect relationship, as established by empirical observation, it will continue to operate in the future since the future will be like the past. Therefore, it is possible to predict and even to control occurrences. Were this assumption not supported, modern science would be in shambles. Of course, this premise actually rests upon an even more fundamental presupposition, namely, we live in an orderly universe or, more simply, we live in a universe with appropriate emphasis on this word

310

itself. Actually, Hume does not really disagree with this analysis of science. His concern is that the assertion of causal necessity as a metaphysical principle is unacceptable. There is only a psychological necessity. What he does, in reality, is to establish the scientific principle of tentativeness on philosophical grounds.

This rigorous application of empiricism does not have serious implications for natural science. But Hume does use it with devastating results in the area of religion. Three major ideas are examined. First, there is the concept of miracle. Traditional Christianity, both Catholic and Protestant, had relied on miracles as providing a major support for the supernatural origin of the faith. Both groups could rely on the biblical narratives for those who accepted the sacred scriptures as divinely revealed. Under Scholasticism, Roman Catholics had sought to establish the view on rational grounds. First, it could be proven that God existed and that he had certain characteristics, especially that of love. Then man was proven to be a divinely created soul which lost its original nature by sin. Since he had his major objective to achieve the eternal Good or God, the condition of the soul prevented him from attaining his fulfillment. He stood in need of assistance which could come only from that divine being who was the embodiment of the power which the soul required. Since God had been proven to be one who loved his creatures, it would be inconceivable for him not to have proferred to man this divine help. Consequently, God had intervened by divine revelation to show man a way to salvation. But how can man have confidence that this revelation is of divine origin? Somehow God would have had to vouchsafe its authenticity. He accomplished it in two ways. First, there were the predictions which had been fulfilled. Both Catholics and Protestants agreed as far as the foretelling in the Old Testament being fulfilled in the New Testament. The latter added a further dimension in asserting that predictions in the New Testament were attained in the Roman Catholic Church. For example, one of the most disputed passages is the following: "And I tell you, you are Peter, and on this rock I will build my church, and the powers of death shall not prevail against it. I will give you the keys of the Kingdom of Heaven, and whatever you bind on earth shall be bound in heaven, and

311

whatever you loose on earth shall be loosed in heaven."[2] Then
in chapter 18 there is substantial material bearing upon church
membership including in vv. 15ff. the procedure for absolution
and excommunication with a repetition of the power vested in
the church with these words: "Truly, I say to you, whatever
you bind on earth shall be bound in heaven, and whatever you
loose on earth shall be loosed in heaven."

The second supportive basis for the genuineness of God's
revelation was in the performance of miracles. Again, it is
in the nature of God as love which would have prevailed on him
to intervene in the normal operations of the universe which
he had created. This intrusion would have been brought about
for the expressed purpose of substantiating the genuineness
of this revelation. Christian Fundamentalists assert that
without miracles the Bible would be only a book of ethics.
But as a disclosure of God's redeeming love, supported by the
evidence of supernatural events, it becomes a way of salvation.
Therefore, both Roman Catholics and Protestants depended heavily on these phenomena as grounds for the verity of the Christian faith. Remove them and it would collapse.

The early pioneers in modern scinnce, especially those who
proceeded along mathematical lines, could only reject the notion of miracles. The mathematical structure of the universe
made a necessary order which could not allow for variations.
Copernicus and Kepler would have had great difficulty with
the statement in Joshua 10:13: "The sun stayed in the midst
of heaven, and did not hasten to go down for about a whole day.
There has been no day like it before or since, when the LORD
hearkened to the voice of man; for the LORD fought for Israel."

The problem was quite different for Hume. For him there
was no natural necessity. A law of nature is nothing more
than a summary of observed regularities whereby we come to
expect future repetitions. Therefore, the very notion of
miracle is an impossible idea. The ordinary person might construe some event as miraculous. From the empirical perspective, it would be just an occurrence which was different than
that which had been experienced previously. If this type of
event were observed, the law of nature would no longer be tenable. The scientist would have to restate it so that it would

provide for the exception. Actually, this procedure has been the course of scientific development. Laws of nature have been formulated. Then subsequent experiences have required that they be modified in order to account for variations. The law may still be generally operative and, therefore, have high probability. Neverthless, it would be less than absolute, and one would anticipate additional exceptions. More to the immediate point, Hume insisted that it is impossible to have a direct observation of a miracle.

From this vantage point Hume examined the so-called miracles which were adduced to demonstrate the divine origin of Christianity. First, we do not have a direct experience of them. Roman Catholics are on firmer ground at this point since they contend that supernatural occurrences have continued in the church, even in recent times. This assertion is especially true as it relates to divine healing. The shrines scattered throughout the world attest to God's continuing ministry. In more recent times the church has taken great care to confirm that cures claimed to be miraculous are, in fact, true works of God. That is, not everyone who comes to Lourdes and proclaims a healing will have it acknowledged by the church as a miracle. Nonetheless, there is the conviction that God's power is still manifesting itself in the church. Protestants have been less than clear on this point. The purpose of miraculous activity, it is asserted, is to substantiate God's revelation. For them it is found only in the Bible. Consequently, post-biblical miracles are not required. Pragmatically, to accept them would add strength to the Roman Catholic Church since it has a long history of these events. If later supernatural acts were acknowledge, it would be difficult to reject the claims made by the Roman Catholic Church that it is the sole channel of God's dispensation. Nevertheless, there is the problem of prayer and God's response to these petitions. Does not the Bible promise that He will hear and answer when man calls upon Him? A person who is ill may seek divine help and may claim a miracle. Even doctors have acknowledge the occurrence of them. The Protestants may respond that there is a difference in that what transpired was in the tradition of the individual priesthood of believers. Therefore, the event took place in the person's own discrete relationship with God; it was not within the church. This factor has been

313

one of the reasons why some Protestants have expressed conster-
nation regarding faith healers. Since the latter are parts of
the institution, the miracles become church events. But, in
more recent years, traditional churches have enlarged upon this
type of service.

Hume directed his attention, however, to biblical miracles.
The empirical approach requires one to go back to the original
experiences. Obviously, this action is impossible. We are
restricted to an assessment of the records which describe these
past events. It is true that accounts of happenings in the
past are accepted. Should we not likewise believe these religious narratives? There is great difficulty, however, since
they are contrary to all of his regular experiences. For example, in our experiences, if a person dies, he stays dead.
We have no report of any exception. Yet, the Bible tells us
that Jesus and others died and returned to life. Hume could
not state that it was impossible for this event to have occurred.
Therefore, he could only conclude that it was improbable.
Certain factors justified this position. They had to do with
the accounts and the persons who made the reports. He proposes
certain questions which should be asked. First, was there a
sufficient number who reported the event independently? Second,
were those who conveyed the information men of good judgment,
education, integrity, and sound judgment? Third, did they
have anything to gain by falsehood or deception? Fourth, did
the events happen publicly so that records could be checked?
Fifth, was there any way whereby probable analogies could be
drawn between the ancient miracles and our own experiences?

When these questions were directed to the biblical miracles,
Hume concluded that one arrived at a high degree of incredi-
bility. Religious fervor frequently tends toward unreliabili-
ty. Accounts of this nature emerge and are preserved and transmitted in order to establish some religious movement. Finally,
different religions set forth and utilize this same kind of
testimony. The Christian religion does not have a monopoly
on miracles. Why not accept the authorities in other faiths
who convey accounts of supernatural activities?

On the whole, then, Hume concludes "that no testimony is
sufficient to establish a miracle, unless the testimony be of

314

such a kind that its falsehood would be more miraculous than
the fact which it endeavors to establish." That is, his argument shows that "a miracle can never be proved, so as to be
the foundation of a religion."

In his consideration of the belief in God, it should be
insisted that he was not trying to prove the nonexistence
of Him. That effort would require an affirmative proposition
and support   by empirical evidence. Hume cannot be classified as an atheist but an agnostic or sceptic - a distinction
which is very often not made by theists. His sole concern
was to demonstrate that the accepted arguments which had
been presented were unsupportable. If one wishes simply
to believe in God, his argumentation is meaningless. The
basic notion involved in this concept, going back to St.
Thomas and ultimately to Plato and Aristotle, involved the
idea of causality. There was a general acceptance of a basic
presupposition that every effect must be accounted for in terms
of a sufficient cause. Now in the universe we experience a
multitude of effects for which we can identify the causes.
Therefore, it would appear that there is ample supportive
evidence for the assumption. Then it was proposed that the
universe as a whole was an effect. In that case, there must
be a sufficient cause which is called God.

Hume begins his rebuttal by asserting that this idea of
First Cause is both logically and empirically unjustifiable.
The latter holds because man cannot produce the evidence
presently to support the causation of the universe. More
importantly, however, is that the explanation is unnecessary.
The universe is composed of a number of effects and each has
its own appropriate cause. The whole is simply a composite
created by the mind out of those individual occurrences. To
explain the whole independently is simply not required.

In fact, however, this notion of First Cause is meaningless.
As he had noted previously, cause and effect are contiguous
That is, two events have to be related in time so as to provide a cause-effect identification. In the particular instance,.
the universe is called the effect produced by the cause, God.
In fact, we have experienced only the former. Observations
has not presented God to us as creator. Therefore, it is im-

315

possible to say whether the universe is cause or effect. It can only be identified as that which exists. To speak of it as an effect is, consequently, to state a meaningless proposition.

But suppose we accepted the universe as an effect. What would it disclose about the cause? Ordinarily, we would examine the cause-effect relationship and determine what there was in the former which produced the latter. As a philosopher of science, this approach was Hume's perspective. He was interested to determine that which was responsible in order that it might be predicted and controlled. In this instance, however, the task was impossible. The phenomena of the universe were so varied that it was difficult to select one property as true of the whole. A commonly held concept identified the universe as comparable to a vast machine - like a clock in its regularity and intricacy. Therefore, the First Cause was thought of as a great clock-maker, a world-making intelligence. Yet, in our ordinary experiences of intelligence, the latter would have its own causality. Simply put, the question emerges, Who caused God? If we think of intelligence, when applied to God, as possessing different qualities than we ordinarily attribute to mind, then the notion becomes meaningless. We have introduced a whole new term. Therefore, from an empirical point of view, proofs for the existence of God and the determination concerning his nature are severely weakened if not totally destroyed.

The third religious proposition which Hume proposed to examine from the standpoint of empiricism was the immortality of the soul. The belief in the continued existence of the person after this present life is well-nigh universal. Is there any proof drawn from human experiences? For the most part, we must answer in the negative. That is, the grave closes the door on the human quest for proof. Yet, the idea persists. What is its source? First, religion has set forth, from different perspectives, that there is a being characterized by perfection. But, in the second place, there is the realization that there is this imperfect world. Surely, there must be another realm wherein the fullness of God can express itself, not only for himself but also for those who are his obedient worshippers. In that next life, they will be able

to participate in an incomparably rewarding existence so that
God's nature can be completely experienced.

Or we may see it from another point of view, the notion
that this God is a just being. Therefore, there must be another realm wherein the scales of justice can be balanced,
where the wicked will receive their just punishment and the
righteous will enter into their appropriate rewards.

It should be observed that this expectation of immortality
rests upon the existence of God. Previous examination has
shown that empirical evidence which has been adduced to support this theory is tenuous. Furthermore, what evidence is
there that there is perfection, including justice? Do we find
it here and now? If we do, then there is no need to seek for
it in another life. Should this desired condition not exist
presently, how can we look forward to it elsewhere? Again, we
are left with no substantive grounds to stand upon.

Hume has taken the fundamental concepts of religion - God,
miracles, and immortality - and has concluded that empirical
evidence for them is lacking. Here he leaves the matter. No
attempt is made to redefine or to seek for other empirical
bases. It would remain for others who sought to meet his
scepticism to accomplish this task.

One of the most certain affirmations which can be set forth
is the unpredictableness of human beings. There continue to
be surprises concerning man's reactions to different occurrences.
The history of modern science reflects this situation. The
Copernican revolution, especially when these earlier theories
had been confirmed by empirical evidence, should have elicited
a loud outcry because it presented a world view which dislodged
man from his central position in the universe surrounded by
the protection of a creative and loving God. Apparently, it
did not occur. It is worthwhile to note that the Bible teaches
the flatness of the earth. Moreover, this belief had been held
by the church through the ages. For example, St. Augustine
argued for this position since the Bible does not refer to
races which are supposed to dwell on the other side of the
earth. Yet, the new astronomy did not call forth any substantial number to engage in a vigorous defense of the prevailing

317

point of view. The penalties and restrictions imposed by the Roman Catholic Church undoubtedly kept the ideas out of general circulation especially since education was still a religious monopoly.

By the time the empirical methodology had established itself, the authority of an all-powerful institution had been severely curtailed in most European countries. Nevertheless, Hume's philosophy, with its destructive examination of long held religious beliefs, apparently elicited no popular opposition. One factor which may have contributed to this lack of hostility was the dynamism which characterized this period. Man was on the move by participating in new adventures. Capitalism was emerging, politics was developing democracy, and diverse Protestant sects were being formed. As a result, the philosophical and scientific emphases supported a tremendous confidence in the human capacity to reach its own successful fulfillment. The idea of progress was the guiding motif. The spirit of optimism was widely prevalent. Given this type of perspective, it is not surprising that Hume's arguments concerning the existence of God would not be particularly disturbing. The deity could be eliminated or, as was the more common position, subordinated to a position of only being the creator of the universe. It left man as the one who stood forth as the central reality in existence.

In the nineteenth century, however, another branch of science attracted attention. It was biology, the study of living forms. It was to make its own contribution to the spirit of naturalism. One of its most distinctive contributions to this outlook was the theory of evolution. Initially, its import was in this specific area of biological species. Eventually, it provided a general theory of reality. In the meantime, however, it was to evoke a decisive change in the relationship between science and religion.

Actually, the theory of evolution was simply a continuation of the preceding intellelctual development. Organic life, with man as its culmination, was a naturalistic explanation similar to Copernicus' theory about planetary movements. Further, it gave support to the optimism created by the idea of progress since it projected new possibilities for human

318

achievements through the evolutionary process. The idea that the"fittest survive" meant that the future held tremendous possibilities for an ever improving creature.

Three factors, however, served to awaken opposition. First, there was the idea that man had evolved from lower forms of life. This backward look, as contrasted with the futuristic notions which had been the scientific approach of the earlier schools, proved to be upsetting since it tended to remove man from his lofty pinnacle. Traditional religion, of course, found this assertion particularly disturbing. The universe had been created by God; and most importantly, the latter had proclaimed, "Let us make man in our image, after our likeness; and let them have dominion. . . ."[3] This account which depicted the exalted origin of man was considered to be infinitely superior to one which had him sharing a common beginning with all living creatures of the earth. In fact, he was described as originating in the primeval slime.

Secondly, and even more disturbing, this theory stood in obvious conflict wihh the Bible, God's own revelation to man. Hume had simply expressed doubt about the accounts of miracles. But he had not sought to put something in their place. Hence, his scepticism simply stood over against the believer's confidence in the narratives; its lack of affirmation could be brushed off with relative ease. The evolutionists, on the other hand, had presented a novel and independent account about creation. Now there were optional explanations. One was forced to choose. It was Darwinism set over against the Bible. But man does not like to be put in a position where he must select among alternatives, especially when some well-established view is contested by a more recently articulated idea.

Thirdly, and most devastating of all from a religious point of view, there was the empirical evidence presented to substantiate the evolutionary notion. The idea of evolution had an ancient vintage since it was developed in the days of classical Greece. Heretofore, however, it had been only a theory which one could accept on the basis of rational arguments or reject with counter reasons. It was simply one point of view opposed by a different one. In the new contest, Darwin had collected substantial evidence to undergird his theory. If it were to be rejected, one would have to accomplish this feat by the same method. What empirical evidence could the biblicists provide to support Genesis?

The evolutionary theory marked a major turning point in the intellectual quest. Not only did it achieve a positive reception in biology, but it opened the door to a much more comprehensive picture of the universe. As it received wider acceptance, other areas of study found that it offered an attractive explanation for their spheres of investigation. Astronomy, geology, psychology, and sociology began to be presented in evolutionary terms. For example, institutions originated in order to meet human needs. It was even applied to religious societies. Therefore, beginning with primitive forms, more complex and higher types of institutions have evolved.

Furthermore, this idea placed the Bible in the same mold. It was not some divinely revealed disclosure of God's plan for salvation but a record of man seeking after the Divine so as to find Him in that frame of reference where human needs are met. To those in the Christian faith, the biblical record unveils the characteristics of God as one with superior qualities so that they continue to challenge human beings. But this provocative account must be expressed in terms which are applicable to man's predicament as it may be expressed in any particular time or circumstance. In other words, the vitality of the Christian faith lies in its ability to form a religious life in terms of the ideas in the Bible not as finalized absolutes but as a creative process which finds implementation in man's continuous evolvement. To put Christianity in some form of a strait jacket, as has been often attempted, is to deny the very essence of Jeuss' own teaching. He said, "I came that they may have life, and have it abundantly."[4] Since life is constantly in a state of flux, the Christian ideals must provide a resource which is capable of responding to the human yearning as it changes from one generation to another.

As the evolutionary principle became more widely authoritative, some new directions of science posed severe problems for religion. Some groups had been able to effect a compromise with Darwinism. They were willing to grant that there had been physical evolution which meant that the human body was not exempt from this process. It could be claimed that it was simply the method by which God had carried out His creative role. Darwin himself had suggested this position. When the body had been properly prepared to receive it, God created the human soul. Hence, there was still a direct act of divine creation. This contention, however, ran contrary to the position asserted by the thoroughgoing evolutionists. They saw the soul as having been the culmination of the evolutionary process. First, there was inanimate substance; second, there was life; and, finally, there was the mind or soul. The latter was simply another ingredient whose function contributed to adaptation and survival.

In the latter part of the nineteenth century, there developed the new science of psychology. As a part of philosophy, the study of the mind had been as old as the latter discipline. Now it sought to utilize the empirical method in order to arrive at a more exact description of human thinking. One of the many schools of psychology was behaviorism. It is usually identified with the name of John B. Watson (1878-1958). The evolutionary theory stated that the mind had come into existence in order to effect a greater ability to survive. The behaviorists followed this point of view with the idea that the mind should be studied on the basis of its behavior. Thereby, it would be subject to the ordinary observations of empirical science and described by its mathematical movements. Every form of mental activity was seen as involving stimulus and response. Stimuli which are external to the brain made an impact which elicited some observable reaction. For example, it had been shown that different parts of this organ controlled separate areas of human activity. Memory was conceived as the accumulated impressions which had previously been made in the physical nervous system. Even thinking was a form of pre-verbalization; that is, certain physical reactions of the larynx occurred which did not issue into speech. The conclusion to this study was to present the mind as a physico-chemical body, subject to the same principles as these two sciences had found in other materialistic phenomena. In other words, the mind was considered as a computer before there was this mechanism.

321

Obviously, this school of thought sent shock waves among most religions and elicited very vigorous responses. Since the mind was identified as simply another part of man's physical composition, it reduced him entirely to a materialistic being with no place for the traditional beliefs in God and immortality.

A later and more influential school of psychology was associated with the name of Sigmund Freud (1856-1939). His earlier studies were devoted to nervous diseases. By employing hypnosis, it was often possible to discover causes for mental disorders and, by bringing them out in the open, to provide cures. Subsequently, it was found that patients could be induced to disclose many forgotten facts and their connection with present difficulties. Usually, these experiences from the past had been painful. Therefore, they had been repressed. Since they retained their dynamic character, they had sought some substituted outlet. Many of these unfortunate experiences had occurred in childhood. It was later learned that dreams disclosed valuable data since they were disguised fulfillment of repressed wishes.

It was recognized that these studies had religious implications. Beliefs embodied the satisfaction of unconscious wishes. They give an account of things which we desire. Faith is a product of the heart, and the beliefs of the religious man are the fulfillments of the deepest desires of the soul. For example, the psychological basis for the belief in God is the childhood sense of dependence on the father. This attitude is composed of a two-fold experience of the father. On the one hand, the father is loved because he provides for and protects the child. On the other hand, he can become angry and punish. As the person grows to maturity, he finds that nature has the same two-fold composition. Therefore, he begins to invest this external power with features of the father figure. In other words, he creates God. Religion was not an attempt to explain the world. It was an effort on the part of man to adjust himself to the world. It was a very practical affair. Ht served human needs. Freud, therefore, asserted that religion was unnecssary in this period of modern science. The latter provided a more certain base for responding to the order of reality.

Another student in this area, Carl Gustav Jung (1875-1961), saw religion as embodying that which is highest in man. But the importance of both men is that they described religion as a psychological or emotional phenomenon. It was not an intellectual order. Their influence has been substantial in that they stimulated the religious organizations to examine faith in terms of meeting man's deepest needs and highest aspirations.

C. THE CURRENT RELATIONSHIP BETWEEN RELIGION AND SCIENCE

Against the background of history wherein the development of modern science has occurred and its association with religion has been determined, a concluding statement is in order to assess the connection which currently exists.

The previous relationships and interconnections are continuing. Many institutions wherein scientists pursue their work, both theoretical and practical, are oriented to, and supported by, religion. While substantial projects are now funded by the government and developed in secular institutions, the contributions of ecclesiastical organizations cannot be minimized. While a few of them place some restrictions on science, because of some concepts embodied in their faith, their opposition is very limited. In general, scientists are not only free to engage in their research but are encouraged to do so. The general principle of academic freedom is widely accepted. While violations do occur, they are more often the result of other conflicts than those between science and religion. Moreover, federal and private grants would usually preclude interference.

There is an even more important factor which supports a close relationship between science and religion. It is the fact that many scientists are dedicated churchmen. They have had close relationships throughout their lives and have participated activily in religious affairs. Other persons in this field of endeavor may no longer have a present attachment, but they have maintained their religious heritage to the extent of continuing to hold to its major precepts. Surveys have been made which confirm that many scientists do

not reject to any great extent the religious understanding of
the universe. These studies have generally indicated that the
scientists who are the most distinguished express themselves
more affirmatively concerning religion than do those individuals
who are not rated as highly.

In general, it can be said that the conflict between science
and religion, as it may continue to exist today, is actually a
striving between parts of the same groups. Some religions reject
some scientific findings or may even be disposed to take a negative attitude toward science itself because of the particular
areas of disagreement. On the other hand, some scientists do
not look favorably on religion. No longer, however, can a general statement be made that there is a conflict between science
and religion. The assessment has to be made in much more restricted terms.

Some differences of attitude concerning this issue can be
observed between Roman Catholics and Protestants. The former's
position has generally been that science will be accepted within limits. But these limits cannot be transcended. When it
does so, it is pseudo-science. In particular, it means that
the findings of science cannot dispute the dogmas of the church.
But, in practice, this church has been able, slowly and de-
liberately, to discover means to reconcile the two areas
when disagreements have first appeared. One of the functions
of the learned men in the church is to seek for ways to enlarge
the understanding of both science and religion so as, if possible, without undermining theology, to harmonize the two. One
particular advantage for them is the fact that they recognize
the Bible can be interpreted by nonliteral techniques. From
the most ancient times, allegorical interpretation has been
permissible. It means that the divine word is often found by
seeking the spiritual meaning of the text. This factor has
precluded many problems.

Historically, the spirit of freedom, which has been a main
principle of Protestantism, has contributed to the encouragement and support of science. It has established an environment wherein inquiry could flourish. It continues to make
this contribution. Like Roman Catholicism, however, too often
its teachings have become so firmly established that it is dif-

324

ficult to adjust when new knowledge requires it. As a result, there has been a vigorous, and sometimes vicious, opposition to scientific findings. The factor which has contributed most seriously has been the literal interpretation of the Bible. It has been a major tradition in Protestantism. On the whole, allegorical interpretation is unacceptable although there are some instances when it is acknowledged. For example, the Bible describes the earth as flat. Very few literalists from any faith insist on this point of view today. Aside from the theory concerning evolution, the most persistent difficulty concerns the miracles of the Bible. While some Protestants have produced understandings which have solved some of the issues, other members of the faith, demanding a literal reading, have refused to follow this form of analysis. The former group, for example, may suggest that the resurrection of Jesus was a spiritual experience of the disciples and others. The second segment vigorously rejects this interpretation and asserts that the rising of the Lord was in a physical body.

It is obvious that there are still areas of disagreements between science and religion. Each has difficulty with certain positions held by the other. But the conflicts are less intense today than in an earlier period. It can be anticipated that the future will witness a continuing diminution of the tenseion. It can be hoped that each side will recognize the values of both and proceed toward a more creative synthesis.

CHAPTER XXI

COORDINATION OF RELIGION AND SCIENCE

Religion must be interrelated to human life in the latter's total dimensions. Historically, the viable religions have accomplished this end by responding to the issues and concerns which were most pressing at the time. They have operated within the context of the most dynamic forces which were shaping the lives of the people. At times, it has, perhaps, been too compromising with these instrumentalities. Nevertheless, it would have been impossible for it to have made its contributions without following this procedure.

This description does not mean that religion has simply adjusted and conformed to the processes to which it was exposed. Rather, it has sought to bring its truths to bear upon life as it was being lived in terms of the determining forces at the time. In fulfilling this general place in society, religion has assumed the most varied forms, structures, programs, goals, values, and meanings.

The history of Christianity has provided substantial evidence for this procedure. Its strength has been due to its ability to respond and to adapt to new challenges brought on by the manner whereby human living was carried out. Consequently, from the beginning, there has been the most varied expressions of the faith. Even though some groups were considered to be false to the truths supported in the mainstream and were excluded, they have continued for a longer or shorter period of time to be viable representations. Even more importantly, they have left an indelible impact on the so-called orthodox sector. The latter may have rejected the positions considered undesirable, but many features of the heretical groups have been retained. As a consequence, it is doubtful that any form of religion which has been found in human history has not been similarly expressed at one time or another in Christianity. It is probably not incorrect to say that Christianity is whatever one wishes to identify by this term. In terms of its existence, it is a comprehensive term. Or,

in the context of Roman Catholic theology, the mortal sin is
to deny the faith.

It is against this background that we see the great challenge in the twentieth century. This period is the age of
science. Unquestionably, this discipline, either directly or
indirectly, is the most determinative influence in human living
in every dimension. Consequently, if religion is to be meaningful and effective, it will have to do so in this sort of
world. It must carry out its role decisively and without hesitation by accepting this fact. Otherwise, it becomes irrelevant. The people of this period are those who have been nurtured in this understanding of the universe. Their outlook
on life has been formed largely by this approach. Their understanding is so scientifically oriented that any presentation
from a different perspective can scarcely be comprehensible.

At the same time, it should be recognized that science alone
is very inadequate in meeting human needs. The greatest danger confronting this age is human confidence in the ability
of science to fulfill life completely. If one seeks to follow
this world view completely, he becomes severely limited in his
apprehension of, and response to, the universe. Meaningless-
ness and purposelessness, conflicts both personal and interpersonal, become the characteristic features with the ultimate
end being a deterioration of human values and an inevitable
loss of individual and social identity. When this occurs,
as it has in the past, the cry of man is for religion to enter into the situation and to extricate man from his own predicament. Consequently, instead of religion being needed less
today, it is more correct to assert for it an even greater
importance. Yet, to be effective, it must respond to the
needs of man where he is, a creature living in an age when
science is the basic factor in experience. The need is for
a coordination of the two. Neither can accomplish the requirements alone.

A. WHAT SCIENCE CAN DO

1. Science can supply a methodology for apprehending. Modern
science makes its most comprehensive contribution at this point
since its tools for inquiry can be utilized in the total realm

328

of human experiences. Even religion can utilize this approach in its own quest for truths. In point of fact, it does so extensively. The real quarrel is not with science. It has proven itself to people generally by the fact that they have given recognition to the many accomplishments which have been achieved by this method. The knowledge explosion in the past several centuries is overwhelming. Further, there is no expectation that there will be any cessation of this process in the ensuing years.

The basic principles, to be distinguished from the particular techniques of investigation, are very attractive. First, science stresses objectivity. Studies are made with the understanding that the evidence will be examined without bias. No effort will be made to force the exploration to bring forth a predetermined result. Consequently, all studies are made with the understanding that the entire operation will be open to public inspection. This means that the scientist must state his problem carefully, set forth the hypothesis or hypotheses which will guide his work, give a full description of the methodological techniques which will be employed in the inquiry, and, finally, subject his conclusions to the most exacting appraisal. All students recognize the exceptional value in this mode of operation. In the natural sciences, there is an easier setting for objectivity since the investigator is focusing attention on natural phenomena toward which he can maintain a greater detachment and independence. In what might be called "people studies," there is is a lessened possibility for this approach. The problems themselves are more complex, less easily measured, and subject to strong proclivities in the one direction or another. But these factors make the scientific contribution of even greater worth since there is the ever-present insistence that objectivity must be sustained.

Associated with the preceding principle, there is the assertion of science that all the evidence must be examined. It is probably this factor which has been a major contributor to the continuing expansion of knowledge. In actuality, there is scarcely any area, no matter how narrowly it is defined, where one can, in fact, fulfill this stipulation. Too many items simply are not recognized as having potential input into the issue at hand. Consequently, the investigator explores the problem as fully as it appears to him. He encompasses every feature which comes within his purview. Subsequently, however, there is the strong possibility that he or someone who is attracted to the issue will discover some other matters which had not been previously considered. Some data may not have been incorporated in the investigation; a different set of circumstances may have been overlooked; new tools or methods for the investigation may emerge. The requirement for a complete investigation contributes substantially to the enlargement of human knowledge.

A third principle of the scientific method which proves to be immeasurably helpful is tentativeness. There can never be any finality. A truth is temporal. It exists only as long as it is not swept away or altered by new evidence. In the advancement of the intellectual life, this notion has been most advantageous. It has meant that man has not become tied to some final or absolute truth. Rather, there is every expectation that new understanding will occur. He is made sufficiently felexible so that adjustments can be made without traumatic experiences. A person who depends upon some infallible dogmas finds it exceedingly distressful when they are called into question. The one who is scientifically oriented both accepts and welcomes new insights even though his previously held ideas are no longer tenable. It should not be thought that the latter individual has no firm truths. On the contrary, he bases his understanding on conclusions which have been adequately confirmed. He will hold to them unless and until they have been shown either to be false or that some other truths have stronger support. Furthermore, his own continuing search for verities provides more than an adequate supply whereby he can live his life confidently and enthusiastically. The problem with the dogmatist is that too often he is so limited in his views that any threat to his positions provides a real menace to his sense of serenity.

Finally, the person who follows the scientific method must be a humble person. On the one hand, he surveys the past and observes that the view of reality has been both highly restricted in its content and viable only for a particular age. For example, he studies the philosophy of Aristotle, one of the really superior students of all times. Nevertheless, it is

330

all too easy to recognize his foibles and mistaken points of view. A Copernicus could revolutionize the picture of the universe; nevertheless, his studies had to be corrected by Kepler. Consequently, the man of science must be willing to accept his own limitations and humbly admit that his successors will undoubtedly amend, to a greater or less degree, his findings. Even more, this person must stand humbly before the vast universe and its monumental problems which are unsolved. As he looks to the future, be can only conclude that the discoveries yet to be made will, in all probability, stand out so far above human findings up to his period of time that future generations might consider him as having lived in what is tantamount to a dark age. Under these conditions, how can science not compel one to stand and express the deepest and most genuine humility?

2. The second achievement of science is the comprehension of reality which it projects. Both the macro-universe and the micro-universe are very much better understood as a result of modern science. While, as previously stated, its very success in disclosing the nature of things points up the vastness of the mysteries not yet unveiled, the grasp in every area of existence is so much greater today than ever before that no one can really question the value of this methodology. By rigidly insisting on empirical evidence, it has projected studies forward with an intensity which has not failed to produce immense results. It has made man more comfortable with his environment because his ignorance of things, which tends to arouse fear, has been relieved somewhat.

Further, the universe is seen as a whole. The discrete parts relate together within a systematic unity. All parts of the natural order are interconnected and, even, interdependent. There is a natural balance which has to be understood and maintained. Science has shown that a new movement in one direction brings a counter movement in another. Human life may be extended through medical science, but the resulting population explosion taxes the resources which are available. Industrialization improves human living, but the pollution which it creates may destroy him. Science has made possible urbanization, but accompanying this phenomenon has been the emergence of social problems of great magnitude. Gradually, the realization of this problem is beginning to demand that it be given attention.

Nevertheless, the comprehension of the universe has been so substantially enlarged that man can proceed much more steadily and confidently even in the face of the enormous unsolved problems. He has a tool which provides him with the means whereby he can pursue his course.

Third, over against the general understanding of the universe, which is theoretical in composition, modern science has made its contributions to man in the practical areas, what is sometimes called applied science. Particularly in the modern period, and especially in the western world, this sector of science has become so predominant that many would mistakenly equate it with the whole field. The lives of all people are affected to some extent.

The two major ingredients are new tools and new sources of energy. These things have so radically transformed our lives that without them we would find it exceedingly difficult to continue. The current energy crisis has brought this issue to our attention in a most insistent manner. When the Arab embargo brought a shortage of gasoline, the reactions of Americans were predictable. Very little was done to find alternate means of movement. Perhaps a few found a solution in walking to some of their destinations; other individuals may have secured a bicycle; a limited amount of car-pooling was accomplished; and some persons turned to public transportation. Most people, apparently, used their ingenuity in securing fuel for their own vehicles. They waited in long lines - literally, for hours; some employed other people to do the chore; gasoline tanks were not allowed to get very low in the amount of fuel; and, evidently, many people violated the law by paying higher prices. Our lives have become so substantially geared to technological science that we are certain that whatever problems may arise, men of science will solve them. We are constantly being reminded that the future for mechanical civilization is not very promising. But it is difficult for these dire warning to be believed. Part of the problem lies in history. The danger signals about some coming hardship have been raised in the past. But the vexing issue

has been solved or disappeared. Not only has the unfavorable
consequence not materialized, but the predictions have served
to stimulate new endeavors which have made additional improvements in the human condition. Therefore, we reason, we shall
overcome again. But the dangers which are being projected are
of such magnitude that it is difficult to see how they can be
fully surmounted.

The achievements of practical science have been accomplished
in four major areas. First, tools and energies have provided
relief to man from arduous toil. What was formerly performed
through personal hands and muscles is now accomplished by mechanical devices operated through physical power from some non-
human source. Second, the length of human life has been extended to the point that it has more than doubled in a relatively
short period of time. The health sciences have really performed miracles. Third, physical comforts have been provided
for this period of longevity. Food, clothing, and shelter
are remarkably superior to comparable products from an earlier
period. Even an ordinary person in the United States enjoys
amenities today which previously would have been luxuries for
the few. This statement is not intended to minimize the deprivation experienced by an all too large group of people even
in the United States, not to mention persons in other parts
of the world. Fourth, technology has provided man with a
vast amount of leisure time and devices which provide the
means whereby it can be enjoyed.

B. LIMITATIONS OF SCIENCE

Modern science has made so many fabulous contributions to
mankind that it is often forgotten that there are severe limitations which it must recognize. First, it is dependent in
the realm of premises. All knowledge, however it is secured,
requires that some assumptions be made. Certain basic principles have to be understood and accepted at the very outset
of an inquiry. This factor becomes even more important in
any systematic quest for understanding since the conclusions
reached are given a very firm credence. In the modern age
of science, the methodology has become so firmly entrenched
that there is a danger due to the fact that its findings will
be accepted without hesitation. But the whole system is no

more firmly grounded than are the preconceptions upon which
it rests.

Premises cannot be proven scientifically. The scientist
can examine and explore the dimensions of them. In all probability, he will have engaged in this process somewhere in his
investigative work. But, fundamentally, these first principles are set forth from a philosophical or rational perception. It is the philosophy of science which essentially provides supportive bases for the investigator. This discipline
is not unrelated to the whole field of philosophy. Since
there are different schools of philosophical thought, diverse
principles about the nature of reality obviously have considerable bearing on the scientific endeavor. While many of these
differences are matters of emphasis rather than diametrical
opposition one to the other, nevertheless the influences upon
the investigator can be considerable. What the scientist experiences will be governed substantially by his philosophy.
One who adheres to a materialistic perspective will observe
things rather differently than an idealist. The direction of
the research will be especially affected by his stance. For
example, one researcher will see existence primarily in terms
of matter while another will observe matter from the standpoint of the uniqueness of the human self.

There is no finalized group of assumptions which is universally accepted but some of the more basic ones are generally
recognized. First, science would be impossible unless it were
accepted that the universe is understandable. Man can scarcely engage in any type of inquiry unless he has confidence that
some comprehension is feasible. Even though he has many disappointments and errors are all too common, he does not give
up because he is certain that persistence will succeed in providing him with knowledge that is dependable. The nature of
the universe precludes a final failure in his efforts. This
confidence is not a blind belief but is based on the accepted
accomplishments which have been made. In the final analysis,
however, it cannot be proven; it must be accepted as a given
principle.

A second presupposition is that knowledge is based on experience. Generally speaking, the scientist defines this

334

concept rather precisely to mean that which is subject to sense examination. A person may set forth a hypothesis as a step in the exploration of a problem based on whatever grounds he wishes to propose. But the final determination of truth can be arrived at only when supportive sense data have been presented. It should be noted, however, that this evidence does not have to do with the thing itself being directly sensed by the investigator. Considerable empirical evidence may be adduced to support some conclusion about something which is beyond direct observation. Especially today, the sophisticated tools available to the scientist enable him to examine areas of the universe which cannot be directly observed. For example, no one has seen a virus. Nevertheless, a considerable amount of knowledge about this form of existence is now available. The basis for this apprehension is empirical evidence.

Third, the scientist accepts the reality of an existence beyond the person. The world which is observed is a real world. It is not a mirage. The latter may be experienced, but it can be distinguished from genuine reality. Hence, the scientist approaches his task with confidence that he is not engaging in some halucinatory operation.

Fourth, to some degree, all scientists accept the concept of causality. Every effect is produced by a cause. Further, the same cause will produce the same effect. In its extreme form this perspective produces a completely deterministic system. Not all scientists today carry the idea to this limit, especially in the area of biology. Here the concept is modified by ideas of potentialities, becoming, and novelties. Even more general, there appears to be some indeterminism in the universe as a whole.

Fifth, following upon the preceding premise, it is generally held that there is a predictive uniformity. When one has discovered the relationship and interconnectedness among certain events, these same processes will hold in the future. In spite of Hume's denial of necessity in a cause-effect relationship, this point of view is an essential one for the modern scientist. Actually, this presupposition provides the primary motivation for his work. There is a desire to control the universe and an assured confidence that it can be accomplished

335

to a considerable extent. Failures only serve as incentives to make another attempt.

The second limitation under which science operates is in the area of value. Theoretically, it is neutral with respect to this issue. How a particular item will be labeled, whether good or bad, science as science cannot answer. Its operations are limited to examination, discovery, revelation, and description. It is quite incapable of determining worth. This factor is very important since some question of value will have already been considered before the scientific operation has been initiated. The scientist will be doing his work with some preconceptions and predispositions about this nonscientific query.

But this consideration sets forth a very important point in this type of investigation. The person who is engaged in the study is more than a scientist. He is a human being dominated by the varied complexities which characterize other persons. The essential nature of man is to be one who evaluates. This factor has led some students to question whether there can be any really objective science. An inquiry has already been partially determined by the nature of the investigator and especially by his sense of value. The latter will have exercised some influence in his recognition of the problem and the subsequent proceedings to solve it.

After the atomic bomb project had proven to be successful, there was an awareness that a hydrogen bomb could probably be made. But there was some delay in initiating the research. Some of the principal persons involved, led by Dr. Robert Oppenheimer, opposed the project. They recognized that great devastation could be accomplished and wondered about the propriety of the undertaking. Recently, Joseph Alsop estimated that probably ninety-five scientists questioned the desirability of proceeding.

At the same time, growing out of the delay, there was raised the question as to whether there was some sinister plot in the foot-dragging which occurred. Even today, the military hawks look upon these individuals with disdain. They are certain that they should not be entrusted with making policy decisions of this nature.

336

But the issue points up, again, that a scientist is first
of all a human being; and this factor has substantial influence
even in his scientific endeavors. As was the case of the hydrogen bomb, once the value question has been resolved, the
scientific methodology is followed. It becomes a dispassionate
search for the answer to the problem at hand.

The third limitation has to do with ends or goals. What will
be done with a discovery? Again, science cannot answer. The
question reverts back to the more comprehensive nature of man.
Herein will be found the basic purposes which will substantially
influence the scientist. We often hear about something "whose
time has come." This phrase suggests that without some meaningful context wherein something can effectively operate, it
is valueless. Science has undoubtedly made many discoveries
which had to wait for a period of time before they could be employed. It is not inconceivable that new insights have been
made before their contributions to man could be recognized
and were, as a result, lost forever. The laboratory is the
place where the research is undertaken. When the solutions
are achieved, they must be brought out onto the scene of human living to find their proper roles in the world.

We live in a world today which is very frightening since
instruments of destruction of very great magnitude are available. Yet, this same modern energy, if some of the baffling
difficulties can be overcome, has the potentiality of usher-
ing in a new day for mankind. It is the question of ends.
Recently, India joined the so-called "nuclear club," thereby adding to the threat to the continued existence of humanity.
But the government of that country went to great lengths in
trying to quiet the fears by insisting that the scientific
success would be employed for peaceful purposes. While it
is doubtful that many people took any comfort in these
assurances, the reponse is indicative of the importance attached to purposes.

Fourth, science is dependent in the realm of the relationships to other areas. In its ordinary role, it is highly
restricted. The most obvious limitation is set by the scientific method itself. Only that can come under investigation
which is subject to empirical verification and is capable of

337

being expressed in exact, that is, quantitative terms. When one attempts to reach beyond this point, science has to bow out and allow other disciplines to take over. There is an isolation in this field. But there is simply too much to the universe to think that science can give all the answers. Water can be analyze into two parts of hydrogen and one of oxygen. But what does this information contribute when one turns to an entirely different world where Jesus says, "I was thirsty, and yo gave me drink?"[1]

Notwithstanding the accolades we have given to science, there is a sense in which it has performed a disservice to mankind at this point. It has emphasized glowingly, and with understandable pride, its tremendous accomplishments with the result that there has been a trend to look with disdain on other fields of inquiry. Students in other areas have been put on the defensive to uphold the worthiness of their disciplines. Further, there has been too often a lack of support for these other investigations. Even now, most research money is allocated to scientific investigations. Consequently, there is an almost inevitable shrinking of life. This approach receives a most complete acceptance in the modern world, and mankind is the poorer for it. The very sickness of our society has been, in large measure, created by the domineering role of modern science. It has become so pervasive that one is almost ashamed to acknowledge interests other than those which embody the sciences. But, surely, we can recognize values, ends, purposes, goals, beauty, justice, love, mercy, interpersonal and group accomplishments. These domains do not fall within the province of scientific inquiry. The actual determination of life's resources in those areas is quite beyond its techniques to explore. Science can tell us that the sun is 93,000,000 miles from the earth, but it can say nothing with respect to the beauty of the sunset.

C. FUNCTION OF RELIGION

Therefore, we come to a final concern, the relationship of religion and science. First, religion today cannot and should not deny the role of science. The latter has so thoroughly established itself in human experience that to attempt a rejection is both futile and foolish. Furthermore, there are many areas of accomplishments which are not alien to the spirit of religion. Actually, the latter has given consideration in its own way to the same quest for knowledge which modern science is doing today. The latter has simply established itself so firmly in its own operations that religion would be foolish to reject the results. For example, biblical cosmology cannot be preferred to the picture of the universe which is now available to us.

Then, too, the scientific methodology can be employed in religion. Its approaches are not without value in pursuing religious questions. Surely, the studies in this area can be appropriately investigated from the standpoint of scientific impartiality. Tentativeness is a quality that is not restricted in its usage.

But the acceptance of science and its methodology does not necessarily require a similar attitude toward the results of science. The history of this discipline should give pause in this regard. Most obviously, scientific conclusions which have been arrived at on some earlier occasions have been either disproved or seriously challenged in later periods. Further, many findings of science are not accepted by all experts in these areas. Consequently, the mere assertion of a scientific position with supportive evidence does not, in the slightest, mean that there is any necessity to give assent.

At the same time, when there is disagreement, religion must give argument on common ground with science. The response to these discoveries must utilize the empirical methodology. Otherwise, the two disciplines operate in separate areas, and there is no communication between them. Science presents its results based on the observable phenomena and grounded on the hypotheses which underlie the intellectual quest. Should religion wish to pursue its search for truth in these matters by using a different method, it has the right to do so. But its results should not be set over against the conclusions derived scientifically and assertions made that the former are correct and the latter are false. Neither can science follow this approach relative to the religious assertions in its own field and applying its own method. In these instances, it would be two separate and independent operations.

339

One could choose between the two whichever was most appealing. Unfortunately, this approach is not usually followed. As it has been demonstrated by the controversy in the evolution dispute, religion asserted the truth of Genesis over against Darwin. In more recent years, there has been a greater effort by supporters of the biblical account to examine it through the techniques of empirical science. Interestingly enough, the gulf between it and the scientific position has been significantly narrowed.

There is another approach which religion might properly take. It would involve the assertion of a sceptical attitude. Since science cannot assert finality, it is certainly not inappropriate for anyone to express doubt concerning some of its findings. This standpoint is a far different one than a categorical denial. Herein lies the difficulty with religion's response to Darwin's theory of evolution. There was a decisive rejection of it because of its contradiction to the accepted biblical tradition. One was confronted with the necessity of choosing between two views set forth as diametrically opposed one to the other.

Suppose, however, the response had developed along this line. Darwin had followed in an ancient and long tradition in the presentation of his theory. Many individuals throughout the centuries had been attracted to it. Unlike his predecessors, however, he has utilized the modern scientific method in his investigation. Hence, he has relied on the discovery of empirical evidence to support the explanation concerning the origin of living creatures. He was quite successful in discovering a substantial amount of supportive data. His theory has been widely hailed as a scientifically proven hypothesis.

We in the religious world are equally impressed by the thoroughness of his work. Nevertheless, our traditional confidence in the Bible as the Word of God forces us to pause in our acceptance of his results. His explanation at this point appears to be totally incompatible with the narrative found in the book of Genesis. This factor puts us in an uncertain position. We are quite aware of the accomplishments which have been wrought by science. At the

340

same time, we know that many scientific explanations are not
sustained and require either a rejection or a revision. Therefore, we reserve our judgment.

Moreover, the rise of this problem has motivated us to examine very carefully the several sides of the matter. An examination of the evidence which Darwin presented may disclose
some weaknesses. It may even be possible to demonstrate that
it is untenable. The Genesis narrative, too, will be reconsidered to see whether it can be supported in the light of the
current scientific ideas.

This type of approach could have been very salutary. It
would have provided a real service to both science and religion.
Most importantly, it would have avoided a general spirit of
animosity whereby too many people in religion think of science
as atheistic and scientists often label religion as obscuran-
tist. For adherents to religion who have moved ahead to adjust to science, there would have been avoided the embarrassment over the bitter confrontation in the earlier period.

The real contribution of religion to science is a positive
one. It must seek to exercise its influence so that the scientific enterprise will not lose a basic perspective. The fundamental characteristic of religion, the centrality of human
personality, must be constantly asserted. Science will have to
be constantly challenged with the perception that everything
which is done should have as its basic motivation to enhance
the status of man. There is no place for any inquiry which
is not ultimately man-centered. This factor is an especially
important one as a result of the limitations which characterize
all endeavors. Priority must be given based on the potential
contributions to the fulfillment of human development.

It should be hastily added that no religious group nor any
similar body should be given any independent authority in making these decisions. But it is not only appropriate but the
duty for men of faith to maintain a continuing interest in
science and to express judgments about its operations. These
assessments will sometimes be mistaken. Oftentimes, it is very
difficult to see initially what human values can be discovered
through some investigations. Furthermore, it is all too easy

341

to have a limited view about the universe so that many great insights of immense value can be missed. Even having recognized these shortcomings, there is no area of life which can have so valuable an impact in guiding human affairs as religion. Its words must be uttered and its voice heard, even in science.

NOTES

N O T E S

CHAPTER I

1. Eccles. 1:2.

2. Religion very often provides opportunities of this nature as will be indicated later.

3. The need for some form of dualistic explanation involving the presence of an evil spirit as the most appropriate explanation has not been too appropriate. It has really produced another deity although the religion inherently denied this possibility. Eventually, the basic deity became sufficiently enlarged so as to accomodate the way of life which was being followed. By that time some new directions had been sighted, and new paths laid out for human experiences. Consequently, the evil power was still there to perform his deceptive work.

4. What has usually happened in the past, when the established religion has become decadent, is that scepticism has resulted. But the number of individuals who would be in a position to express this point of view would be limited. Further, these individuals ran the risk of being persecuted by the established religious order or even the political organization.

CHAPTER II

1. Cf. Ruth Benedict, Patterns of Culture. New York: The New American Library of World Literature, Inc., 1934.

2. One of the unfortunate characteristics of our society is the fact that we operate as a right-handed society. All the rules of etiquette are so designed. Fortunately, we have discarded the practice of trying to force the child to change his mode of handling objects when he is inclined to be left-handed. Perhaps, in time, we shall learn to adjust to this phenomenon in the total experiences of life.

3. Sometime ago Leonard Bernstein devoted one of his pro-

grams to an analysis of modern music of the popular variety. Through the eyes of his expertise, one could perceive the possibilities for some of it becoming a permanent accretion to our culture.

4. I hesitate to use the word "peace" since it tends to convey a notion of finality in one's orientation to life, and this position is categorically denied as being possible.

5. Actually, what is being described here as a forthright form of religious determinism has been followed indirectly in the past history of the several religions. Unfortunately, the inclination to assert final and irrevocable absolutes has made the task a more tortuous one. It has been necessary to make some rather abstruse delineations from the standpoint of interpretation in order to extricate a position from a no longer tenable stance. But the accomplishment has been wrought nonetheless and that notwithstanding the fact that institutional pressures have frequently been heavily weighted against the change. In the last analysis, the social structure has been revamped, if necessary, in order to do what had to be done.

6. Mt. 5:15f.

7. Ps. 34:8.

8. The decline of influence emanating from religious institutions has been observed. It may well be that what we are seeing is the change in the process of these social forces. In an earlier day, they could impose their will from the standpoint of the great fears inculcated. Today, however, these fears are largely absent.

CHAPTER III

1. In a study made in 1975, it was found that Americans had become so disillusioned that they could not identify those who might be considered as statesmen.

2. The cynic has been quoted as saying, "The church was sent forth into the world to do good, and in the course of the centuries it has done very well."

3. Cf. 1 Cor. 5:10.

4. Judg. 21:25.

5. Judg. 7:20.

6. Mk. 10:45.

7. The biblical story concerning the conflict of Abraham and his nephew Lot gives a very striking account of a group which had become too large. Gen. 13.

8. It has been stated that during recorded history only 248 years have been without war.

9. For the past quarter of a century in America, we have witnessed the eruption of considerable racial discord. The basic cause appears to be the fact that the Black population has not been given the requisite freedom so as to relate to the American society. They have been repressed educationally, economically, politically, and socially. On the other hand, when demands are made that Americans abide by the laws, pay taxes, serve in the armed forces, make economic purchases, and otherwise participate in the affairs of life, the burden imposed on the Black citizens has been substantially heavier than that on other parts of the body politic. Consequently, they have been objects of oppression on the two sides of the social order. Finally, by sheer grit and determination, some of these people have secured a sufficient know-how and motivation to bring the people to an awareness of their deprivation. A slow and painful evolution has become operative. After having broken some of the barriers, it appeared to some that more forceful and revolutionary steps were required. While many gains have been achieved far more rapidly than would have been possible otherwise, the costs may prove to be very great for the full Americanization of the Blacks. Antipathies have been built up which may take many years, or even generations, to eradicate. In many respects, this development is quite ironical. Many historians see in the American Civil War one of the most unnecessary and destructive conflicts in human history. The evolutionary process was already moving toward the emancipation of the Blacks long before the outbreak of hostilities. Given time and patience, the gall of slavery would have been removed. But too many people were impatient. The result was that a form of sectionalism came into being which has continued for over a century to be an impediment to the development of an American culture. It is tragic that the Blacks were a major

347

factor in the first instance; and now we see them again at the center of this latest episode.

10. The twentieth century has seen the divergent religions in America - and to some extent in the world - working feverishly to achieve that form of religion which will be expressive of the American way of life. Conceivably, it is possible that some form of union among the major religious groups could take place. Seemingly insuperable hurdles have appeared to stymie this process. Nevertheless, we do observe an underlying oneness in the general nature and function of religion in this country. It grows out of the interacting among the varied groups with the inevitable influence of each one on the other. This creation will be accelerated by the fact that an increasing number of our professional schools of religion are losing their unique denominational features. The subjects studied, the contents mastered, the description of the function of religion are similar wherever one studies.

11. One is inclined to question the strategy of Khruschev in removing Stalin as one of the idols of Russian Communism. But the problem here, as in traditional religion, is that it is sometimes difficult to transfer the sense of adoration of a person from the past so as to meet the demanding needs of the new era. One may call Jesus "Lord" and do not the things which he commanded.

CHAPTER IV

1. Modern technology has lessened substantially the importance of these factors. For example, Japan is very limited in resources for industrial productivity. Nonetheless, it has become one of the major nations of the world in this area. Similarly, irrigation projects have transformed deserts into lush agricultural regions. In a more positive sense, however, we see in these matters influences determining culture. The control of petroleum by certain countries will contribute a closer correlation among countries with the inevitable cultural interactions. In the western part of the United States the control of rivers is having repercussions in our relationships with Mexico.

2. Roderick McLeish, "Youth in Dissent: Rebellion or Renewal? The Reader's Digest, XCII, 553, May, 1968, p. 79.

348

3. It has been suggested that the reason for the success of the American Revolution was the fact that the leaders subordinated passion to thought, serious thought to political principles and institutions.

4. Gen. 4: 1-16.

CHAPTER V

1. The discovery of the Tasaday in the Philippines has been an exciting venture for anthropologists since these people appear to have been living their lives totally isolated from advanced societies.

2. Mt. 12:25.

3. Mk. 8: 36.

4. It may be worthy of note that there are encouraging signs that this operation is being carried forward with an ever increasing acceleration. Increasingly, men and women are given positions of leadership in the religious communions only after they have received substantial training in various educational institutions. Further, there are more and more efforts being put forth to update the training periodically. Of course, the facilities which are now available for a continuing enlargement of the affairs of men are more widely available than every before.

5. 1 Cor. 1:14.

CHAPTER VI

1. Lk. 12:52.

2. Mt. 7:26f.

3. One of the attractive features of the Salvation Army is to be found in its motto, "A man may be down but he is never out." The work which this organization does among the outcasts of society can be based only on an extraordinary appreciation about the inherent worth of human personality.

4. Among groups of this type in the United States, the amount which is contributed to the organizations will be substantially greater per capita than among other religious bodies.

5. A newspaper recounted tha fact that two college professors, husband and wife, had committed suicide. A note was discovered which explained the basis for the action. It seems that they had asked the question concerning a reason for existence and could find none. The only appropriate response, therefore, was to eliminate themselves.

6. Lk. 6:39.

7. Mt. 5:13f.

8. It may well be that a share of the blame must be placed on those who do have an appreciation for knowledge. They have been "motivated." Why is it that this same incentive cannot be developed in other individuals? Oftentimes, we try "gimmicks." What is needed is an understanding of what can develop within people an urge to engage in that area of life which many people find so very interesting and desirable. Many individuals think that we live in a very fascinating world with all the features of its physical and social composition. There is an insatiable thirst for greater knowledge. Yet, there are those who shrug their shoulders at the very mention of something more than the score of the latest ball game. It would seem, therefore, that a greater effort ought to be given to the search for that which instills this desire for knowledge.

9. It has been said that this attitude is found among many students in our schools and colleges. One simply does not want to be identified as a superior student lest it incur rejection by his peers.

CHAPTER VII

1. Gen. 3:7.

2. The Greek story of Pandora's box involves essentially the same implications.

3. Jn. 18:38.

350

4. Modern logic, with its emphasis on symbolism, has made the operations of these rules more flexible and has enlarged the scope of their application.

5. See Chapter XXI for a discussion of this problem.

CHAPTER VIII

1. Acts 17:22.

2. It is not too difficult to see a strong similarity between this point of view and that which is described in the parable of the Prodigal Son. Even the slave in the house of the father was in a more enviable position than the son in his present status.

CHAPTER IX

1. Mt. 5:48.

CHAPTER X

1. When the tribal chieftain reached the age when he had served his people as long as he was capable, he was sometimes executed. The power had to be transmitted to someone else who would be able to sustain the group. The individual life really was of secondary importance.

2. 1 Sam. 13:8ff.

CHAPTER XI

1. Since this statement was written, the United States Supreme Court has reestablished legal grounds for the death penalty and, thereby, made the state and its citizens into

murderers. Moveover, the act is the most reprehensible type, premeditated.

2. This area will be more fully discussed in Chapter XV.

3. Some business men have stated forthrightly that they would prefer to engage in business relationships with one who was not a Christian rather than the person who did identify himself with this faith.

4. This problem is handled most vigorously by the apostle in his Corinthian correspondence. To see the two positions most effectively contrasted one with the other, one should read I Corinthians 11-12 and, then, follow with I Corinthians 13.

5. It should be noted that morality itself has been subjected to a very devastating attack as an area which can be examined from the standpoint of the scientific method. Logical positivism has asserted that ethical statements are unlike factual statements. For the latter, one looks for evidence which will serve as proof for their truth or falsity. In the instance of moral propositions, however, there is no evidence. Rather one has simply given his attitude toward a particular virtue or vice. These are emotional expressions which can be subjected only to psychological examination.

CHAPTER XIII

1. It may be suggested that we have reached a stage in technology which poses the possibility that man will again become subject to new forces. The devices which he has created seem oftentimes to be bent upon enslaving the creator.

CHAPTER XIV

1. It is worthy of note that the total wealth of American churches has been estimated to be greater than the combined

worth of American Telephone and Telegraph Company and the five
largest oil companies.

2. For example, it has been noted that about one billion dollars in Protestant pension funds have been invested in corporations doing the bulk of American military production. Since
these figures were published, however, some efforts have been
made to dispose of these investments.

3. Davida Crabtree, "The Order of the Day." United Church
Herald, March, 1970, p. 8. Copyright A. D. Used by permission.

4. Slowly emerging is a technique which immediately is even
more alarming; it is terrorism. Civilization is so exposed to
the sophisticated tools which can be used that one wonders if
it can be stopped.

CHAPTER XV

1. On a recent radio program, it was noted that welfare recipients have developed a practice of reporting the nonreceipt
of their checks with the result that duplicates are sent. Then
they cash both of them. Naturally, there has been a loud outcry as a result of this revelation. Were this form of theft
to be eliminated entirely, however, the amount saved would
amount to only a few thousand dollards. At the same time, it
was stated that studies have shown that the fraud perpetrated
by retail establishments in such things as giving short weights
runs into the millions. The general attitude, however, is a
shrug of the shoulders with the old advice that the buyer
should beware. In a sense, it might even be commendable since
it can be considered to be good business provided one does not
become apprehended. Is it surprising that our society is
manifesting a rapid deterioration of simple honesty and personal
integrity and a total unconcern for the other person?

2. Gen. 25:29ff.

3. Mt. 16:26.

4. Hos. 8:7.

5. Mt. 23:10-12.

6. "No one will be saved outside the church."

7. "In spite of all differences, Baptists and Roman Catholics have much in common," declared a Roman Catholic scholar while addressing a group of Baptist seminarians.

8. Von Ogden Vogt, Cult and Culture. New York: Macmillan Publishing Company, Inc. Copyright 1951 by Von Ogden Vogt. P. 93.

9. In some countries, especially West Germany, industrial democracy appears to be developing more rapidly.

CHAPTER XVII

1. When an established order comes to be accepted as comical, its days are numbered. That is, more formal efforts to effect changes, such as rational analysis or power struggles, may be essentially ineffectual. The traditional patterns of social operation will persist.However, when there develops an open attitude of levity, the structure of the society will be severely undermined. We can see illustrations at this time. Church councils were held to attempt a revitalization of the ancient institution Reform movements arose to provide a critical evaluation. Greater significance, however, may be attached to Dante's Divine Comedy and Boccachio's Decammeron. When institutions fail to retain the respect of its constituents, its power to order human life is substantially weakened. Today (March 1, 1974), we see an example of this. The Nixon administration is under heavy attack from many quarters. But it is doubtful that anything is so thoroughly devastating as the political cartoons by Herblock or the pictures showing Rose Mary Wood, the President's personal secretary, in a ridiculous pose as she attempts to explain the tape erasures.

2. A commentator recently observed, as a result of his stay in a hospital for cancer patients, that every effort is made to prevent terminal patients from dying before some appropriate

time. They are watched carefully to see that they do not have opportunity to commit suicide. Even more strange is the fact that they are limited in the amount of pain-killing drugs lest they cause death. Obviously, the whole question of euthanasia arises in these matters. But one is forced to ask this question: Have we really advanced very far from barbarity?

3. In reality, it may be questioned whether he has really provided for it.

4. Obviously, this position compromises his general thesis. It means that religion is superior to the state.

5. It was expressed in the phrase, cuius regio, eius religio.

6. "Concession and Agreements" of 1676.

7. Since the primary function of the state is to evaluate controversies and to redress injuries, there may be implied the possibility of government interference. Even Roger Williams had stressed that freedom of religion did not mean license.

CHAPTER XVIII

1. The General Assembly of the United Nations on December 10, 1948 adopted a "Universal Declaration of Human Rights." Articles 2 and 18 express the concept of religious freedom.

2. One of the difficulties in the effort to restore prayer in the school system is that of determining the type of prayer to be offered. For many Christians, it would be inappropriate to pray if it did not reflect the doctrine of the Trinity. Should it happen, as would be true in most communities in the United States, that Trinitarian Christians (some would insist that there are no others) constituted the majority, would there not be strong pressures to produce this type of prayer? Even now, it is very embarrassing to many members of the educational communities when Christian ministers offer this type of prayer at commencements since it is known that nonChristians are present.

CHAPTER XIX

1. Since this statement was originally written, the school has ceased operating the station where the training was provided.

2. 1 Sam. 9:9.

3. This history of the past raises a current question. Can it be said that today the western world is moving in a similar direction? The twentieth century, with its rapid developments in the natural sciences and technologies, has been characterized by an extreme optimism. The inevitability of progress has been the dominant motif. The problems which had confronted man from the most distant times would be solved. Diseases would be conquered; education would become universal so that every person could fulfill his personal aspirations; social ills would be overcome, etc. Increasingly, we are becoming doubtful and uncertain; pessimism is replacing optimism; a lack of confidence in our institutions is widely expressed; man is turning inward to seek his own way; and, to climax it all, there are emerging the new religions which offer man solace by promising him personal salvation. This latter is especially seen in the renewed emphasis on apocalypticism. Even Kohoutek has been seen as the harbinger of some cataclysmic occurrence. In other words, do we see a repetition of the ancient historical period? Will this mood result in a decline of science itself?

4. It should be noted that in this period the universe was still considered as closed and limited.

5. Centuries later, this story was repeated in the work of Charles Darwin. Theories of evolution had existed long before him. But he presented the empirical evidence.

CHAPTER XX

1. Preserved Smith, A History of Modern Culture. New York: Henry Holt and Company, 1930, Vol. I, p. 40.

2. Mt. 16:18f.

3. Gen. 1:26.

4. Jn. 10:10.

CHAPTER XXI

1. Mt. 25:35.

SELECTED BIBLIOGRAPHY

SELECTED BIBLIOGRAPHY

INTRODUCTION

Adolfs, Robert, The Grave of God; Has the Church a Future?
New York: Harper & Row, 1967.

Basilius, Harold A., Contemporary Problems in Religion. Detroit:
Wayne University Press, 1956.

Bayne, Stephen Fielding, Space Age Christianity. New York:
Morehouse-Barlow, 1963.

Beker, Johan Christiaan, The Church Faces the World.
Philadelphia: Westminster Press, 1960.

Bower, William Clayton, Moral and Spiritual Values in Education.
Lexington: University of Kentucky Press, 1952.

Burr, Nelson Rollings, Religion in American Life. New York:
Appleton-Century-Crofts, 1971.

Cailliet, Emile, Christian Approach to Culture. Nashville:
Abingdon-Cokesbury Press, 1953.

Callahan, Daniel J., The Secular City Debate. New York:
Macmillan, 1966.

Coe, George Albert, What Is Religion Doing to our Consciences?
New York: C. Scribner's Sons, 1943.

Dawson, Christopher Henry, Enquiries into Religion and Culture.
Freeport, New York: Books for Libraries Press, 1968.

Edwards, David Lawrence, Religion and Change. New York: Harper
& Row, 1969.

Fabry, Joseph B., The Pursuit of Meaning: Logotherapy Applied
to Life. 1968.

Greenslade, Stanley Lawrence, The Church and the Social Order.
London: SCM Press, 1948.

Guyau, Jean Marie, The Non-Religion of the Future. New York:
Schocken Books, 1962.

Harvey, George Leonard Hunton, Church and the Twentieth Century.
New York: Books for Libraries, 1936.

Herzog, Arthur, The Church Trap. New York: MacMillan, 1968.

Hook, Sidney, Religion in a Free Society. Lincoln: University
of Nebraska Press, 1967.

Hough, Lynn Harold, Christian Criticism of Life. New York:
    Abingdon-Cokesbury Press, 1936.
Johnson, Paul Emanuel, Christian Love. New York: Abingdon-
    Cokesbury Press, 1951.
Kaufmann, Walter Arnold, The Faith of a Heretic. Garden City,
    New York: Doubleday, 1963.
Kegley, Charles W., Protestantism in Transition. New York:
    Harper & Row, 1965.
Kraemer, Hendrik, World Cultures and World Religions: The Com-
    ing Dialogue. Philadelphia: Westminster Press, 1960.
Lee, Robert, Cities and Churches:Readings on the Urban Church.
    Philadelphia: Westminster Press, 1962.
Luccock, Halford Edward, Christian Faith and Economic Change.
    New York: Abingdon Press, 1936.
Macintosh, Douglas Clyde, Social Religion. New York: C.
    Scribner's Sons, 1939.
McKown, Harry Charles, Character Education. New York:
    McGraw-Hill Book Company, 1935.
Maritain, Jacques, Christianity and Democracy. New York:
    Books for Libraries, 1972.
Marty, Martin E., The New Shape of American Religion. New
    York: Harper, 1959.
Marty, Martin E., Varieties of Unbelief. New York: Holt,
    Rinehart and Winston, 1964.
Metz, Johannes Baptist, Theology of the World. New York:
    Herder and Herder, 1969.
Mortimer, Robert Cecil, Christian Ethics. London and New
    York: Hutchinson's University Library, 1950.
Niebuhr, Helmut Richard, Christ and Culture. New York:
    Harper and Row, 1956.
Nottingham, Elizabeth Kristine, Religion and Society. Garden
    City, New York: Doubleday, 1954.
Richardson, Alan, History, Sacred and Profane. Philadelphia:
    Westminster Press, 1964.
Szczedny, Gerhard, The Future of Unbelief. New York: G.
    Braziller, 1961.
Theology and Church in Times of Change. Philadelphia:
    Westminster Press, 1970
Tillich, Paul, The Future of Religions. New York: Harper
    and Row, 1966.
Trueblood, David Elton, Alternative to Futility. New York:
    Harper, 1948.

Trueblood, David Elton, Predicament of Modern Man. New York
    and London: Harper and Brothers, 1944.
Wallis, Wilson Dallam, Culture Patterns in Christianity.
    Lawrence, Kansas: Coronado Press, 1964.
White, Leslie A., The Science of Culture. New York: Grove
    Press, 1958.
Wicker, Brian, Toward a Contemporary Christianity. Notre Dame,
    Indiana: University of Notre Dame Press, 1967.
Winter, Gibson, Suburban Captivity of the Churches. New York:
    Macmillan, 1962.

RELIGION AND PHILOSOPHY

Cobb, John B., A Christian Natural Theology. Philadelphia:
    Westminster Press, 1965.
DeWolf, Lotan Harold, A Theology of the Living Church. New
    York: Harper & Row, 1968.
Edman, Irwin, Landmarks for Beginners in Philosophy. New York:
    Holt, Rinehart and Winston, 1960.
Frank, Erich, Philosophical Understanding and Religious Truth.
    London and New York: Oxford University Press, 1945.
Hartshorne, Charles, The Divine Relativity. New Haven: Yale
    University Press, 1948.
Hick, John, Faith and the Philosophers. New York: St. Martin's
    Press, 1964.
Lynch, Lawrence, A Christian Philosophy. New York: C. Scrib-
    ner's Sons, 1968.
MacGregor, Geddes, Readings in Religious Philosophy   Boston:
    Houghton Mifflin, 1962.
Novak, Michael, Belief and Unbelief. New York: Macmillan,
    1965.
Smith, John Edwin, Reason and God. New Haven: Yale University
    Press, 1961
Williams, Daniel Day, What Present-Day Theologians are Think-
    ing. New York: Harper & Row, 1959.

363

RELIGION AND ETHICS

Davis, Charles, A Question of Conscience. New York: Harper
    & Row, 1967.
Fletcher, Joseph Francis, Situation Ethics. Philadelphia:
    Westminster Press, 1966.
Forell, George Wolfgang, Christian Social Teachings. Garden
    City, New York: Anchor Books, 1966.
Gardner, Edward Clinton, Biblical Faith and Social Ethics.
    New York: Harper & Row, 1960.
Harkness, Georgia Elma, Christian Ethics. New York: Abingdon
    Press, 1957.
Kelsey, George D., Racism and the Christian Understanding of
    Man. New York: C. Scribner's Sons, 1965.
Orr, Horace E., Christian Ethics for Practical Living. Phila-
    delphia: Westminster Press, 1961.
Robinson, John Arthur Thomas, Christian Morals Today. Phila-
    delphia, Westminster Press, 1964.
Rowland, Stanley J., Ethics, Crime, and Redemption. Pholadel-
    phia: Westminster Press, 1963.
Schweitzer, Albert, Reverence for Life. New York: Philosophi-
    cal Library, 1965.

RELIGION AND ECONOMICS

Balk, Alfred, The Religion Business. Richmond: John Knox
    Press, 1968
Bennett, John Coleman, Christian Values and Economic Life.
    Freeport, New York: Books for Libraries Press, 1970.
Carter, Paul Allen, The Decline and Revival of the Social Gos-
    pel. Ithaca, New York: Cornell University Press, 1956.
Fichter, Joseph Henry, Religion as an Occupation. Notre Dame,
    Indiana: University of Notre Dame Press, 1961
Gollwitzer, Helmut, The Christian Faith and the Marxist Criti-
    cism of Religion. New York: C. Scribner's Sons, 1970.
Hecker, Julius Friedrich, Religion Under the Soviets. New
    York: Vanguard Press, 1927.
Kendall, Guy, The Social Application of Christianity. London:
    Duckworth, 1948.
Knight, Frank Hyneman, The Economic Order and Religion. New
    York and London: Harper and Brothers, 1945.
May, Henry F., Protestant Churches and Industrial America.
    Octagon, 1963.

Moberg, David O., The Church as a Social Institution. Engle-
    wood Cliffs, New Jersey: Prentice-Hall, 1962.
Rasmussen, Albert Terrill, Christian Responsibility in Economic
    Life. Philadelphia: Westminster Press, 1965.
Troeltsch, Ernst, Social Teachings of the Christian Churches.
    New York: Macmillan, 1931.

RELIGION AND POLITICS

Cripps, Sir Richard Stafford, Towards Christian Democracy.
    Westport, Conneticut: Greenwood Press, 1970.
Cullman, Oscar, The State in the New Testament. New York:
    C. Scribner's Sons, 1956.
Goerner, Edward Alfred, Peter and Caesar. New York: Herder
    and Herder, 1965.
Jerrold, Douglas, Future of Freedom: Notes on Christianity
    and Politics. Freeport, New York: Books for Libraries
    Press, 1968.
Kelley, Alden D., Christianity and Political Responsibility.
    Philadelphia: Westminster Press, 1961.
Lee, Robert, ed., The Church and the Exploding Metropolis.
    Richmond: John Knox Press, 1965.
Marrin, Albert, ed., War and the Christian Conscience: From
    Augustine to Martin Luther King, Jr. Chicago:
    Regnery, 1971.
Marxism and Christianity. New York: Humanities Press, 1968.
Meyer, Donald B., The Protestant Search for Political Realism,
    1919-1941. Berkeley: University of California Press,
    1960.
Morgan, Richard E., The Politics of Religious Conflict: Church
    and State in America. New York: Pegasus, 1968.
Pichon, Charles, The Vatican and Its Role in World Affairs.
    Westport, Connecticut: Greenwood Press, 1969.
Smith, Elwyn Allen, Church and State in Your Community.
    Philadelphia: Westminister Press, 1963.

365

RELIGION AND SCIENCE

Barbour, Ian G., Issues in Science and Religion. Englewood
    Cliffs, New Jersey: Prentice-Hall, 1966.
Heim, Karl, Christian Faith and Natural Science. New York:
    Harper, 1957.
Heisenberg, Werner, Physics and Philosophy: the Revolution in
    Modern Science. New York: Harper, 1958.
Jones, William Thomas, The Sciences and the Humanities: Con-
    flict and Reconciliation. Berkeley: University of
    California Press, 1965.
Lodge, Sir Oliver Joseph, Man and the Universe. New York:
    George H. Doran, 1920.
Malinowski, Bronislaw, Magic, Science, and Religion, and
    Other Essays. Boston: Beacon Press, 1948.
Peacoke, Arthur Robert, Science and the Christian Experiment.
    London and New York: Oxford University Press, 1971.
Rust, Eric Charles, Science and Faith. New York: Oxford
    University Press, 1967.
Spinks, George Stephens, Psychology and Religion. Boston:
    Beacon Press, 1965.
Stuermann, Walter Earl, Logic and Faith: A Study of the Re-
    lations Between Science and Religion. Philadelphia:
    Westminster Press, 1962.
Walsh, James Joseph, Catholic Churchmen in Science. Freeport,
    New York: Books for Libraries Press, 1966.